THE DECLINE OF THE MUGHAL EMPIRE

Oxford in India Readings
DEBATES IN INDIAN HISTORY AND SOCIETY

Series Editors: SABYASACHI BHATTACHARYA, B.D. CHATTOPADHYAYA,
RICHARD M. EATON

RAZIUDDIN AQUIL (*Editor*)   *Sufism and Society in Medieval India*

FINBARR BARRY FLOOD (*Editor*)   *Piety and Politics in the Early
                                    Indian Mosque*

BISWAMOY PATI (*Editor*)   *The 1857 Rebellion* (OIP)

SCOTT C. LEVI (*Editor*)   *India and Central Asia*
                                    Commerce and Culture, 1500–1800

BHAIRABI PRASAD SAHU (*Editor*)   *Iron and Social Change in Early India*

SEEMA ALAVI (*Editor*)   *The Eighteenth Century in India*
                                    (OIP)

AMIYA P. SEN (*Editor*)   *Social and Religious Reform*
                                    The Hindus of British India (OIP)

DAVID N. LORENZEN (*Editor*)   *Religious Movements in South Asia
                                    600–1800* (OIP)

G. BALACHANDRAN (*Editor*)   *India and the World Economy
                                    1850–1950* (OIP)

BIDYUT CHAKRABARTY (*Editor*)   *Communal Identity in India*
                                    Its Construction and Articulation in
                                    the Twentieth Century (OIP)

KAUSHIK ROY (*Editor*)   *Partition of India*
                                    Why 1947?

THE DECLINE OF
THE MUGHAL EMPIRE

edited by
MEENA BHARGAVA

OXFORD
UNIVERSITY PRESS

OXFORD
UNIVERSITY PRESS

Oxford University Press is a department of the University of Oxford.
It furthers the University's objective of excellence in research, scholarship,
and education by publishing worldwide. Oxford is a registered trademark of
Oxford University Press in the UK and in certain other countries

Published in India by
Oxford University Press
22 Workspace, 2nd Floor, 1/22 Asaf Ali Road, New Delhi 110002, India

First Edition published in 2014
Digitally Printed in 2025

ISBN-13: 978-0-19-809056-4
ISBN-10: 0-19-809056-0

Typeset in Adobe Garamond Pro 10.5/13
by Sai Graphic Design, New Delhi 110 055
Printed in India by Manipal Technologies limited, Manipal

Contents

Series Editors' Note

The Debates in Indian History and Society series focuses on the diversity of interpretations in historical discourse. The series addresses widely debated issues in South Asian History (including contemporary history) through edited volumes centring on sharply focused themes or seminal writings which have generated arguments and counter-arguments resulting in worthwhile debates. In this context, the debates represent not simply differences in opinions but also offer important interpretative frameworks which result in them acquiring a certain historiographic status. The approach encourages the interrogation of history, as distinct from presenting history as a collection of 'given' facts. The aim is to bring to readers significant writings, interpretations and to open to students bridge heads into research.

The present volume addresses one of the most vexed questions of South Asian historiography—how to understand the decline of the Mughal Empire, which by any measure was one of the most powerful and wealthy empires in world history? What, exactly, had happened? What is meant by 'decline'? What was it that was experiencing a decline, and from whose perspective? What is the evidence? When did it begin?

Scholars have debated these issues ever since the early nineteenth century, when British colonial historians sought to understand the nature of the huge north Indian state they had replaced during their notorious 'fit of absent-mindedness'. As Indian history itself evolved through the nineteenth and twentieth centuries, so did historians' interpretative frameworks for understanding Mughal decline. Theories of that decline also changed as new or different sorts of data fell into historians' hands. The result is a remarkably wide range of historical explanations, making for one of the liveliest debates in all of South Asian historiography. This volume presents the reader with samples of different approaches to this enduring question, written by leading scholars from around the world.

SABYASACHI BHATTACHARYA
B.D. CHATTOPADHYAYA
RICHARD M. EATON

Introduction

Meena Bhargava

The Mughal Empire has been a fascinating and overwhelming chapter in the history of India, whether one considers its power, its wealth, its stability, its extent, its character, or its decline in the eighteenth century. It is the latter that has engaged historians for over three decades in contentious debate. Many propositions and counter-propositions have been made. It may be pertinent to pose a question: what does 'decline'— one of the most value-loaded and emotional concepts in historical analysis—actually mean? Certainly, the notion of decline envisages a prior state of perfection, efflorescence, harmony, and cohesion, in contrast to corruption, moral degradation, and loss of ethical values, principles, and customs. Historians therefore wish to understand the phenomenon of change and its causes. For instance, social decay, deterioration of the previous order, and brief or long spells of chaos and disorder are all considered to be causes of decline.[1] Conscious, then, of the different meanings of the term, and the emotions it can arouse, we look at the kind of responses that the decline of the Mughal Empire has evoked over the years.

Was it merely a deterioration of power over a period of roughly thirty to fifty years, or did the empire's decentralizing tendencies become more apparent and aggressive during these years? Did the decline of the Mughal Empire lead to a 'dark age' when 'the gates were opened to reckless rapine, anarchy and foreign conquest'?[2] Notwithstanding the decline, 'intricate layers of interconnections and continuities'[3] prevailed, although changes or restructuring within the Mughal structure remained equally significant.

While the weakening and collapse of the Mughal Empire overshadowed much of the eighteenth century, it was by no means the only phenomenon of that period. Regional political structures emerged and thrived amidst the waning of Mughal power. In these provincial and regional political configurations, Mughal institutions generally continued. Yet some, like Hyderabad, were able to move beyond Mughal patterns of governance even while maintaining the fiction that they were Mughal dependencies. Ultimately, however, as Munis Faruqui argues, Hyderabad emerged as neither a poor imitation nor a miniature version of the Mughal Empire.[4] These developments suggest that the disintegration of the Mughal Empire meant neither the eclipse of political authority nor the economic stagnation of the entire society. The economy visibly moved in new directions, leading to decentralization and economic density at local levels, which remained integrated by networks of trade and monetary transactions. The period also acquired significance as it coincided with the rising power of the East India Company. As European influence grew, the regions came into contact with institutions that threatened to erode the foundations of the erstwhile social order,[5] and which heralded the unmistakable rise of a new one as an *inqilab*—a world turned upside down.[6]

In view of these historical processes, should we then follow Frank Perlin and call this phase the 'late pre-colonial period' of Indian history and rescue it from its long-standing characterization as a chaotic or 'black' century?[7] Or should we perhaps use the term 'Early Modern' for these pre-colonial centuries? Sanjay Subrahmanyam argues that this is necessary not merely for reasons of justice to the history of the period, but also for reaching a better understanding of the colonial intervention.[8] Maybe there is also a need, as several scholars have argued, to re-think this era 'whose core was the eighteenth century, but whose antecedents were earlier and whose consequences extended well into the nineteenth century'.[9]

The present volume, however, attempts something more modest, which is to identify the divergent views and debates that surround the withering of the 'mammoth imperial banyan tree',[10] and to focus on the different paradigms or assumptions that have shaped interpretations of the decline of the Mughal Empire. A few core issues or groups of issues that form the basis of the debate can be identified here, namely: (a) the personality and religion of the Mughal emperors, in particular the religious policy of Aurangzeb (or 'Alamgir, r. 1658–1707), which alienated large sections of the population; (b) the nature of the assignment system, or the *jagirdari* system, which was intrinsically exploitative of peasants; (c) the role of bankers and merchants and their failure to support the empire fiscally or commercially; (d) cultural, scientific, or other transregional forces, since three large empires (Mughal, Safavid, and Ottoman) all faced their decline at roughly the same time; and (d) the failure of the centre to retain the loyalty of regional elites.

PERSONALITY AND THE RELIGIOUS POLICY OF THE MUGHAL EMPERORS

The decline of the Mughal Empire, together with its courtly pomp and luxury, its rituals of power, and its enormous wealth, was described in some detail by contemporary European travelers, in particular Francois Bernier (d. 1688). These accounts influenced the perceptions of early historians of Mughal India—both British imperialist and Indian nationalist historians of the late nineteenth and early twentieth centuries—and their characterization of the eighteenth century. Indeed, these historians tended to conflate developments of eighteenth century India with developments in the Mughal Empire. They also held the empire's administrative and religious policies and the weak personalities of the post-1707 emperors and their nobles responsible for the decline. Imperialist historians, starting with James Mill (d. 1836), described pre-colonial society as backward, and as having plunged into even deeper chaos after the death of Aurangzeb, resulting in the fragmentation of the empire into disorderly successor states that threatened to erode and disrupt the trade practices of the East India Company. This in turn compelled the Company to assume direct administrative powers, transforming it from a merchant company into a territorial power. Describing the eighteenth century as a 'dark era', imperialist historians argued that order and modernization could have been introduced into India only after the establishment of British rule in India. Justifying the British conquest of India, utilitarian and evangelical writers also (but differently than James Mill) saw it as a moral mission of 'enlightened' Britain to bring progress and development to the Indian subcontinent. Even Marx could not avoid this colonial teleology. He used his formulation of an 'Asiatic Mode of Production' to describe conditions in pre-colonial India, suggesting that it was British capitalism that had relieved India of these backward practices, thereby ushering it 'into history'.[11]

Writing the political history of the Mughal Empire after the death of Aurangzeb, William Irvine in the early 1920s explained the empire's decline by posing questions that were personality-oriented — How was the work of Akbar and Shahjahan, Man Singh, and Mir Jumla undone? Why did the seemingly flourishing state of Aurangzeb fall down like a house of cards only thirty-one years after his death? In reviewing the history of these thirty-one years, Irvine concluded that the flawed character of the emperors had corrupted the nobility and was therefore the primary cause of imperial decline. The nobles, he suggested, found that their careers were not open to talent and that loyal and useful service was 'no security against capricious dismissal and degradation'.[12] Irvine added, 'When the emperor was a sluggard or a fool, he ceased to be the master and guide of the nobility. (Their) selfish struggle necessarily ranged the nobles in factions, each group or bloc trying to push the fortune of its members and hinder the success of its rival groups.'[13]

Apart from holding the degenerative character of the emperors and the nobles responsible for the decline, Irvine also accused Aurangzeb of alienating the Hindus and the Shi'is. Unlike Akbar (r. 1556–1605), who had made the 'first beginnings of the conversion of a military monarchy into a national state' by hiring the services of 'Hindu warrior tribes', Aurangzeb annexed Jodhpur after the death of Jaswant Singh, invaded Mewar, 'incessantly destroyed temples', and imposed the *jaziya* tax. These actions not only alienated the Rajput clans but convinced all other Hindu races of India that they had 'no lot or part in the Mughal state and that for the preservation of their honour and liberty of conscience, they must look elsewhere'. This provided an opportunity for the empowerment of the Marathas, who appeared 'as heaven sent' to the Rajputs and the Bundelas, earlier the staunch supporters of the Mughals. 'A Rama slaying Ravana or Krishna slaying Kansa' is the feeling, Irvine observed, that breathes in every line of the odes to Shivaji by the Hindi poet Bhushan. According to Irvine, Bhushan voiced the unspoken thoughts of millions of Hindus all over India, who by the end of the seventeenth century regarded the Mughal government as 'Satanic' and therefore refused to cooperate with it.[14]

Irvine was in some respects the mentor of Jadunath Sarkar.[15] Writing in the 1930s, Sarkar used the same tools of assessment as Irvine did to understand developments in the eighteenth century. Characterizing the period as politically chaotic and economically crisis-ridden, he focused on Aurangzeb's religious policy and Deccan campaigns as the principal reasons for Mughal decline. Although he acknowledged that Aurangzeb's reign may have showed signs of being the greatest Indian empire of pre-British days, Sarkar felt that signs of the empire's incipient decline and disruption were unmistakable. Unrelenting towards Aurangzeb, he held that well before the invasions of Nadir Shah (1739) and Ahmad Shah Abdali (1761), 'the Padishah [proved] to be an impotent shadow of royalty and Delhi the mere memory of past greatness, long before the Maratha confederacy hid beneath its super-imposed sway the regular monarchy of the land'. Years before the death of Aurangzeb in 1707, argued Sarkar, the Mughal Empire had become financially bankrupt, its administration had declined, and its institutions and society faced irreversible decay.[16] Aurangzeb's Deccan campaigns, moreover, intensified these political woes: 'the emperor, his court and family, the bulk of the army and all his best officers live there for a quarter century and Hindustan sinks back to a place of secondary importance'. The generals and soldiers stationed in the Deccan in 'enforced exile' sighed to return to their homes in the north. Sarkar cited the examples of a homesick noble who apparently offered the emperor one lakh of rupees to spend a year in Delhi, or of Rajput soldiers who grieved over the diminishing of their breed 'by reason of their life-long stay in Deccan away from home and family'. And yet, though his Prime Minister had convinced the emperor of the military successes in the Deccan and urged him to move back to Delhi, Aurangzeb remained adamant in his obstinate resolve to 'root out' the Marathas. The emperor's unyielding behaviour on the issue of Deccan, asserted Sarkar, resulted in political disorder and lawlessness in most parts of India, while the administration in north India fell into 'decay at the withdrawal of the master's eye and the ablest officers'. For Sarkar, this marked 'the first rudimentary beginnings of that political, economic and cultural breakdown ... rightly given the name of the "Great Anarchy" to the eighteenth century in northern India.'[17]

It was not just political issues that distinguished Aurangzeb from Akbar, or that contributed to the collapse of the 'grand edifice' built by Akbar. Aurangzeb's ideology and religious practices, argued Sarkar, marked a profound shift from Akbar's syncretism, leading to a fanaticism that alienated Sikhs and Hindus—Rathor, Bundela, Maratha—who rebelled against Mughal authority. Elaborating on the religious policies of Aurangzeb, Sarkar argued that the 'Quranic polity made life intolerable for the Hindus under orthodox Muhammadan rule', that schools of Hindu learning and Hindu places of worship were demolished, that Hindu fairs were prohibited, that the Hindu section of the population was subjected to special fiscal burdens 'in addition to being made to bear a public badge of inferiority', and that the service of the State was closed to them.[18] Evaluating the impact of Aurangeb's religious policy, Sarkar wrote, 'the only life that the Hindus could lead under Aurangzeb was a life deprived of the light of knowledge, deprived of the consolations of religion, deprived of social union and public rejoicing, of wealth and self-confidence that is begotten by the free exercise of natural activities and use of opportunities—in short, a life exposed to constant public humiliation and political disabilities ... Heaven and earth alike were closed to him as long as he remained a Hindu'.[19]

For Sarkar, such policies made Aurangzeb 'the worst ruler imaginable of an empire composed of many creeds and races, of diverse interests and ways of life and thought'.[20] The emperor's orthodox Sunnism produced a Hindu reaction and induced Hindus into constant revolt and disturbances. They deteriorated in intellect, organization and economic resources and thereby weakened the State of which they formed more than two-thirds'.[21] So, concluded Sarkar, when Aurangzeb 'closed his aged eyes in death (1707) ... decline had unmistakably set in: Indo-Mughal civilization, whose agent was the Empire of Delhi, was now a spent bullet, its life was gone, it had no power for good left in it'. But the empire did not dissolve immediately after Aurangzeb's death; the central government stood intact. It was, in fact, the succession of 'weaklings and imbeciles' on the throne that perpetrated the decline. 'The dry rot in the heart of the Mughal State' manifested itself when the imperial capital was attacked by Baji Rao's cavalry in 1737, followed by the invasion of Nadir Shah and the 'utter collapse of the Government of Delhi in 1738'.[22]

Irvine's and Sarkar's explanation for the decline of the Mughal Empire hardly takes us beyond the perspective of the seventeenth and eighteenth century Persian chroniclers. Nonetheless, there is a difference, in the sense that both Irvine and Sarkar also see evidence of a 'Hindu reaction' in the anti-Mughal revolts of Rathors, Bundelas, Marathas, and Sikhs. Muzaffar Alam, however, advances a contrary view, arguing that the rebels and 'disturbers' mentioned in contemporary sources were identified either by their class—namely as zamindars—or by their caste, clan, or region.[23]

Twentieth century historians like Ishwari Prasad, S. R. Sharma, and Jagdish Narayan Sarkar[24] subscribed to the Irvine-Sarkar interpretation of Mughal history. Ishwari Prasad argued that the reaction against the spirit of toleration begun in the reign of Shahjahan became more pronounced under Aurangzeb, when the administration acquired a theocratic character. Aurangzeb, he said, gave ample evidence of his bigotry when he demolished schools and temples of the Hindus, forbade their religious teachings and practices, and revived the *jaziya* tax 'with the object of curbing the infidels and of distinguishing the land of the faithful from an infidel land'. Prasad also blamed Aurangzeb for inducing conversion to Islam by offering incentives and cherished posts to those Hindus who renounced their religion. 'The state', he observed, 'became a large missionary institution which extended its favour to renegades and made liberal promises irrespective of merit and efficiency ... Aurangzeb lost all sense of proportion in the glare of religious zeal', arousing the defiance and wrath of the Hindus and rendering conciliation between the two communities impossible. This led to 'a cruel misunderstanding and a sanguinary conflict between the opposing forces, which paved the way to complete ruin.'[25] It may be true that Aurangzeb attempted to associate the Mughal state with Islamic orthodoxy, but to suggest—as Jagdish Narayan Sarkar, Prasad, and Sharma do—that this alienated only the Hindus, or that the Hindus alone were the trouble-makers, or that the 'Hindu reaction' was the primary major cause of the decline, is untenable. Much evidence shows that Muslim officials and nobles also reacted against such imperial policies. For example, Muzaffar Alam argues that Muslim holders of *madad-i ma'ash* stipends created problems of equivalent stature for the empire.[26]

The above-mentioned interpretation emphasizing the personality, religious ideology, and religious practices of the Mughal emperors—particularly Aurangzeb—was based on colonial views. James Mill's *The History of British India,* published in 1817, divided Indian history into Hindu, Muhammadan, and British periods, though Sir William Jones (d. 1794) had already propounded the idea of a Hindu and Muslim India. This Orientalist view of history imposed a rigid structure on the history of India, that is, a history of two foreign rules—one, Islamic, tyrannical, and despotic; the other, European and benevolent—preceded by an era of indigenous governance. Inspired by his 'utilitarianism', Mill defined the pre-colonial period in India not simply by the religion of the ruling dynasties. He also held that India had no vision of science, rationality, and enlightenment until it was incorporated into the British Empire. Such an explanation of history, which ignored processes of change and evolution in an extremely pluralistic Indian society, dominated the writing of Indian history well beyond the mid-twentieth century.[27] The notion that Hindus during the 'Muslim' (medieval) period suffered under Muslim tyranny was also a colonial construct used to justify European rule, so that the British could then be projected as having freed the Hindus from severities and persecutions. Moreover, depicting Hindus and Muslims as warring communities both legitimized the British presence in India and prevented the two communities from uniting against their foreign rulers.[28]

THE ASSIGNMENT SYSTEM

The above-mentioned interpretation, derived from a personality-based, ideology-prone analysis, was challenged and virtually displaced in the late 1950s and early 1960s with a series of publications by historians from Aligarh University. These scholars provided a systemic perspective on the Mughal Empire, focusing on the state as a 'revenue sponge or fiscal mechanism'[29] and explaining imperial decline by linking it to the Mughal assignment system. Satish Chandra speaks of the 'jagirdari crisis', while Irfan Habib talks of an 'agrarian crisis', that is, a crisis in the distribution of *jagirs* (revenue assignments), a decline in production and revenue, and Mughal exploitation. Other historians, like Tapan Raychaudhuri, explain the actions of the Mughal state as 'the uncomplicated desire of a small ruling class, for more and more material resources.... (T)heir economism was simple, straightforward and almost palpable ... there was no containing it until it collapsed under the weight of its own contradictions'.[30]

The significance of the Mughal assignment system and its implications were first observed by Francois Bernier, a French physician who visited the court of Aurangzeb in the seventeenth century. Bernier had argued that the frequent transfers of jagirs had left a disastrous impact on the *jagirdars/mansabdars* (nobility), who felt deprived and had no incentive to improve the land or its production. Instead, they appropriated large amounts for themselves, leaving the land and agricultural production completely depleted and exhausted, with no concern for the peasants. Commenting on the behaviour of the jagirdars towards the peasants, Bernier wrote of

the tyranny of Timariots [landholders], Governors, and Revenue Contractors—a tyranny which even the monarch, if so disposed, has no means of controlling in provinces not contiguous to his capital—a tyranny often so excessive as to deprive the peasant and artisan of the necessaries of life and leave them to die of misery and exhaustion ... a tyranny, that drives the cultivator of the soil from his wretched home to some neighbouring state ....[31]

Bernier found the cause of this 'execrable tyranny' in the frequent transfers of jagirs. Stressing the apprehensions of the jagirdars, Bernier remarked, 'We (*jagirdars*) may be deprived of it (*jagir*) in a single moment, and our exertions would benefit neither ourselves nor our children. Let us draw from the soil all the money we can, though the peasant should starve or abscond, and we should leave it, when commanded to quit, a dreary wilderness.'[32]

Bernier made these statements in a letter written in the late 1660s to Jean Baptiste Colbert (d. 1683), the finance minister of France's King Louis XIV. His proposition of the 'crisis' in the Mughal assignment system first impressed W. H. Moreland, and then Irfan Habib and Athar Ali. This prompts us into a compelling query: why was Bernier's hypothesis on the assignment system so eagerly accepted for developing the argument for an 'agrarian crisis', whereas his theories about the limited nature of Mughal power— namely, that 'The empire of the Great Mogol comprehends several nations, over which he is not absolute master'[33] —was dismissed or counter-argued? Perhaps his commentary, as he addressed his correspondents in France, had a rhetorical purpose.[34] A member of the French landed gentry class, Bernier probably wished to criticize revenue farming as a principle—a practice prevalent in France then—and instead advocate for an indispensable, urgent need for security in private property in land. Believing that such security was absent in India, Bernier identified that absence as a serious defect in Mughal India, one that he did not wish to see repeated in France. Thus, he may have wished to influence Colbert's revenue policies. In this way, argues Sanjay Subrahmanyam, Mughal India served as 'the screen on which he presented his views of what would happen to France if certain despotic and tyrannical policies were followed'.[35]

Accepting the arguments laid out by Bernier, W. H. Moreland, in several works published in the 1920s, stressed the exploitative nature of the Mughal revenue assignment system. Like Jadunath Sarkar, he held Aurangzeb responsible for the adversities in the empire. Drawing upon the account of William Hawkins, a visitor in the court of Jahangir (r. 1605–27), Moreland suggested that changes in revenue assignments were so frequent that 'a man could not continue half a year in his living, but it is taken from him, and given unto another'. Consequently, it was the 'assignee's interest to extract the utmost possible sum from each successive grant'.[36] Elaborating on the impact of the assignment system, he noted the increasing pressure on the peasantry, in particular during Aurangzeb's reign. Moreland observed that the standard of cultivation was determined not by the peasants but by the assessor, 'whose momentary interest was that it should be as large as possible, and who was authorized to enforce his views if necessary by flogging'.[37] Apart from this insistence on bringing large areas under cultivation, the state demand was increased from one-third of the gross produce to one-half, amounting to an enhancement of 50 per cent. The administrative pressure on the peasants, observed Moreland, increased so tremendously that it affected the productive resources of the empire, completely exhausted the potential of agricultural production, and impoverished the country to such an extent that it led to the empire's decline. These ideas are discussed in the excerpts that have been included in this volume from his book *From Akbar to Aurangzeb: A Study in Indian Economic History* (1923).

Apart from giving credence to the writings of Bernier, Hawkins, and several other foreign travellers, Moreland's writings were also influenced by the controversy between the apologists and the critics of British rule. To them, the question was whether Indians were better off under the previous rulers (Mughals) or under the British. Moreland's major concerns were: (a) to compare national wealth and income in India at the death of Akbar with that of early twentieth century British India, (b) to refute the notion of a pre-colonial 'golden age', and (c) to establish that India's economy under the British was an improvement, even if small, on the period of Akbar in terms of per capita output and consumption. His views were also influenced by his long posting as a revenue official in the United Provinces, where he constantly opposed state interference in trade, high land revenue assessments, and the 'luxurious expenditures' of landowners. Moreland, it appears, wished to suggest that Mughal despotism and heavy taxation smothered tendencies towards private property in land, that domestic trade was sporadic and scanty, and that foreign trade was largely based on the exchange of precious items until the Europeans stimulated and expanded Indian textile exports.[38]

In the 1960s, the debate on the decline of the Mughal Empire took a swerve towards the left with a series of publications from Aligarh University that reiterated the long-held opinion on the eighteenth century as politically chaotic and crisis-ridden. These included Satish Chandra's *Parties and Politics at the Mughal Court, 1707–1740* (1959), Irfan Habib's *The Agrarian System of the Mughal Empire, 1556–1707* (1963), M. Athar Ali's *The Nobility under Aurangzeb* (1966), and Noman Ahmad Siddiqui's *Land Revenue Administration under the Mughals, 1700–1750* (1970). Shifting away from individuals and personalities, these historians focused on institutions. They also identified social groups with certain material interests, and associated imperial rise and decline with tensions arising from systemic, rather than psychological contradictions. Drawing a kind of a diagram of tensions between the emperor, the jagirdars/mansabdars, the zamindars, and the *raiyat*s (peasant), they argued that if these groups were maintained in equilibrium, they could establish order and stability.[39] But if they were left uncontrolled, or if the grip on them were loosened, the result could be disorder and instability. In another line of argument, historians like S. Nurul Hasan emphasized the tensions between the state and the rural-based 'gentry', or zamindars, in order to understand the mechanism of the Mughal state, particularly during the period of decline after 1700.[40]

Published in 1959, Satish Chandra's *Parties and Politics at the Mughal Court* was the first serious attempt to understand the decline of the Mughal empire by studying its structural flaws. He argued that the stability of the empire as a centralized state had depended on the efficient working of the ranking (*mansab*) and jagirdari systems. But these institutions failed to function effectively by the reign of Aurangzeb, whose political problems were accompanied by a crisis of the jagirdari system. Although the emperors had evolved a number of administrative devices to facilitate the proper functioning of the *mansabdari* (ranked nobility) system, these practices failed to overcome a basic administrative problem, namely, that the available revenue surplus was insufficient to finance wars of one kind or another, or to fulfill the needs of the ruling class according to its expectations. Further, a rise in the requirements of the ruling class without a corresponding rise in agricultural production —despite evidence of a continual expansion of the cultivated area during the seventeenth century—resulted directly or indirectly in growing economic pressure on the producing class. Thus, symptoms of a crisis in the jagirdari system began to appear already during the latter years of Jahangir's reign. Ranks (*zat* and *sawar*) that in principle corresponded to a jagirdar's required cavalry contingents failed to reflect the total number of horsemen or horses that jagirdars actually maintained. Shahjahan (r. 1628–58) tried to mitigate the crisis by introducing certain reforms. For one, he created a norm that a noble must maintain at least one-third of the number of cavalry indicated by his sawar rank. For another, government support of jagirdars was scaled down proportionately by paying salaries for ten, eight, six, or even four months in the year. Most of the nobles evidently received salaries for only eight or six months. Thus, Chandra argued, appearances were maintained, while the reality was sought to be managed by disbursing the available resources more widely.

And yet, Shahjahan could not resolve the financial crisis, for resources could not keep pace with growing expenses and increasing demands. Consequently, when Aurangzeb reviewed the situation at the end of the thirteenth year of his reign, in 1670, he realized that the empire was in the midst of a revenue-deficit. Accordingly, he urged cuts in expenditures, emphasized simplicity, imposed fresh taxes, and issued advisories to his nobles to extend and improve cultivation. Yet he too failed to solve the financial crisis. As a result, there were inordinate delays in the granting of jagirs, and when they were ultimately granted, they could yield only a fraction of the sanctioned pay. The jagirdars, observed Satish Chandra, failed to realize their full salaries from the jagirs allotted to them, particularly in the areas around Agra, the borders of Rajputana, and parts of the Deccan where agriculture had rarely reached a large surplus. A flight of the peasants from their lands was the first apparent sign of the growing crisis, which later took the form of violence and armed uprisings. The uncertainty of income from the jagirs demoralized the administration. Many mansabdars resisted maintaining the required cavalry contingents or kept a much smaller number than required, whereas others—especially in the lower grades—demanded salaries in cash (*naqd*) instead of jagirs, or farmed out their jagirs to different middlemen. Chandra thus argued that by the end of Aurangzeb's reign the jagirdari system had reached a state of acute crisis heralding a complete breakdown. The problem, he concluded, was at root a systemic one, which no mere cuts in expenditures and administrative devices for expanding cultivation could solve. In fact, a basic improvement in the situation was beyond the competence of any one king.[41]

As he discovered new archival sources, Satish Chandra argued that with the growth of central authority, there developed a system of checks and balances to prevent one group of people from encroaching on the duties of another. As a result, various sections of society, including the cultivators, began to look to the central government rather than to the local government or the zamindars for the redressal of their grievances. This led to a triangular or tripolar relationship between the jagirdars (representing the central government), the zamindars, and the cultivators. This, Chandra argued, was an important factor in stabilizing the Mughal Empire—a marked feature in the first half of the seventeenth century—which could thrive as long as the central government managed to convince zamindars and cultivators that it was more profitable for them to look to the central government for support in resolving their grievances than to resist it. But it was a delicate social balance that could be easily disturbed by a variety of factors, such as the effects of serious struggles for power at the centre, discontentment in the nobility, challenges to the empire by regional chiefs, large-scale local migrations, or conflicts based on caste, religion, or ethnicity. The issue of 'tripolar' relationships was further investigated by Muzaffar Alam, who added a fourth dimension in the form of *madad-i ma'ash* (stipend) holders and a large number of indigenous elements such as Shaikhzadas in Awadh and Khatris in Punjab. As classes who drew on imperial funds, they also contributed to defining the nature of the struggle for control of resources during this period.[42]

A social and economic crisis appeared as early as the first half of the seventeenth century—the so-called period of stability—in the form of a growing gap between the revenue (*jama*) required to support the *mansabdars* (ranked nobles) and available state income (*hasil*). By Shahjahan's reign (1628-58), the situation had become so serious that the emperor had to introduce the rule of one-third/one-fourth and *mahwar* (month-scales), which aimed at reducing the emoluments and the obligations of the mansabdars so as to bridge the gap between their salary requirements and the available revenue. Consequently, by 1655, a mansabdar's cash salary could not be more than eight monthly or less than four monthly. Chandra argues that lowering of the effective share of the nobles in the agricultural surplus reflected a social and economic crisis which the Mughal ruling class attempted to resolve by different administrative means. But even these measures could not resolve the basic problem, i.e., the growing inadequacy of available revenue. The gap between the jama (revenue demand) and the hasil (collected revenue) continued to widen, since the central government was unable or unwilling to make any drastic changes in the existing agrarian relations based on the above-mentioned triad, namely, the state, the *zamindars*, and the cultivators. This was probably because the government depended on the support of the *zamindars* and the dominant landowning castes at the village level. Chandra adds however, that there was no shortage of *paibaqi*, that is, land reserved for assignment as jagirs to the mansabdars. Instead, the problem was a shortage of productive (*sair-hasil*) jagirs, which imperial officers (*mutasadolis*) demanded, leaving the mansabdars to manage less productive jagirs, or those in rebellious areas where collection was difficult because of recalcitrant zamindars. Moreover, although many jagirs were waste land (*viran*) where virtually no revenue could be collected, mutasaddis nonetheless demanded the payment of feed for animals (*khurak-i dawab*) from the jagirdars, and if they resisted, they were imprisoned. Chandra thus argues that the struggle for productive jagirs became 'a matter of life and death' for the mansabdars, and that this struggle gave imperial officers an opportunity to indulge in corrupt practices, including frequent transfers. This had the worst impact on the smaller mansabdars.

So, it was not the shortage of *paibaqi* that affected the descendants of mansabdars (*khanazads*), but rather the delay in granting jagirs to the new entrants, as well as a shortage of productive jagirs. Chandra thus suggests a clear distinction between *be-jagiri* (a lack of jagirs), which affected the new entrants rather than the existing incumbents, and the crisis in the jagirdari system. Central to the growth of the latter, observes Chandra was its non-functionality, that is, its inability to assist in the maintenance of law and order or to collect the central government's share of the land revenue over large parts of the empire. This, in due course, had repercussions on the rest of the empire. The jagirdari system, in his opinion, was a complex phenomenon that was linked to the structure and working of the village society and the Mughal system of administration both at the central and at local levels. As the product of a complex interplay between social and administrative factors, the crisis of the jagirdari system led to a general breakdown in the eighteenth century.[43]

Satish Chandra took another 'fresh look' at the jagirdari crisis in an essay that has been included in this volume. He observes that some recent studies see the jagirdari crisis as merely a financial-cum-administrative crisis, rather than a deep-seated social crisis. In this context he comments on the work of Athar Ali and J. F. Richards, emphasizing the importance of Mughal documents of the Deccan, especially the mass of documents in the Inayat Jung Collection. Even a cursory look at these documents reveals a number of complaints about lack of paibaqi. They also reveal that 'due to *be-jagiri* (lack of jagirs) people were dying everyday'. Chandra argues that the jagirdari crisis, which grew rapidly during the first half of the eighteenth century when the struggle between centripetal and centrifugal forces reached a new phase, must be understood in a larger socio-cultural context. Created in the sixteenth century, the jagirdari system had to sustain a socio-political situation that was undergoing rapid change during the eighteenth century. As long as the system worked, it could keep in check the centrifugal forces represented by the zamindars and allow for administrative centralization. Arguing thus, Satish Chandra holds that his main thesis on the jagirdari crisis still remains valid. As he says, 'the linking of the crisis of the *jagirdari* system with a deepening social crisis and increased factionalism in the ruling class leading to a break-up of central polity still remains at the core of the Mughal crisis of empire'.[44]

In his seminal work *The Agrarian System of Mughal India,* Irfan Habib explained the decline of the Mughal Empire and the political and the social unrest that followed it in fiscal terms. He pointed to the inherent flaws in the Mughal method of collecting *kharaj* (land revenue). On one hand, Mughal policy had set the revenue demand high so as to secure the greatest military strength for the empire; on the other hand, jagirdars were acutely insecure in their assignments since they could be transferred any moment. For that same reason, they squeezed the maximum from their jagirs even if it proved detrimental and ruinous to the peasantry and destroyed the latter's revenue-paying capacity. Following Bernier's suggestion, Habib argued that the frequent transfer of jagirs left no incentive for the jagirdars to pursue 'a far-sighted policy of agricultural development'. In fact, it led to 'a reckless exploitation of the peasantry' and a heavy burden on the peasants, encroaching upon their basic means of livelihood. To escape exploitation and oppression, peasants refused to pay the land revenue and fled the fields, making 'peasant migrations ... a general feature of the agrarian life of our period'. Such tendencies, says Habib, led to an 'agrarian crisis' in the eighteenth century and the ultimate collapse of the empire. The zamindars were yet another class that posed a danger to law and order by refusing to pay the revenue and had to be subjugated by either the *faujdar* (local commandant) or the jagirdar. Their conflict with the imperial authorities was over the size of their share in the land revenue, that is, the surplus produce. The peasants and the zamindars frequently collaborated in the struggle against the Mughal government, although Habib notes that the zamindars' leadership was not uniformly established over all peasant uprisings; nor did peasants support all rebellious actions taken by zamindars. Nonetheless, the two most successful anti-Mughal revolts – those of the Marathas and the Jats—were led by men who aspired to be zamindars. Habib first raised these issues in 'The Agrarian Causes of the Fall of the Mughal Empire',[45] a two-part article that has been reproduced in this volume. Like most systems of oppression, argues Habib, the Mughal Empire became its own grave-digger. The forces pitted against it were so constituted that the state failed to provide an alternative or a new order. To the contrary, these forces dissolved India's administrative unity that the 'fallen' empire had represented, 'devastated the towns, throttled trade and commerce and thus created ideal conditions for foreign conquest'.[46]

Habib's arguments are derived from a wide use of Persian sources and reflect a Marxist perspective, yet they betray the influence of Bernier and of W. H. Moreland's model. What Moreland presented as Oriental Despotism, Habib categorized as class-based exploitation. He argued that the entire commercial structure of the Mughal Indian economy was largely parasitical, relying upon a system of direct agrarian exploitation by a small ruling class. He also argued that practically no rural market existed for urban crafts, and that rural monetization resulted almost entirely from the need to transfer surplus agricultural produce to the towns. Thus, asserting that the main external charge on the peasants was the state's revenue demand, Habib agrees with Moreland that 'next to the weather, the administration was the dominant fact in the economic life of the country'.[47] So, concludes Habib, when an agrarian crisis developed, it was bound to extend to the entire structure of the Indian economy. The empire's restricted capitalistic development became apparent in the eighteenth century, when merchant capital was denied a large market. The empire was thus left with no choice but to atrophy. With these developments, any features that may have appeared capitalistic during the heyday of the Mughal Empire receded into the background.[48]

Athar Ali accepted Habib's model of a fiscally centralized state, although he attributed the decline not to an exorbitant land revenue demand but to the shortage of jagirs. He observed that the jagirdari system had worked with tolerable efficiency till the middle of Aurangzeb's reign, but that because of the increasing pressure of the Deccan wars on the empire's financial resources, and the dislocation of the administration caused by the absence of the emperor and his court from northern India, the complicated mechanism for the assignment of jagirs lost its efficiency. Athar Ali argues that Aurangzeb's last years 'saw the first stage of the disorganization; but it was the beginning of the end'. The crisis was felt in the form of insufficient jagirs. Quoting the contemporary historian Mamuri, Athar Ali says, 'A world became *jagirless* and there was no *paibaqi* left', meaning that there were no areas left for assigning jagirs.[49] Compelled by the scarcity of paibaqi, the emperor resumed the jagirs of some nobles so that he could give them to others. This situation was caused by the influx of Deccani nobles to whom Aurangzeb had granted mansabs on a large scale in order to attract them to the Mughal camp. But the scarcity of paibaqi lands adversely affected the working of the jagirdari system and made it difficult for the new mansabdars to get jagirs. According to Athar Ali, they had to wait for four to five years since the orders for transfers of jagirs were not duly respected. As a result, resentment and growing factionalism amongst the nobility continued to fester till the very end of Aurangzeb's reign. Although the jagirdar might not have had rebellious intentions, he understood that if he relinquished his jagir, another jagir might never be assigned to him, and 'once this happened, all was over not only with the *jagirdari* system, but with the Mughal Empire'.[50]

For almost fifteen years, until a 1975 symposium on Mughal decline, formulations based on the interpretations of Satish Chandra, Irfan

Habib, and Athar Ali had held centre stage. But at that symposium Michael N. Pearson, John F. Richards, and Peter Hardy proposed alternative understandings for the decline. According to Hardy, when the works of Chandra, Habib, and Athar Ali are read together, the analyses of the growing weakness of the empire were 'almost Newtonian in their force and simplicity'. From the works of these three Aligarh historians it is possible to draw 'a diagram of tensions' between the emperor, the mansabdars/jagirdars, the zamindars, and the cultivators. If the elements of this diagram were upheld in a balanced manner, order and stability would exist across the empire, but if allowed to pull free, they would create disorder.[51] Lavish assignments combined with the military successes of the Marathas created a shortage of *paibaqi*, or land available for assignment to nobles. Consequently, the resources to support the military contingents became inadequate, and the number and effectiveness of the Mughal forces fell, rendering the Mughal military machine increasingly unable to control the military and the rural aristocracy (the zamindars).[52]

Criticizing this argument, Hardy proposed a greater attempt at reintegrating ideological with economic and institutional considerations, but not in the old simplistic terms of citing Aurangzeb's bigotry and his deliberate undoing of 'the beginnings of such a national and rational policy which Akbar had set on foot', as Jadunath Sarkar had argued.[53] Both Michael Pearson in 'Shivaji and the Decline of the Mughal Empire' and John Richards in 'The Imperial Crisis in Deccan' (both included in this volume) raised questions concerning ideology. And, while accepting the 'diagram of tensions' sketched by the Aligarh historians, they proposed modifications to the direction and reading of those tensions. They also felt that important modifications were required in the time-scale to explain imperial decline.

In his article, John Richards re-examines the reasons for the declining imperial authority in the Deccan during the two decades following the conquests of Bijapur and Golconda in 1686 and 1687 respectively. Based on Mughal archival sources and his exhaustive research on Mughal rule in Golconda between 1687 and 1724, Richards offers an alternative explanation for the failure of the Mughal Empire in Deccan. He accepts Satish Chandra and Athar Ali's argument about the 'economic squeeze' following the conquests of Bijapur, Golconda, and the Maratha kingdom by Aurangzeb between 1686 and 1689; and that the shortage of paibaqi contributed to factional conflict within the nobility. But he argues that certain assumptions that underlie this explanation are not plausible since they imply a sense of inevitability and an irreversible sequence of events, namely, that as soon as the Deccan was conquered and the Deccani nobles were absorbed as mansabdars, the jagir shortage inevitably led to the crisis. And while he agrees with Satish Chandra and Athar Ali that the Mughal noble was deeply attached to his economic and monetary status and that the strength of the empire depended on efficient and loyal nobles, he argues that the imperial system depended on various other groups whose loyalty was equally important. Based on evidence from the Deccan, Richards notes that despite the sudden increase in the number of Mughal nobles, the empire need not have collapsed for the shortage of funds. The problem was the emperor's failure to secure his southern frontiers and to exploit the considerable resources of Bijapur and Golconda that could have covered his additional expenditures. Moreover, in his eagerness to expand, Aurangzeb attacked such areas in the Deccan that had remained protected from outside invasions. Consequently, the emperor could neither assimilate the Maratha, Bedar, Gond, or Telugu warrior chiefs into the imperial elite nor establish political ties with them as tributary chiefs or zamindars. Too, a lack of protection and security from the Mughal government demoralized mansabdars in the Deccan, who virtually refused to obey imperial *farmans* after 1700. By 1711–12 zamindars there had resorted to open revolt.

Thus Richards argues against the shortage of jagirs as a prime motor of decline, and instead holds Aurangzeb's strategic objectives responsible for the disorder in the Deccan. The shortage of jagirs in the 1690s was not a condition caused by a shortage of territory. Rather, it was a partly 'artificial' condition caused by the emperor's decision to put potentially revenue-yielding lands under *khalisa* – that is, lands whose revenues went straight to the central treasury and not to jagirdars—while the least promising areas were placed in paibaqi. Richards estimates that if the emperor had allocated and utilized the jagirs discreetly, the annexation of Bijapur and Golcunda could have enhanced the annual imperial revenues by at least 23 per cent. Hyderabad could also have generated increased annual revenues, since its districts showed an increase in annual revenue by 26 per cent, though only in the khalisa areas. Yet the emperor continued to transfer paibaqi districts to khalisa, instead of granting jagirs from khalisa.[54]

In his article 'Shivaji and the Decline of the Mughal Empire', M. N. Pearson finds substance in Athar Ali's argument about insufficient jagirs (be-jagiri) but disagrees with Athar Ali's calculation of the rate of increase in Aurangzeb's nobility, and also with his division of Aurangzeb's reign into periods of unequal length. Yet Pearson acknowledges that even when Athar Ali's calculations are corrected, there still remains a large increase in the number of nobles in the late seventeenth century. In his view, trouble for the empire began in the last few years of Aurangzeb's rule, and its root cause lay in the emperor's move towards the south, a move that itself revealed a central weakness in the empire. Being a final desperate attempt to crush a formidable Maratha enemy that had inflicted humiliating defeats on the empire, 'the move was not expansionist, it was entirely defensive, a product of desperation, not of free Mughal choice'. Even though they were stationed in the Deccan, the Mughals failed to defeat the Marathas. It was these protracted wars that produced the signs of decline, namely, an imbalance between the number of jagirdars and the jagirs available, peasant revolts, and disloyal nobility.

Pearson asks: if these were the circumstances that the move towards the south produced, why was it undertaken at all? His answer lies in the composition of the Mughal nobility, the nature of the nobles' relationship to the empire, and the impact that Maratha successes up to 1666 had on them. To explain his point, Pearson makes several assumptions about the nature of the Mughal state and its nobility. He argues that Mughal rule was 'very indirect' and that the subject population was divided by language, kin, caste, occupation, locality, religion, and so on. The core of the empire, argues Pearson, was composed of only a small number of men, that is, the mansabdars, who were bound to the emperor by direct patronage ties and were the only ones in whom the concept of the Mughal Empire 'outweighed other primordial attachments'. The continuance of this patronage depended neither on religion nor on race, but on military success; the nobles followed the emperor as a person and 'this person had to be a winner'. In such a system, the only way an individual could be made loyal to the emperor was by integrating him into the mansabdari system. As a result, only the mansabdars were loyal to the empire, while all other subjects were loyal to the social groups to which they belonged, and not to the empire or the emperor. Pearson then examines the impact of the Mughals' failure to defeat the Marathas. Aurangzeb and his nobility felt compelled to respond to the military challenges of Shivaji (r. 1674–80), whose rejection of his own mansabdar status, his escape from Mughal custody, his attack on Shaista Khan, and his sack of the key Mughal port of Surat had all made the 'tragedy' of Aurangzeb inevitable. In effect, the emperor had mobilized his entire army to pursue a personal vendetta against the successors of a single, demonized Maratha chieftain. So for Pearson, the fundamental problem was the Mughals' failure to evolve a more impersonal political system.[55]

Commenting on the articles of Pearson and Richards, Peter Hardy insisted on the importance of the study of military technology and the military ethos to explain Mughal decline. It might help, he says, to explain the working of one of the 'real' options available to the emperors ('real' because Akbar had adopted it for some time)—namely, the option of paying most salaries in cash (*naqd*) by extending the area of khalisa land rather than that of jagirs. Or, Hardy asks, in view of the ethos of the nobility, was it more prestigious to be paid by jagir than in cash? Noting the growing factionalism amongst the nobles during the last years of Aurangzeb's reign (as documented by Satish Chandra and Athar Ali), Hardy suggests that we explore how important the mansabdars were in formulating policies by the various princely contenders for the throne, and whether the rank and size of the sanctioned contingents of mansabdars were proportionate to their political influence. He further asks, if Mamuri and Khafi Khan were aggrieved by the khanazads losing out to the new appointees from the Deccan in the allocation of jagirs, were those writers referring to the allocation of jagirs in Deccan alone, or did these also include jagirs in Hindustan (north India)? Hardy also suggested that the military history of the period should be evaluated to confirm whether the deficiency in numbers of cavalry contingents against the Marathas was of decisive importance. Also, was it possible that lightly armed cavalry would have been of greater value against the Marathas, as opposed to the traditional Mughal heavy cavalry? Was the preference for the use of heavy cavalry attributable to social, rather than to military conservatism—'to a feeling that service in the Mughal dragoons was the only fit form of military service for a gentlemen'? And if the Maratha light cavalry posed the main tactical threat to the Mughal armies, what steps were taken to resist it? What was the state of musket technology in Mughal India? While a historian of military technology might provide a better understanding of these matters (many of them have since the time Hardy wrote), a gerontologist, added Hardy, may give new insights into the behaviour of Aurangzeb, who was in extremely old age when the empire witnessed its decline.[56]

Hardy also disagreed with Pearson's proposition that the empire declined because it failed to evolve a more impersonal structure. Muzaffar Alam also noted that, while the personal achievements and failures of the emperors certainly affected the nobles (*umara*), one cannot, on the basis of the contemporary evidence, accept Pearson's suggestion that the absence of an impersonalized Mughal bureaucracy was the source of all failure. Not only the small group of nobles but also the zamindars, the village and *qasba*-based madad-i ma'ash holders, and a very large number of lower-level officials from different regional and local communities were integrated intimately into the framework of the empire. It was on balancing these diverse interests that the stability of the empire rested. Alam concedes that the imperial system could not override the landholders' primary attachments to local groups, particularly those of kin, clan, and caste; yet the empire required a coordinating agency between conflicting communities and indigenous socio-political systems at different levels. In a way, he argues, the empire's strength lay in the inability of local communities to mobilize beyond certain narrow limits. Political integration, therefore, remained inherently defective. It was conditional and rested on the coordination of the interests and political activities of different social groups. Having no hereditary lands that they could consolidate or bequeath, and with their resources under the surveillance of the government, the nobles depended on the emperor for their position and power. In fact, they were mere salaried officials who represented the emperor at various levels. Yet the nobility nurtured tensions. The principle of transfer of jagirs prevented them from building a personal base, although it strengthened the imperial organization. The nobles resisted the implementation of this principle, which in many cases remained unenforced in the seventeenth century, giving rise to more permanent estates (*jagir-i mahal-i watan*). These long-term jagir holdings, Alam states, further strengthened the nobility.[57]

ROLE OF BANKERS AND MERCHANTS

Some scholars have considered the social basis of the fiscal system and the role of bankers and merchants during the eighteenth century as the reason for the decline. In her essay 'The "Great Firm" Theory of the Decline of the Mughal Empire', Karen Leonard observes that while scholars have proposed many theories for the decline of the Mughal Empire, they have neglected the bankers—*sahukars*, *shroffs*, and *mahajans*—particularly those in the 'great firms', who played critical roles in the Mughal political system. The reason for this neglect, she states, perhaps lies in the nature of the sources. Moreover, many who wrote about the bankers and merchants in Mughal India did so from a Marxist perspective and turned the 'data into a fairly rigid framework'. Most writers described the bankers and other financial and merchant groups in India as 'segmental' rather than 'strategic' elites, who stood outside the governing structures and played no political role in decisions that affected society. They were analysed as 'hinge' groups, 'largely autonomous and apolitical' and 'passive and parasitic beneficiaries of the conditions established by a strong imperial government'. Leonard, however, analysing the organization and volume of economic activities of great indigenous banking firms and their participation in politics during the Mughal and early British period, suggests that these firms played a significant role in the decline of the empire. She uses the term 'great firm' to describe a business firm engaged in a variety of enterprises, with several branches, often based on one 'household'. The banking firms, she argues, were crucial to the financial functioning of both the central government and individual mansabdars, jagirdars, zamindars, and *talukdars*, all of whom directly depended upon them. When the 'great firms', being 'indispensable allies' of the Mughal state, began diverting both credit and trade from Mughal authorities to regional powers, the empire began to unravel. Between 1650 and 1750, argues Leonard, the banking firms' growing engagement in revenue collection at regional and local levels surpassed their provision of credit to the central government. As a result, the empire's central structure suffered even while many banking firms and merchants witnessed expansion and diversification.[58]

Through her emphasis on the role of the 'great firms', Leonard extended the observations of Philip Calkins and M. N. Pearson, who studied the political roles of merchants in Bengal and Gujarat respectively.[59] However, neither Calkins nor Pearson suggested that the Mughal financial system depended on the merchants' credit, or that the stability of the empire was derived from merchant participation. Critical of Leonard's exaggerated emphasis on the role of bankers, Alam, too, doubts the extent of merchants' political participation, since contemporary Persian sources, despite occasional references to Khatris as 'nobles' (umara) and 'notables' (a'yan), provide little information about the 'conventionally non-political urban groups'. He does, however, acknowledge that *sahukars* (big merchants) and some artisans had supported the Mughals against the Sikhs in the early eighteenth century, suggesting that the trading community was engaged in active political participation in some parts of Mughal India. Too, the interests of the merchants were possibly connected to the prosperity and stability of the ruling class and the markets that they fostered. Similarly, they may have shown a keen interest in politics when they felt threatened by the impending imperial decline.[60]

Responding to Karen Leonard's rather provocative essay, John F. Richards dismissed her hypothesis as lacking in documentation and as an implausible argument to explain the 'puzzling aspects' of Mughal decline. He acknowledged that various private banking firms contributed significantly to the restructuring of the imperial system by rulers of regional successor states in the eighteenth century, and that these firms grew in power and importance owing to their ties with European trading companies. But he insists that no available evidence indicates that these 'great firms' played a similar role for the Mughal imperial system in the sixteenth and the seventeenth centuries. He further argues that the Mughal system, constrained by its centralized power, perhaps could not adapt to the rapidly changing socio-economic circumstances of the early eighteenth century, some of which were produced by the successes of the imperial system as it expanded. In this context, Richards cites the case of Hiranand Sahu and his son Manikchand, of the prosperous house of Jagat Seth. Yet, he says, no evidence points to the type of banking enterprise, its scope, or its possible connection with the Mughals and the British East India Company. It was only with Bengal's transition to a regional polity that the banking house of Manik Chand could flourish in a way not possible under the 'centralized imperial administration' of the seventeenth century. Nor is there evidence that the withdrawal of this firm's indispensable services might have contributed to Mughal decline. At best, private banking firms such as this one contributed to imperial decline only indirectly—by providing essential financial services to new regional rulers of the early decades of the eighteenth century. Richards adds that in the seventeenth century there may have been occasional cases of merchants with enormous wealth, but even the wealthiest of these men were not direct participants in the imperial system, much less 'indispensable allies of the Mughal state'. Their services were limited and dispensable. Private bankers or moneychangers did not control or manage imperial treasuries and mints. Nor did private entrepreneurs collect imperial revenues. Rather, in large commercial centres Mughal emperors imposed limits on indigenous markets by formally sanctioning traders or headmen for each specialized market and by recruiting an officer from the local commercial community to collect urban taxes, alongside imperial officials.[61]

Sanjay Subrahmanyam and C. A. Bayly, however, disagree with Richards's proposition of 'centralization through state power', which implies that the fiscal integration under Aurangzeb was mediated by the Mughal treasury and the great households rather than by bankers. They also note that Richards assumes the existence of a huge inter-regional commodity and agro-based trade that balanced the flows of treasure, of which the provinces were deprived. But if such were the case, they argue, there must have been merchants who controlled the trade. Where, then, were such merchants, they ask, and how did they finance their trade? Moreover, if it is assumed that the change came early in the eighteenth century, where did great merchant corporations with vast resources, influence, and well-developed culture of book-keeping and subcontinental credit come from?

Probing such questions, Subrahmanyam and Bayly discuss the important role in the Mughal system played by 'portfolio capitalists', or merchants 'able to straddle the worlds of commerce and political participation'. These large-scale entrepreneurs utilized not only their own capital but also that of small-scale operators, who served as conduits for indirect investment. In northern India, great merchant families emerged and became important over the first half of the eighteenth century. For instance, the enterprise established by the Marwari merchants Manikchand and Fatehchand in Bengal, later called the house of Jagat Seth, was the most conspicuous among a series of significant networks of

Gujaratis, Multanis, and Agarwals. These networks had evidently been developing over generations. Apart from these were the Benares Agarwals and the Kashmiri Mul. The period also coincided with the dominance of Gujarati merchants in Bengal's external trade, once the mansabdars withdrew. Evidence from Benares and Bengal also reveals the deep involvement of merchant capital in the conduct of revenue farms and other enterprises controlled by larger portfolio capitalists and the state. Belonging to the military and administrative set-up, portfolio capitalists of the early eighteenth century were generally Muslims or Kayasthas who were willing to perform functions that the great merchant families were either unable or unwilling to perform. Unlike the great merchants, these men had access to, and control over the military labour market; hence, they could comfortably engage in political matters without relenting on their credit. Noting that such men 'commanded the state in matters of revenue', Subrahmanyam and Bayly argue that perhaps such great houses were already firmly placed in the administration of the jagirs of the mansabdars even before the beginning of the eighteenth century, and that the disintegration of the Mughal system in early eighteenth century served further to consolidate their power. This would suggest that merchant capital and 'portfolio capitalists' had begun to intervene in agricultural production and to control labour and trade, a process that marked the emergence of many 'new' zamindars of the eighteenth century. In this way, merchant capital made a significant contribution to state and military finance, which subsequently facilitated the rise of the English East India Company.[62]

OTHER TRENDS—CULTURAL AND SCIENTIFIC

In his article 'The Passing of the Empire: The Mughal Case', Athar Ali has questioned discussions of Mughal decline that do not consider wider historical contexts. He argues that the first part of the eighteenth century witnessed the decline of not only the Mughal Empire, but also the Safavid Empire, the Uzbek Khanate, and the Ottoman Empire. Moreover, this was no coincidence, but a combination of miscellaneous factors (perhaps common to these empires) that led them all to their disintegration. Their decline may have preceded the military impact of colonial powers like Britain and Russia, but the emergence of Europe as the centre of world commerce between 1500–1700, its domination of the New World, and its monopoly of commerce passing the Cape of Good Hope, subverted states and societies of Asia even before its military coercion was felt. While Europe became a major market for Asian luxury manufactures and high-value products, Iran lost its position as the principal market for Indian commodities, and India and Iran together could no longer sustain their hold over Chinese exports. Such developments, Athar Ali observes, severely disturbed the economies of Asian states, causing a decline that was 'not only relative; it could not but be absolute as well'. The financial difficulties of the ruling classes intensified with the rise in the costs of luxury items. As the income of ruling elites became increasingly inadequate, they indulged in agrarian exploitation. When this failed or proved counter-productive, they resorted to factionalism to achieve personal advantages, resulting in endless civil wars.

These activities, says Athar Ali, sounded the death knell of the great Asian empires. Moreover, even as there was a spurt of urban growth in Europe, facilitated by its new science and technology, the pace of such developments in Asia was slow and limited. Mughal India, for instance, made no attempt to design new artillery weapons; the manufacture of guns and muskets remained a mere craft that displayed no evidence of the influence of new science and technology. Consequently, by 1700 it remained outdated. He also notes the Mughals' intellectual and technological aridity, which prevented towns and cities from becoming the 'safety-valves' that could grapple with the agrarian crises. As a result, Mughal cities remained 'parasitical' and dependent on expropriating an agrarian surplus, while the empire as a whole, despite its professional army, faced incessant resistance from zamindars and peasants. Athar Ali thus argues that the failure of the Mughal Empire was derived from a 'cultural' failure, which it shared with other Asian states. This failure tilted the economic balance in favour of Europe and deprived those states of the ability to deal with their agrarian crises. These economic effects contributed to political and military disasters, while an 'intellectual stagnation' gripped the entire Asian world.[63]

Rejecting Athar Ali's suggestion of the intellectual and technical barrenness of the Mughal elites, I. G. Khan drew attention to the technical life of the average Mughal mansabdar. He argued that the Mughal emperors encouraged nobles to become technocrats, as is evident from the chapters in the *Ain-i Akbari* concerning metal purification, alloying, canon casting, handgun boring devices, and geared wagons that ground grain as they moved. The *Ain-i Akbari* also describes the new syllabus, introduced in the 1580s, for school-going boys. Comprising subjects that were usually taught, like logic, prosody, disputation, and recitation of the Qur'an, the syllabus also featured disciplines such as agriculture, land measurement, medicine, mathematics, algebra, and household management, which included a variety of managerial and pragmatic skills. Such a syllabus, writes Khan, provided a foundational basis for the careers of nobles who joined the Mughal bureaucracy as military, civil, and revenue officials. In this context, he cited the emotional outburst that Aurangzeb, in 1661, directed at his teacher Mulla Saleh. It seems that the newly crowned emperor was discontented at being trained in a specialized theological-scholastic syllabus. On the other hand, he expressed satisfaction when the technical and reason-based (*falsafi*) syllabus for elite education was revised and strengthened by the *Dars-i Nizamiyya* of Mulla Nizamuddin Sahalvi at Lucknow's Firangi Mahal.

Elite youth in the Mughal Empire thus had access to more technical roles than was evident in their *madrasa* syllabi. This, argues Khan, indicates that within the Mughal system there were opportunities, avenues, and resources for technical intervention and even innovation.[64] Complementing the argument of Khan, and critical of Athar Ali, Richard Barnett observes that, just as in the 'high Mughal period', the courtiers of Muhammad Shah 'Rangila' (r. 1719–48) and of other regional courts were interested in disciplines of technology like metallurgy, chemistry, agrarian management, cost-accounting, mathematics, astronomy, craft-related sciences and hydrology—if not science. Therefore, characterizing the eighteenth century as a 'cultural failure of the Islamic World' amounts not only to 'prefiguring modernity' and judging historical societies by contemporary standards, but also to legitimizing the British opinion on pre-colonial history: 'after all, they had to have some "improving" ideology to justify their colonial exploitation'. He thus warns against the Whig interpretation of history.[65]

Marshall G. S. Hodgson conceded that while one can speak of the cultural and social stalemate in the Islamic empires during the eighteenth century, the argument that there was a decline of Islamic culture cannot be accepted in absolute terms. He urged the need to understand the evolution of that culture in a larger, world historical context, in which all the Islamic empires were confronted with 'modernity' between 1600 and 1800. Europe's commercial expansion and its search for new markets, its introduction of new military and economic systems, and its innovations in science and technology ultimately affected the internal workings of Asian societies and state systems.[66]

Regarding the crises in the Mughal, Safavid, and the Ottoman empires, Christopher Bayly completely rejects arguments of cultural stagnation, military decline, and elite debauchery. Instead, he attributes these crises to a variety of internal political factors. He argues that the peace and stability that imperial authorities in these states had provided contributed to a deepening of commercial networks, an expansion of urbanization, and a dominance of landed classes. These developments, however, generated a new economic and social order that later weakened the empires and ultimately 'wasted and muscled out the previous institutions and accoutrements of rule'. According to Bayly, a combination of 'accommodating indigenous capitalism' and fiscal weakness unsettled these centralized bureaucracies. As this happened, new commercial and landed classes merged into vibrant regional and provincial formations.[67]

The Ottoman state enjoyed a span twice as long as the Mughals (1526–1857) and three times that of the Safavids (1501–1720). Like the latter two, the Ottoman Empire was both an early modern state and a relic of the medieval past. Yet it also survived into the twentieth century; as Alam and Subrahmanyam note, the Ottomans seemed to move in 'slow motion' as compared to the other dynasties and states. The phase of Ottoman consolidation continued for over a century, while 'Ottoman decline' in conventional historiography began with the Battle of Lepanto (1572) and continued for another three centuries as the 'sick man of Europe', 'enviously eyeing its healthier neighbours to the west'.[68] This contrasts with the quick *coup de grace* of the Safavids or the 150-year-long Mughal 'twilight'. Alam and Subrahmanyam therefore suggest a comparison between the eighteenth and nineteenth century transitions in the Ottoman Empire and the processes of 'regional centralization' in the late Mughal period.

John Richards, on the other hand, argues that the 'general crisis' that is said to have occurred in Western Europe, the Ottoman Empire, China and Japan in the first half of the seventeenth century was not apparent in India at any point in the seventeenth century. At that time, all of these regions except India witnessed political instability, war, population decline, urban stagnation, economic crises, falling prices, depleted stocks of precious metals, and climate changes. Most of the Indian subcontinent, by contrast, experienced peace and order in this period: Mughal sovereign territory continued to expand, resources continued to flow to the state, and imperial culture continued to diffuse throughout South Asia. By the mid-seventeenth century no Indian ruler (except at Mysore) could assert autonomous power or complete independence from the Mughal emperor. At the same time, India saw a period of moderate but steady population growth and rising productivity[69]. Nonetheless, some European historians have cited a seventeenth century 'general crisis' in which agricultural, demographic, climatic, economic, military, and political factors were all inter-related. Some explained it as the crisis of the transition to capitalism; for others it was that of the absolutist state, and for yet others it stemmed from climatic and environmental factors.[70]

Contrary to this, according to Richards it was not until the early eighteenth century that India experienced the sort of political crises, warfare, disease, and economic disruption that accompanied Mughal imperial decline. In the last two or three decades of Aurangzeb's reign, imperial treasuries were presumably depleted when the emperor was engaged in his 'draining wars' against the Marathas in the Deccan. In actuality, argues Richards, the imperial treasuries were well stocked at this time, as is evident from the appropriations that took place during the war of succession in 1707–09. When Prince Muazzam (later Bahadur Shah) captured Agra, his officials found 240 million rupees in coined and un-coined gold and silver, a sum considerably greater than the reserves of specie at Akbar's death. Richards admits that by the early 1700s, just prior to Aurangzeb's death, several Mughal nobles were struck by impoverishment in the absence of potential jagirs. Nevertheless, he says, recovery was possible. Had Bahadur Shah lived longer, had the empire not been subjected to two wars of succession in 1712–13, and had Farrukhsiyar (1713–19) succeeded in controlling his king-makers—the Sayyid brothers—revenues would likely have resumed their inward flow. Instead, all the reserves of the empire were squandered in Farrukhsiyar's rebellion. The six-year hiatus spent in political struggle that ended with his execution allowed the Marathas to consolidate their power over large parts of the Deccan. Between 1711 and 1719, power rapidly drained from the centre to the empire's constituent regional units, such that by the time of the emperor Muhammad Shah

(r. 1719-48) and his successors, the emperor no longer remained the sole arbiter and dispenser of legitimate authority. If not symbolically, at least effectively, the empire was no longer the centralized polity it had earlier been, and by the mid-eighteenth century one can already see the process of political reconstruction that followed the empire's dissolution. Mughal India thus continued to decline and to display the symptoms of a 'general crisis' that had been noticed during the Deccan famines of 1703–4. So, Richards contends, the Mughals' eighteenth century crisis was the product of new forces and new connections to which the Indian subcontinent had been subjected.[71]

An interesting perspective on this matter has been added by Rosalind O'Hanlon, who provides a gendered dimension to the disintegration of Mughal service morale after the late seventeenth century. Examining gender identity and norms of manhood in Mughal political and religious discourses, O'Hanlon argues that a concern with the meanings of ideal manhood cut through these discourses and through medieval Perso-Islamic political culture generally, serving to connect kingship, norms for statecraft, and imperial service. These links had already existed in the moral thought and political theory of the Delhi Sultanate. But from the late sixteenth century on, gendered idioms of kingship were developed in new ways. Akbar and his courtiers attempted to strengthen the associations between imperial service and ideal manhood, making these a more public and explicit part of court culture. Bodily and sexual codes for imperial servants were reworked to emphasize the possibilities for moral and human perfection in the 'homologous worlds' that men occupied as governors—namely, the worlds of kingdom, household, and body. These eclectic norms for ideal manhood were expected to cut across all differences of law, religion, caste, and region, with the imperial service being the best and perhaps the sole way for its realization. This Mughal strategy sought to create a new model of north Indian patriarchal and heterosexual male virtue that differed from that of the Iranian-influenced courts of the Deccan.

O'Hanlon argues that Mughal officials negotiated these bodily codes and used wider idioms of sexual difference in their understanding of imperial authority and imperial service. These codes and idioms, she suggests, changed between the early seventeenth century and the first decades of the eighteenth century—a period marked by the high point of Mughal power and its crisis and disintegration. During Aurangzeb's prolonged, twenty-six year absence from the north, while he campaigned in the Deccan, important implications emerged for the wider cultural authority of Mughal imperial service. As existing loyalties and salaries were put under strain, an older ethic of service, obligation, and reward lost much of its meaning, while the older model of the imperial servant as embodiment of ideal manliness fractured. Although some of its fragments became a part of the new and powerful notion of man as 'sophisticated gentleman connoisseur', this did not gel with the ethic of absolute personal subordination to the emperor. To the contrary, the inner dynamic that connected body, moral self, and environment in this thought suggested an overriding concern with the individual and with 'self-cultivation as both ambition and reward'. Such ideas, asserts O'Hanlon, gained prominence in the first half of the eighteenth century as the emperor's personal authority ebbed. The decline of the emperor's power and authority thus 'coincided with the remarkable flowering of a wider and overtly celebratory urban culture of pleasure at the imperial capital'.[72]

REGIONAL ELITES

The above discussion would suggest that the eighteenth century was a gloomy period for the Mughal Empire. However, while the argument for 'cataclysmic change'[73] and imperial disintegration seems apparent at first glance, we should guard against such generalizations or exaggerations. During the first half of the eighteenth century, Delhi was shaken by political turmoil, dissipation of resources, court politics, and factionalism amongst the nobility, as Muhammad Shah and his successors dealt with the Marathas and invasions by Nadir Shah and Ahmad Shah Abdali. Whereas the people of Delhi surely felt 'a sense of being under permanent siege',[74] such feelings were not necessarily shared beyond the capital. Political decentralization at the centre was accompanied by economic reorientation in the regions, each with its own particular political trajectory. Having successfully carved out their own 'autonomous homelands',[75] regional groups left the imperial authorities in Delhi and Agra with a 'mere ceremonial residue of power'.[76] Therefore, one should not project the experiences of Delhi or Agra onto India as a whole in this period.

Indeed, we might ponder whether the Mughal administration had ever performed effectively, even at its prime. We might also question the extent to which Mughal traditions and institutions survived the eighteenth century collapse of imperial power. Here, one may note the observations of Alam and Subrahmanyam on the nature of the Mughal state prior to the eighteenth century. They argue that the empire continuously evolved between 1530 and 1750, and did not achieve its perfection even by 1600. Moreover, its incorporation of new regions entailed accommodation to countless local factors, implying that imperial control over the regions was uneven rather than uniform. The Mughal state, therefore, appeared a 'patchwork quilt' rather than a 'wall-to-wall carpet'.[77] If this was the case, then the emergence of regional states and kingdoms in the eighteenth century was not necessarily a 'political revolution',[78] as has been argued. Regional identities were the 'product of a complex interaction between region and empire',[79] and in this process both were redefined. To Jos Gommans, regional centralization was already 'pre-cooked' in the late seventeenth century process of 'zamindarization'. That is, many of the new regional rulers of the eighteenth century came from zamindar backgrounds that had either suppressed or cooperated with their local gentry in order to resist imperial authorities. Ultimately, the political and military expansion of the East India Company in the late eighteenth and early nineteenth centuries stimulated the processes of zamindarization and regional centralization.[80]

Several scholars writing since the 1980s have been concerned less with Mughal 'decline' as such, and more with understanding an evolutionary pattern of change. Hence, they see more continuity than discontinuity between the Mughal Empire and the regional states, or between the regional states of the eighteenth century and those of early British rule. While they acknowledge the 'immortality' of Mughal achievements, they are not obsessive about the loss of empire. Rather, they value the rise of different social and political formations, which by the 1720s, as Richard Barnett argues, 'emerge as young plants where before grew only the mammoth imperial banyan tree'.[81] The new scholarship on eighteenth and early nineteenth century India has thus provided a realistic understanding of the historical problems of the period, and an impetus for research that is free from 'Eurocentric, dogmatic, prefiguring, Mughal-centric and essentialist viewpoints, and [is] increasingly concerned with actual indigenous Indian pragmatism and realism from the ground up—a heterogeneous vision with multiple discourses and much tolerance of ambiguity'.[82]

In short, the fortune or misfortune of the Mughal Empire cannot be considered the sole determining factor for understanding the historical processes in the eighteenth century. Nor is it possible, in view of newly analysed data, to accept the idea of a pan-Indian decline, or of a stagnant economy that lacked sufficient initiative and potentiality to grow. In fact, the eighteenth century no longer appears as a 'dark valley in the shadow of towering empires'.[83] In this context, one may revisit Frank Perlin's questioning the 'established orthodoxy' that political decentralization in the eighteenth century was synonymous with decline. Instead, political decentralization accompanied 'a broader process of localization in the distribution and organization of power—of its multiplication or complexification'.[84] In other words, the politics of the eighteenth century was more remarkable for its decentralization than for its decline, while its economy and society were buoyant. It was precisely that period's pulsating, throbbing 'tributary commercialism', as David Ludden suggests, that made India look appealing and engaging to the European companies.[85]

The patterns mentioned above are visible in the works of several scholars who have written on eighteenth and nineteenth century South Asia, beginning in the early 1960s with Bernard Cohn's study of the Banaras region.[86] Scholars subsequently extended the inquiry to other regions, including Bengal,[87] Maharashtra,[88] parts of peninsular India,[89] and elsewhere.[90] In his article 'The Formation of a Regionally Oriented Ruling Group in Bengal, 1700–1740', Philip Calkins studied the role of merchants and bankers in the delta's politics, concluding that the decline of Mughal imperial power brought a rather orderly transformation in the political structure of Bengal's provincial system, and not chaos, decadence, or even administrative inefficiency. That system actually grew stronger, not weaker, after the death of Aurangzeb. As the Mughal Empire weakened, political power shifted from the centre to the province. This was accompanied by a shift in the balance of power within the province. The power of imperial mansabdars in Bengal declined since they could no longer depend on the support of the central government. At the same time, a group of larger and stronger zamindars emerged to assume governing responsibilities and entered into partnership with the Mughal Emperor. This coalition, Calkins observes, reached its final form when the larger commercial and financial interests within Bengal began financing the administrative reforms that accompanied these power shifts.[91]

It is thus clear that historians of eighteenth century India have contributed much to our understanding of the period.[92] Whatever their differences, these historians have set aside the notion of a static, stagnant, traditional India during the eighteenth century. Instead, they have highlighted (a) the emergence of secure power bases with their robust agrarian and commercial sectors, (b) the continuing links between merchants and markets, leading to the creation and growth of towns;[93] (c) the East India Company's interaction with the indigenous military labour market[94] and its negotiations with 'native' sepoys to acquire strength and sustenance;[95] (d) the Company's adoption and redefinition of prescribed systems of rule, rank, status, and gender to accommodate its own political purposes;[96] and (e) the significance of Unani medicine as a science[97] or as a cultural process that shaped social change.[98] These developments took place while the central institutions of the Mughal Empire continued to disintegrate, or at least well before the consolidation of the East India Company. In general, these arguments stress the flexibility and adaptability of India's society and economy, revealing this period's relative stability and commercial growth.

Muzaffar Alam also sees economic stability and growth in the regions for the earlier half of the eighteenth century, though this was accompanied by a political crisis as old relationships between the empire's different constituents were politically realigned. The period also witnessed a heightened sense of regional identity, which further propelled political and economic decentralization. Though advantageous to both zamindars and merchants, the flourishing economy engendered conflict among various local groups, as each tried to maximize its profits at the expense of the others. Paradoxically, the 'restabilization' of the regions was achieved almost wholly within the Mughal institutional framework, even while the central government was collapsing. Although by the 1720s the symptoms of political disintegration at the center had become apparent, the regions remained integrated with the center through trade and monetary transactions. Consequently, economic and monetary institutions of the seventeenth century that had contributed to the expanded network of commerce and credit markets survived the collapse of the Mughal Empire and kept the 'erstwhile' empire interconnected even during the eighteenth century's political turmoil. Alam thus argues that despite the shift from the control of peripheries by the centre in the seventeenth century to the control of the centre by the peripheries in the eighteenth century, the 'myth and influence' of Delhi remained unfazed. No region could match, far less replace, Delhi's symbolic power in this period.[99]

Based on his work on seventeenth century Punjab, Chetan Singh wonders whether the Mughal empire was ever centralized. Taking up the Mughal policy of transferring imperial officials periodically so as to prevent them from becoming locally entrenched, Singh argues that even though medieval chronicles imply that the Mughal 'bureaucracy' was prevented from developing a regional power base, this was far from the truth. The appearance of certain names as appointees to various positions in the Punjab suggest that though transfers often occurred, officials either remained within the region or were transferred back frequently. This was considered a way of utilizing the regional experience of these officials, though such appointments may also have been driven by political considerations. In any event, the system of transfers did not prevent officials from building strong regional ties, especially in the case of influential mansabdars. Particularly towards the latter part of the seventeenth century, as imperial supervision was relaxed such patterns led to friction between officials. Furthermore, the hierarchy, designations, and functions of subordinate officials in the local administration did not remain constant throughout the seventeenth century, suggesting the system's flexibility. Such flexibility was also noticed in the creation and functions of local commandants, or *faujdars*, since the reorganization of the *faujdari* was often affected by the personal influence of mansabdars. According to Singh, this regionalization of administrative functionaries indicates that while the Mughal state outwardly appeared highly centralized, regional diversity as is seen in seventeenth century Punjab could hardly have been accommodated within a rigid and centralized 'bureaucratic' structure. In fact, for its very survival, the empire had to incorporate regional landed elites into its administration. Dismissing the notion of a 'high degree of Mughal centralization' as an illusion, Singh argues that developments in eighteenth century Panjab can be traced back to the seventeenth century and to the emergence and long-term survival of regional administrative elites.[100]

Christopher A. Bayly has advanced the notion of a certain unity in north India's political economy from about 1740 to 1830. The political turbulence of the eighteenth century did not herald the dissolution of the Mughal polity or the collapse of its political culture, he argues, but rather the emergence of regional dynastic rulers who pioneered processes of growth and regeneration. 'Indeed', he writes, 'the Mughal Empire did not fall, it was simply swallowed by a larger political organism'. Political decentralization had boosted the growing economic vitality of regional and local powers that gained autonomy between 1735 and 1762. It also encouraged the growth of a rooted service gentry and a homogeneous merchant class that operated around small towns far from the imperial capitals. India's so-called 'Black Century' thus witnessed the redeployment of merchant capital, rather than its destruction. Even though the mid-nineteenth century witnessed a change in state formation and a modification of the corporate institutions of mercantile classes, India's merchants and service gentry continued to flourish well into the nineteenth century and dominated the commercial and political life of the later colonial period.

Bayly also suggests that the disturbed conditions of the eighteenth century contributed to the homogeneity and independence of urban solidarities, which in turn led to the development of both nationalism and religious communalism in the later nineteenth century. The growth of urbanism, mercantile activity, and service people was influenced by external trade that had remained buoyant throughout the eighteenth century and continued to increase after 1780. India's mercantile and urban society also responded to the trends of its peasant economy, which included (a) an expansion of agricultural production in the eastern Ganges valley in the eighteenth century, (b) growth in agricultural yield and commercialization stimulated by cash crop production, (c) incentives to patterns of consumption provided by the market and the political order, and (d) revenue extraction that drew together townsmen and rural bazaars.[101]

Similar arguments have been made by David Ludden, Burton Stein, Nicholas Dirks, David Washbrook, Sanjay Subrahmanyam, Andre Wink, Stewart Gordon, among others. In his essay 'The Slow Conquest:

Administrative Integration of Malwa into the Maratha Empire, 1720–60'
(excerpts from which are reproduced in this anthology), Stewart Gordon
has studied the actual process by which the Mughal province of Malwa
became Maratha. He notes that while many historians have dismissed
the eighteenth century as an 'unsavoury hiatus between the collapse of
the Mughal Empire and the rise of British domination', several issues
emanating within that century command our attention. Among these
is the role of Mughal successor states in developing regional languages
and a regional consciousness, and in promoting economic and social
mobility. In this context, he writes of the conquest of Malwa by the
Marathas, who, as Gordon explains, typified the period and left a 'most
complete administrative record, permitting the broadest questions and
the most detailed answers'. He also studies the continuities and changes
in Malwa after 1738, when a Mughal *sanad* granted the plateau to the
Marathas. The victory of the Marathas, says Gordon, was 'an impressive
show of strength to local *zamindar*s, and contractual tribute relations
promptly began'. By 1745, the Marathas controlled the towns and
roads; their garrison troops walked the ramparts in search of marauders;
their civilian officials conducted surveys, collected revenue, tried cases,
and regulated bazaars, while the *Peshwa* and his *kamavisdar*s committed
themselves to the economic revival of the province that they had once
plundered. While the Maratha administration in Malwa appeared
'suspiciously Mughal'—their legal apparatus, and their rural and urban
police resembled their Mughal counterparts in both terminology
and function—it was also different. Some rural characteristics were
permanently altered, while urban features were changed even more
profoundly. By 1760 Malwa was successfully conquered and integrated
into a Mughal successor state—namely, the Maratha state.

While seeking to identify continuities rather than ruptures in the
transition to colonialism, this vast body of literature also suggests
that the critical changes that Bayly located in the 1830s, the 'age of
reforms', had been anticipated in the eighteenth century itself. That
is, the East India Company continued to borrow from indigenous
structures even as it reinvented and reformulated them to legitimize its
political sovereignty.[102] The impact of the colonial state was felt not in
the mid-eighteenth century but much later in the second quarter of the
nineteenth century. By the mid-nineteenth century, when prices had
shown an upward trend and economic expansion had resumed, it was

evident that India was being governed in ways very different from those of the eighteenth century, and that it was moving in new directions. Such changes might or might not have initiated something that can be called a revolution or the beginning of modernity, but they certainly heralded a break with the continuities that were rife throughout the eighteenth century.[103]

As we try to understand the decline of the Mughal Empire, it may be pertinent to raise questions of the kind that Richard Barnett does: Was there really a systemic civilizational failure, or simply the conclusion to a great era of imperial success? Is it reasonable to presume that such a success could be sustained forever? The responses to these queries also come from Barnett. Dismissing the notion of 'failure', he prefers instead 'an almost inevitable conclusion to a lasting, dazzling civilizational achievement', and emphasizes the need to liberate ourselves from the elite Mughal view of 'imperial segmentation, which was naturally one of lamentation'.[104] It is also necessary to guard against the prejudiced perspective of a 'crisis' following the weakening of the empire. The first half of the eighteenth century was 'unfortunate in that it was sandwiched between the political glory of the Great Mughals and the humiliation of colonial rule'.[105] In their urge to fulfill their vested interests, the British portrayed the period as bleak and sought justification in the works of Persian chroniclers who had also presented the era as one of total chaos and failure.[106] But, warns Alam, these chroniclers were the protégés of nobles who, as beneficiaries of the Mughal state, had suffered much when Mughal provinces resisted central authority and became increasingly autonomous. With their focus riveted on the Mughal throne and the person of the emperor, these chroniclers tended to identify the decline of the imperial structure with the decline and decay of the entire society.[107]

It emerges quite clearly from this discussion that no one factor can explain the decline of the Mughal Empire. However, we must acknowledge the wide range of scholarship that has contributed to new and different perspectives, as compared to earlier formulations on the Mughal Empire. Perhaps the best way to evaluate the fate of the empire is to consider the local and regional ties of Mughal elites, and thereby to focus on the study of regions themselves. For despite the decline of the centre, the Indian economy and polity showed resilience, growth and development. It was neither static nor stagnant, nor in a dilapidated state.

NOTES

1. See Andrea Hintze, *The Mughal Empire and Its Decline: An Interpretation of the Sources of Social Power* (Aldershot: Ashgate, 1997), p. 7.

2. J. N. Sarkar, *Fall of the Mughal Empire, 1739–1754*, Vol. I (New Delhi: Orient Longman Ltd., reprint, 1997, first edition 1932); Irfan Habib, *The Agrarian System of Mughal India, 1556–1707*, second revised edition (New Delhi: Oxford University Press, 1999, first published, Bombay: Asia Publishing House, 1963); also see his 'The 18th Century in Indian Economic History', *Proceedings Indian History Congress*, 56th Session, Calcutta, 1995, pp. 358–78; M. Athar Ali, 'The Passing of Empire: The Mughal Case' and 'Recent Theories of Eighteenth Century India', both in M. Athar Ali, *Mughal India, Studies in Polity, Ideas, Society and Culture*(New Delhi: Oxford University Press, 2006), pp. 337–49, 350–60.

3. Farhat Hasan, 'Forms of Civility and Publicness in Pre-British India', in Rajeev Bhargava and Helmut Reifeld (eds), *Civil Society, Public Sphere and Citizenship: Dialogues and Perceptions* (New Delhi: Sage Publications, 2005), p. 87.

4. Munis D. Faruqui, 'At Empire's End: The Nizam, Hyderabad and Eighteenth Century India', in *Modern Asian Studies*, Vol. 43, No. 1, 2009, p. 7.

5. Meena Bhargava, *State, Society and Ecology: Gorakhpur in Transition, 1750–1830*, Revised Edition (New Delhi: Primus Books, 2014, first published New Delhi: Manohar, 1999), p. xviii.

6. P. J. Marshall (ed.), 'Introduction', in *The Eighteenth Century in Indian History, Evolution or Revolution?*, Oxford in India Readings, Themes in Indian History (New Delhi: Oxford University Press, 2003), p. 1; Rajat Kanta Ray, 'Indian Society and the Establishment of British Supremacy, 1765–1818', in P. J. Marshall (ed.), *The Oxford History of The British Empire*, II, *The Eighteenth Century* (Oxford: Oxford University Press, 1998), p. 508.

7. See Burton Stein, 'Eighteenth Century India: Another View', in Meena Bhargava (ed.), *Exploring Medieval India, Sixteenth to Eighteenth Centuries: Culture, Gender, Regional Patterns*, Vol. II (New Delhi: Orient Blackswan, 2012), p. 337.

8. Sanjay Subrahmanyam, *Explorations in Connected History: From the Tagus to the Ganges* (New Delhi: Oxford University Press, 2005), pp. 2–5.

9. Burton Stein, 'Eighteenth Century India', p. 337.

10. Richard B. Barnett (ed.), 'Introduction', *Rethinking Early Modern India* (New Delhi: Manohar, 2002), p. 22.

11. Burton Stein, 'Eighteenth Century India', p. 339.

12. William Irvine, *Later Mughals, 1719–1739*, Vol. II (Calcutta: M. C. Sarkar & Sons, 1922), pp. 307, 311–12.

13. Ibid., p. 313.

14. Ibid., pp. 309–10.

15. See Rajat Kanta Ray, 'Inventing History, Discovering the Past: A Sketch of Indian Historiography, 1760s to 1990s', *Contemporary India*, Vol. I, No. 2, April–June, 2002, pp. 7–8.

16. J. N. Sarkar, *History of Aurangzib*, Vols I & II (New Delhi: Orient Longman Ltd., 1975, first edition 1912), pp. xi–xiii.

17. J. N. Sarkar, *History of Aurangzib, Northern India, 1658–1681*, Vol. III (New Delhi: Orient Longman Ltd., 1972, first edition 1928), pp. 1–2.

18. J. N. Sarkar, *History of Aurangzib*, Vol. V (New Delhi: Orient Longman Ltd., 1974, second edition 1952), pp. 370–71.

19. Ibid., p. 371.

20. J. N. Sarkar, *Anecdotes of Aurangzeb*, reprint (Calcutta: M.C. Sarkar & Sons, 1988), p. 20, cf. Muzaffar Alam and Sanjay Subrahmanyam ed., *The Mughal State*, 1526–1750, Oxford in India Readings, Themes in Indian History (New Delhi: Oxford University Press, 1998), p. 58.

21. J. N. Sarkar, *History of Aurangzib*, Vol. V, p. 371.

22. J. N. Sarkar, *Fall of the Mughal Empire, 1739–1754*, vol. I (New Delhi: Orient Longman Ltd., reprint, 1997, first edition 1932), p. 2.

23. Muzaffar Alam, *The Crisis of Empire in Mughal North India, Awadh and the Punjab, 1707–48* (New Delhi: Oxford University Press, 1986), p. 2.

24. See, Ishwari Prasad, *The Mughal Empire* (Allahabad: Chugh Publications, 1974); S. R. Sharma, *The Religious Policy of the Mughal Emperors* (New Delhi: Munshiram Manoharlal Publishers, 1988); Jagdish Narayan Sarkar, *A Study of Eighteenth Century India* (Calcutta: Saraswati Library, 1976).

25. Ishwari Prasad, *A Short History of Muslim Rule in India: From the Advent of Islam to the Death of Aurangzeb* (Allahabad: Indian Press Ltd., second edition 1939), pp. 647, 654–56, 686–96, 701, 737.

26. Muzaffar Alam, *The Crisis of Empire in Mughal North India*, p. 3.

27. See, James Mill, *The History of British India*, in H. H. Wilson (ed.), 10 Vols (London: James Madden, 1858); Javed Majeed, *Ungoverned Imaginings: James Mill's The History of British India and Orientalism* (Oxford: Clarendon Press, 1992); Harbans Mukhia, '"Medieval India": An Alien Conceptual Hegemony?', *The Medieval History Journal*, Vol. 1, No. 1, January–June 1998, pp. 91–105; also, Harbans Mukhia, 'Communalism and the Writing of Medieval Indian History—A Reappraisal', in Harbans Mukhia (ed.), *Perspectives on Medieval Indian History* (New Delhi: Vikas Publishing House, 1993); also Harbans Mukhia, *The Mughals of India* (Oxford: Blackwell Publishing, 2004, first Indian reprint, 2005), p. 9; Richard M. Eaton (ed.), *India's Islamic Traditions, 711–1750*, Oxford in India Readings, Themes in Indian History (New Delhi: Oxford University Press, 2003), pp. 9–11; Ronald Inden, *Imagining India* (Oxford: Basil Blackwell, 1990), pp. 45–6.

28. For details, see Romila Thapar, Harbans Mukhia, and Bipan Chandra, *Communalism and the Writing of Indian History* (New Delhi: People's Publishing House, third reprint, 1981); Bipan Chandra, *Communalism in Modern India* (New Delhi: Vikas Publishing House, 1984), pp. 209–36; Romila Thapar, Irfan Habib, and P. S. Gupta, Symposium on 'The Contribution of Indian Historians to the Process of National Integration', *Proceedings Indian History Congress*, 24th session (New Delhi, 1961), pp. 345–61.

29. Muzaffar Alam and Sanjay Subrahmanyam (ed.), *The Mughal State*, p. 12.

30. Tapan Raychaudhuri, 'The State and the Economy: The Mughal Empire', in Tapan Raychaudhuri & Irfan Habib (eds.), *The Cambridge Economic History of India*, vol. I, *c.1200–c. 1750*, New Delhi: Orient Longman (in association with Cambridge University Press), 1984, p. 172.

31. Bernier, 'Letter to Monseigneur Colbert, Concerning Hindustan', in Francois Bernier, *Travels in the Mogul Empire, AD 1656–1668*, tr. Archibald Constable (New Delhi: S. Chand & Co., 1968, first published, London: Oxford University Press, 1891), p. 226.

32. Ibid., p. 227.

33. Ibid., p. 204–05.

34. Sanjay Subrahmanyam, 'The Mughal State—Structure or Process? Reflections on Recent Western Historiography', in *The Indian Economic and Social History Review*, Vol. 29, No. 3, 1992, p. 309.

35. Ibid.

36. W. H. Moreland, *From Akbar to Aurangzeb: A Study in Indian Economic History* (New Delhi: Oriental Books Reprint Corporation, 1972, first published, London: Macmillan & Co., Ltd., 1923), pp. 249–50.

37. Ibid., p. 254.

38. Christopher A. Bayly, 'State and Economy in India over Seven Hundred Years', *The Economic History Review*, Vol. 38, No. 4, November 1985, p. 585.

39. Peter Hardy, 'Commentary and Critique', *Journal of Asian Studies*, Vol. xxxv, No. 2, February 1976, p. 257.

40. S. Nurul Hasan, 'Zamindars under the Mughals', in S. Nurul Hasan (ed. & introduced by Satish Chandra), *Religion, State and Society in Medieval India* (New Delhi: Oxford University Press, 2005), pp. 135–150; also see, Muzaffar Alam and Sanjay Subrahmanyam (ed.), *The Mughal State*, p. 56.

41. See, Satish Chandra, *Parties and Politics at the Mughal Court, 1707–1740* (New Delhi: Oxford University Press, fourth edition, 2002, first published, New Delhi: People's Publishing House, 1959), especially pp. 29–39.

42. Muzaffar Alam, *The Crisis of Empire in Mughal North India*, pp. 110–22.

43. Satish Chandra, 'Review of the Crisis of the *Jagirdari* System', in Satish Chandra, *Medieval India, Society, the Jagirdari Crisis and the Village* (New Delhi: Macmillan India Ltd., 1982), pp. 61–75; also his, *Essays on Medieval Indian History* (New Delhi: Oxford University Press, 2003), pp. 128–142.

44. Satish Chandra, 'The Jagirdari Crisis: A Fresh Look', in Satish Chandra, *State, Society and Culture in Indian History* (New Delhi: Oxford University Press, 2012), pp. 119–128.

45. Irfan Habib, 'The Agrarian Causes of the Fall of the Mughal Empire', Part I & II, *Enquiry*, Nos 2 & 3, September 1959 & April 1960.

46. Irfan Habib, 'The Agrarian Causes of the Fall of the Mughal Empire', Part II, *Enquiry*, No. 3, April 1960, p. 78.

47. Irfan Habib, 'The Eighteenth Century in Indian Economic History', in Seema Alavi (ed.), *The Eighteenth Century in India*, Debates in Indian History and Society (New Delhi: Oxford University Press, 2002), p. 60; also his, 'Potentialities of Capitalistic Development in the Economy of Mughal India', in Irfan Habib, *Essays in Indian History, Towards a Marxist Perception* (New Delhi: Tulika, fourth reprint, 2001), pp. 180–232.

48. Irfan Habib, 'Potentialities of Capitalistic Development in the Economy of Mughal India', pp. 231–32.

49. M. Athar Ali, *The Mughal Nobility under Aurangzeb* (New Delhi: Oxford University Press, new revised edition, 1997), p. 92.

50. Ibid., pp. 93–4.

51. Peter Hardy, 'Commentary and Critique', p. 257.

52. Ibid.

53. Ibid., pp. 259–60.

54. John F. Richards, 'The Imperial Crisis in the Deccan', *Journal of Asian Studies*, Vol. xxxv, No. 2, February 1976, pp. 237–256 (reproduced in this volume).

55. M. N. Pearson, 'Shivaji and the Decline of the Mughal Empire', *Journal of Asian Studies*, Vol. xxxv, No. 2, February 1976, pp. 221–35 (reprinted in this volume).

56. See, Peter Hardy, 'Commentary and Critique', pp. 257–63.

57. Muzaffar Alam, *The Crisis of Empire in Mughal North India*, pp. 5, 13–14.

58. Karen Leonard, 'The 'Great Firm' Theory of the Decline of the Mughal Empire', *Comparative Studies in Society and History*, Vol. 21, No. 2, April 1979, pp. 151–67 (included in this volume).

59. Philip Calkins, 'The Formation of a Regionally Oriented Ruling Group in Bengal, 1700–1748', *Journal of Asian Studies*, Vol. 29, No. 4, August 1970, pp. 799–806 (also reproduced in this volume); M. N. Pearson, *Merchants and*

Rulers in Gujarat (Berkeley: University of California Press, 1976); also his 'Political Participation in Mughal India', *The Indian Economic and Social History Review*, Vol. 9, No. 2, June 1972, pp. 113–31.

60. Muzaffar Alam, *The Crisis of Empire in Mughal North India*, pp. 8–9.

61. See, John F. Richards, 'Mughal State Finance and the Premodern World Economy', *Comparative Studies in Society and History*, Vol. 23, No. 2, 1981, pp. 285–308.

62. Sanjay Subrahmanyam and C. A. Bayly, 'Portfolio Capitalists and the Political Economy of Early Modern India', in Sanjay Subrahmanyam (ed.), *Merchants, Markets and the State in Early Modern India* (New Delhi: Oxford University Press, 1990), pp. 242–65.

63. M. Athar Ali, 'The Passing of the Empire, The Mughal Case', in M. Athar Ali, *Mughal India: Studies in Polity, Ideas, Society and Culture*, pp. 337–349 (reproduced in this volume).

64. See Iqbal Ghani Khan, 'Technology and the Question of Elite Intervention in Eighteenth Century North India', in Richard B. Barnett (ed.), *Rethinking Early Modern India*, pp. 257–288.

65. Richard B. Barnett, 'Introduction', Richard B. Barnett (ed.), *Rethinking Early Modern India*, p. 21.

66. Marshall G. S. Hodgson, *The Venture of Islam: The Gunpowder Empires and Modern Times*, Vol. 3 (Chicago: University of Chicago Press, 1974), pp. 134–222.

67. See Christopher A. Bayly, *Imperial Meridian: The British Empire and the World, 1780–1830*, Studies in Modern History (London & New York: Longman, 1989), pp. 16–73.

68. Muzaffar Alam and Sanjay Subrahmanyam, (eds), *The Mughal State*, pp. 5–12.

69. John F. Richards, 'The Seventeenth-Century Crisis in South Asia', *Modern Asian Studies*, Vol. 24, No. 4, 1990, pp. 625–38.

70. Anthony Reid, 'The Seventeenth-Century Crisis in Southeast Asia', *Modern Asian Studies*, Vol. 24, No. 4, 1990, p. 639.

71. John F. Richards, 'The Seventeenth-Century Crisis in South Asia', pp. 625–38.

72. Rosalind O'Hanlon, 'Manliness and Imperial Service in Mughal North India', *Journal of the Economic and Social History of the Orient*, Vol. 42, No. 1, 1999, pp. 47–93; also see, John F. Richards, 'The Formulation of Imperial Authority under Akbar and Jahangir', in Meena Bhargava (ed.), *Exploring Medieval India, Sixteenth to Eighteenth Centuries—Politics , Economy, Religion*, Vol. I (New Delhi: Orient Blackswan, 2010), pp. 183–224; also his 'Norms of Comportment among Imperial Mughal Officers', in Barbara Daly Metcalf (ed.),

Moral Conduct and Authority: The Place of Adab in South Asian Islam (Berkeley: University of California Press, 1984), pp. 255–89.

73. P. J. Marshall, 'Introduction', in P. J. Marshall (ed.), *The Eighteenth Century in Indian History*, p. 4.

74. Muzaffar Alam and Sanjay Subrahmanyam (ed.), *The Mughal State*, p. 69.

75. Jos Gommans, *Mughal Warfare, Indian Frontiers and High Roads to Empire, 1500–1700*, Warfare and History Series (London & New York: Routledge, Taylor & Francis Group, 2002), p. 203.

76. Ibid.

77. Muzaffar Alam and Sanjay Subrahmanyam (ed.), *The Mughal State*, p. 57.

78. P. J. Marshall, 'Introduction', *The Eighteenth Century in Indian History*, p. 5.

79. Muzaffar Alam and Sanjay Subrahmanyam (ed.), *The Mughal State*, p. 68.

80. Jos Gommans, *Mughal Warfare, Indian Frontiers and High Roads to Empire, 1500–1700*, p. 203.

81. Richard B. Barnett, 'Introduction', *Rethinking Early Modern India*, p. 22.

82. Ibid.

83. Sugata Bose and Ayesha Jalal, *Modern South Asia: History, Culture, Political Economy* (New Delhi: Oxford University Press, 1998), p. 48.

84. Frank Perlin, 'The Problem of the Eighteenth Century', in P. J. Marshall (ed.), *The Eighteenth Century in Indian History*, p. 54.

85. See, David Ludden, 'World Economy and Village India, 1600–1900: Exploring the Agrarian History of Capitalism', in Sugata Bose (ed.), *South Asia and World Capitalism* (New Delhi: Oxford University Press, 1990), pp. 159–77.

86. Bernard Cohn, 'The British in Benares: A Nineteenth Century Colonial Society'; also his 'Political Systems in Eighteenth Century India: The Benares Region', in Bernard Cohn, *An Anthropologist among the Historians and Other Essays* (New Delhi: Oxford University Press, reprint, 1994), pp. 422–62, 483–99.

87. Philip Calkins, 'The Formation of a Regionally Oriented Ruling Group in Bengal'; P. J. Marshall, *Bengal: The British Bridgehead, Eastern India, 1740–1828* (Cambridge: Cambridge University Press, 1987); see also his *East India Fortunes: The British in Bengal in the Eighteenth Century* (Oxford: Oxford University Press, 1976); Neeladri Bhattacharya, 'Colonial State and Agrarian Society', in Burton Stein (ed.), *The Making of Agrarian Policy in British India, 1770–1900* (New Delhi: Oxford University Press, 1986, reprint), pp. 113–

49; Sushil Chaudhury, *From Prosperity to Decline: Eighteenth Century Bengal* (New Delhi: Manohar, 1995); Rajat Datta, *Society, Economy and the Market: Commercialization in Rural Bengal, c. 1760–1800* (New Delhi: Manohar, 2000); Tilottama Mukherjee, 'The Coordinating State and the Economy: The Nizamat in Eighteenth-Century Bengal', *Modern Asian Studies*, Vol. 43, No. 2, 2009, pp. 389–436.

88. Frank Perlin, 'Of White Whale and Countrymen in the Eighteenth Century Maratha Deccan: Extended Class Relations, Rights and the Problem of Rural Autonomy under the Old Regime', *Journal of Peasant Studies*, Vol. 5, No. 2, 1978, pp. 172–237; Andre Wink, *Land and Sovereignty in India: Agrarian Society and Politics under the Eighteenth Century Maratha Svarjya* (Cambridge: Cambridge University Press, 1986); Stewart Gordon, *The Marathas, 1600–1818*, The New Cambridge History of India, Vol. II, No. 4 (Cambridge: Cambridge University Press, 1993).

89. David Ludden, *Peasant History in South India* (New Delhi: Oxford University Press, 1993, second edition); Nicholas Dirks, *The Hollow Crown: Ethnohistory of an Indian Kingdom* (Cambridge: Cambridge University Press, 1987) ; Burton Stein, 'State Formation and Economy Reconsidered', *Modern Asian Studies*, Vol. 19, No. 3, July 1985, pp. 387–413; R. E. Frykenberg, 'Company Circari in the Carnatic c. 1799–1859: The Inner Logic of Political Systems in India', in R. G. Fox (ed.), *Realm and Region in Traditional India* (Durham: Duke University Press, 1977).

90. Muzaffar Alam, 'Eastern India in the Early Eighteenth Century "Crisis": Some Evidence from Bihar', *The Indian Economic and Social History Review*, Vol. 28, No. 1, 1991, pp. 43–71; Dilip Menon, 'Houses by the Sea: State Experimentation in Malabar, 1760–1800', in Neera Chandoke (ed.), *Mapping History: Essays Presented to Ravinder Kumar* (New Delhi: Manohar, 2000), pp. 161–86; Karen Leonard, 'The Hyderabad Political System and its Participants', *Journal of Asian Studies*, Vol. 30, No. 2, May 1971; Kate Brittlebank, *Tipu Sultan's Search for Legitimacy: Islam and Kinship in a Hindu Domain* (New Delhi: Oxford University Press, 1997); Chetan Singh, *Region and Empire: Punjab in the Seventeenth Century* (New Delhi: Oxford University Press, 1991); David Washbrook, 'Progress and Problems: South Asian Economic and Social History, c. 1720–1860', *Modern Asian Studies*, Vol. 22, No. 1, 1988; Tapan Raychaudhury, 'The Mid-eighteenth Century Background', in Dharma Kumar and Meghnad Desai (eds), *The Cambridge Economic History of India*, Vol. II (New Delhi: Orient Longman, 1984), pp. 3–35.

91. Philip Calkins, 'The Formation of a Regionally Oriented Ruling Group in Bengal (reprinted in this volume).

92. Christopher A. Bayly, *Rulers, Townsmen and Bazaars: North Indian Society in the Age of British Expansion, 1770–1870* (New Delhi: Oxford

University Press, 1992); Muzaffar Alam, *The Crisis of Empire in Mughal North India*; Richard B. Barnett, *North India Between Empires: Awadh, the Mughals and the British, 1720–1801* (New Delhi: Manohar, 1987); Michael H. Fisher, *A Clash of Cultures: Awadh, the British, and the Mughals* (New Delhi: Manohar, 1987); P. J. Marshall, 'Economic and Political Expansion: The Case of Oudh, 1765–1804', *Modern Asian Studies*, Vol. 11, No. 4, 1975, pp. 465–82; Meena Bhargava, *State, Society and Ecology: Gorakhpur in Transition, 1750–1830*.

93. Christopher A. Bayly, 'Town-Building in North India, 1780–1830', *Modern Asian Studies*, Vol. 9, No. 3, 1975, pp. 483–503; P. J. Marshall, 'Economic and Political Expansion: The Case of Oudh'.

94. Dirk H. Kolff, *Naukar, Rajput and Sepoy: The Ethnohistory of the Military Labour Market in Hindustan, 1450–1850* (Cambridge: Cambridge University Press, 1990).

95. Seema Alavi, *The Sepoys and the Company: Tradition and Transition in Northern India, 1770–1830* (New Delhi: Oxford University Press, 1995); also see her, 'The Company Army and Rural Society: The Invalid Thanah, 1780–1830', *Modern Asian Studies*, Vol. 27, No. 1, February 1992, pp. 147–78.

96. Radhika Singha, *A Despotism of Law: Crime and Justice in Early Colonial India* (New Delhi: Oxford University Press, 1998).

97. N. Qausar, 'Politics, Culture and Colonialism: Unani's Debate with Doctory', in B. Pati and M. Harrison (eds), *Health, Medicine and Empire: Perspectives on Colonial India* (New Delhi: Orient Longman, 2001).

98. Seema Alavi, 'Medical Culture in Transition: Mughal Gentleman Physician and the Native Doctor in Early Colonial India', *Modern Asian Studies*, Vol. 42, No. 5, 2008, pp. 853–97; also see her, *Islam and Healing: Loss and Recovery of an Indo-Muslim Medical Tradition, 1600–1900* (New Delhi: Permanent Black, 2007).

99. Muzaffar Alam, *The Crisis of Empire in Mughal North India*, excerpts from the 'Introduction' and the 'Conclusion' are reprinted in this volume.

100. See, Chetan Singh, 'The Structure of Administration', in his book *Region and Empire: Panjab in the Seventeenth Century*, pp. 30–56 (reproduced in this volume).

101. Christopher A. Bayly, *Rulers, Townsmen and Bazaars*, excerpts from the chapter 'Prologue: War and Society in Eighteenth-Century India' and the 'Conclusion' are reprinted in this volume.

102. Seema Alavi (ed.), *The Eighteenth Century in India*, Debates in Indian History and Society (New Delhi: Oxford University Press, 2002), pp. 35–6.

103. P.J. Marshall, 'Introduction', in P. J. Marshall (ed.), *The Eighteenth Century in Indian History*, p. 36.

104. Richard B. Barnett, 'Introduction', in Richard B. Barnett (ed.), *Rethinking Early Modern India*, p. 20.

105. Muzaffar Alam, *The Crisis of Empire in Mughal North India*, p. 9.
106. Ibid.
107. Ibid., pp. 9–10.

From *From Akbar to Aurangzeb*
*A Study in Indian Economic History**

W.H. MORELAND

THE ECONOMIC INFLUENCE OF THE ADMINISTRATION

Indian Administrative Systems

... In the India of our period the working of the administration was, next to the rainfall, the most important factor in the economic life of the country. It acted directly on the distribution of the national income to an extent which is now difficult to realise, for in practice the various governments disposed of somewhere about one half of the entire gross produce of the land, and they disposed of it in such a way that the producers were left with a bare subsistence or very little more, while the energies of the unproductive classes were spent in the struggle to secure the largest possible share. The reaction on production was inevitably unfavourable: producers were deprived of the natural incentive to energy, because they could not hope to retain any material proportion of an increase in their income; men of ability or talent were discouraged from producing, and attracted by the very great prizes to be won in the struggle for distribution: it was better to be a peon than a peasant....

... An Indian peasant might thus find himself under a master of one of five different classes: a farmer of the revenue, a salaried official, a *jāgīrdār* in temporary possession, a private person or corporation with a longer and possibly a permanent tenure, or, finally, a *zamindār*; and the powers of his master were so great, and the chances of superior interference so

* Excerpts from W.H. Moreland, *From Akbar to Aurangzeb: A Study in Indian Economic History*, New Delhi, Oriental Books Reprint Corporation, 1972, pp. 233, 237–8, 246–7, 248–50, 255–9, 267. First published in 1923, Macmillan and Co. Ltd., London.

small, that his welfare depended principally on the master under whom he happened to come....

... The peasant holding land, in an assigned tract might be either fortunate or unfortunate according to the nature of the assignment. When the grant was intended to be durable, and the grantee could pursue a constructive policy, the peasants might be comparatively well off, as appears to have been the case in Farid Khan's *jāgīr* near Benares in the sixteenth century, or under Shaista Khan in Bengal at the close of our period; but when assignments were changed frequently, as in the reign of Jahangir, the temporary possessor thought only of extracting as much as the peasants could pay, or in the words of Hawkins, "he racketh the poor to get from them what he can, who still thinketh every hour to be put out of his place."[1] The peasant whose land was included neither in a farm nor in an assignment was in theory fortunate, since his master had less direct incentive to oppress him, but in practice the lack of effective supervision made oppression possible; and though our information on the subject is necessarily defective, it appears to be probable that those peasants were best off who held land from a *zamindār* of an old-established family. It must not be inferred that the life of such peasants was idyllic, but such evidence as that of Bernier, indicates that the average of oppression was lower under *zamindār*s than under either officials or assignees....

Administrative Changes in the Mogul Empire

... It is beyond dispute that Akbar was far superior as an administrator to Jahangir or Shahjahan in their later years, or to Aurangzeb in the greater part of his reign;[2] we should be justified therefore in inferring that the same standard would have been worked more oppressively in 1660 than in 1600, and when we find that a new standard had come into existence in the interval, itself much more oppressive than the old, the conclusion becomes irresistible that for the masses of the people our period was one of growing impoverishment....

... Whatever the system of assessment might be, Akbar desired that the officials should be paid cash salaries instead of receiving assignments of land, and he insisted that, wherever possible, they should deal directly with the individual peasant cultivators. Our knowledge of the activities of his successors is incomplete on many points, but it is possible to show that these two principles disappeared in the course of the next half century; assignments multiplied, the farming system spread, and the growth of what may be called summary settlements of the revenue gave increased scope for tyranny within the village. These three changes all point to deterioration in the position of the ordinary peasant; in addition we have evidence of increasing pressure to extend the area under crops beyond the economic possibilities of the time; and lastly, we have the standard of assessment raised from one-third of the gross produce to one-half. The cumulative effect of these measures cannot be stated in precise figures, but the facts appear to justify the conclusion that the small margin left by Akbar was swept into the Imperial treasury or the pockets of officials, and that a very large proportion of the peasants were brought dangerously near to the bare level of subsistence. The evidence of these changes must now be set out.

In regard to assignments, it must be remembered that this method of remunerating officials was of old standing: Akbar endeavoured to abolish it, but there are indications that he was not entirely successful, and, when his personal influence was removed, the system quickly regained its previous vogue. The frequent references to assignments in Jahangir's *Memoirs* show that they were normal incidents of his administration, and the same inference can be drawn from the experience of William Hawkins at his Court. If the practice of payments in cash had been at all common, it would almost certainly have been followed in the case of a foreign visitor, but as a matter of fact Hawkins found that, as soon as he had been appointed to an official position under the Emperor, he had to join in the scramble for assignments which he describes so vividly. His narrative shows further that at this time changes of assignment were frequent; a man could not 'continue half a year in his living, but it is taken from him, and given unto another'; and consequently it was the assignee's interest to extract the utmost possible sum from each successive grant. Terry also noted the frequency of transfers, saying that officials were usually removed annually, and, while Hawkins' language is probably exaggerated, there is no reason to doubt the substantial truth of his account.

The practice of granting assignments was continued by Shahjahan, as can be seen from Peter Mundy's account of his journey through the Gangetic plain, in the course of which he notes the numerous assignments through which he travelled. According to him, transfers were at this time less frequent, being made at intervals of three or four years, but about the same period van Twist noted their frequency in Gujarat, and some incidental remarks in the commercial correspondence suggest that, with the weakening of the Emperor's will, this source of danger to the peasants increased. It is clear that under Shahjahan a very large proportion of the revenue was assigned. In the careful account of the Empire about 1650 given in Abdul Hamid's *Badshahnama*, the total revenue is shown as 880 *karors* of *dams*, while the *khālisa*, or portion available for the Imperial treasury, was 120 *karors*; on this basis, nearly seven-eighths of the revenue at this period was received by assignees or other intermediaries, and a still larger proportion appears in statistics of the reign of Aurangzeb. The ordinary peasant was therefore subject to an assignee rather than an official collector....

... In order to realise the deterioration in the position of the ordinary peasant, it is necessary to bear in mind that the revenue, though it was assessed on the gross produce, had in fact to be paid out of the net income, that is to say, out of the produce which remained after defraying the expenses of cultivation and the cost of maintaining the peasant and his family. In a previous work[3] I suggested that something like half the gross produce must have been recurred to maintain the "representative" peasant as an efficient cultivating unit with a small margin to meet losses in unfavourable season; on this view the effect of enhancing the revenue to one-half of the produce was to bring the peasant dangerously near to the level of subsistence in ordinary times, and to leave him practically nothing to make his life worth living, while even moderate losses might be ruinous. Under Akbar's regulations, the distribution of the gross produce of the soil was nearly one-half for necessary expenses, one-third for the State, and a margin of one-sixth or a little more for the peasants' comforts and luxuries, or for unfavourable seasons: under Shahjahan, nearly one-half was for necessaries, one-half, or more, for the State and intermediate claimants, and practically nothing was left at the disposal of the peasant. Judging by modern experience, Akbar allowed the peasant just about the minimum required to keep agriculture going, but Shahjahan did not; and, arguing merely from the official regulations, we should expect to find that the industry was becoming unpopular, and that men who found the life not to be worth living were deserting it for other forms of employment.

There is direct evidence that this change had in fact set in before the end of our period. Many of the detailed provisions contained in

Aurangzeb's orders indicate that peasants were absconding to an extent which seriously embarrassed the administration, but the fact is brought out most clearly in Bernier's *Letter to Colbert*, which was based on his experiences about the year 1656. In this letter, after commenting on the severity of the Mogul officials, he goes on:

Thus it happens that many of the peasantry, driven to despair by so execrable a tyranny, abandon the country, and seek a more tolerable mode of existence, either in the towns, or camps; as bearers of burdens, carriers of water, or servants to horsemen. Sometimes they fly to the territories of a Raja, because there they find less oppression, and are allowed a greater degree of comfort.

Further on he writes of the tyranny

that drives the cultivator of the soil from his wretched home to some neighbouring State, in hopes of finding milder treatment, or to the army, where he becomes the servant of some trooper. As the ground is seldom tilled otherwise than by compulsion, and as no person is found willing and able to repair the ditches and canals for the conveyance of water, it happens that the whole country is badly cultivated, and a great part rendered unproductive from the want of irrigation. The houses, too, are left in a dilapidated condition, there being few people who will either build new ones, or repair those that are tumbling down. The peasant cannot avoid asking himself the question, "Why should I toil for the tyrant who may come tomorrow and lay his rapacious hands upon all I possess and value, without leaving me, if such should be his humour, the means to drag on my miserable existence?" The Timariots,[4] governors, and revenue contractors on their part reason in this manner: "Why should the neglected state of this land create uneasiness in our minds? And why should we expend our money and time to render it fruitful? We may be deprived of it in a single moment, and our exertions would benefit neither ourselves not our children. Let us draw from the soil all the money we can, though the peasant should starve or abscond, and we should leave it, when commanded to quit, a dreary wilderness.'

These somewhat lengthy quotations are justified by their importance, for they state as observed facts the inferences which have been drawn from official regulations and other indirect evidence. The concentration of the authorities on immediate gain, their severity to the peasants, the compulsory cultivation, the neglect of agriculture, the desertion of the land for other employments, the gradual impoverishment of the country, all these features were sufficiently obvious to attract the attention of a foreign observer. It has occasionally been suggested that Bernier was inclined to exaggerate, but each fact alleged by him, though not the magnitude of each fact, follows almost necessarily from the changes known to have been introduced in the administration; and the concurrence of the two lines of evidence justifies the conclusion that by the end of Shahjahan's reign the economic system of the Mogul Empire had been strained almost to breaking-point, because the burdens on the principal industry were becoming unbearable and that production was ceasing to be worthwhile, because the life of the producer was ceasing to be worth living.

The foregoing observations relate to the area of the Mogul Empire as it stood at the beginning of our period, and they require to be supplemented by a brief account of the changes in the southern territory acquired by Shahjahan. In the course of the struggle to maintain the independence of the kingdom of Ahmadnagar, Malik Ambar introduced a revenue system obviously modelled on that of Akbar, but it did not survive the downfall of the kingdom. This region suffered terribly from the famine of 1630, and for twenty years or so it remained in a deplorable condition, with a falling revenue demand, which was still far in excess of the collections. When Prince Aurangzeb became Viceroy of the Deccan in 1653, he found that the area which had formerly belonged to Ahmadnagar could not pay even for the local administration. The Emperor sent repeated orders to extend cultivation so as to increase the revenue, and the administration was reorganised under Aurangzeb's revenue officer, Murshid Kuli Khan, who reintroduced the methods of assessment approved by Akbar. The results lie outside our period, but the fact is significant that the two outstanding administrators in this region should have taken Akbar's regulations as their model. The same inspiration is apparent in the system applied by Sivaji to the dominion which he secured, and it is noteworthy that at first he followed Akbar in claiming only one-third of the gross produce, though the proportion was subsequently raised to two-fifths.

It is important, however, to distinguish Sivaji's dominions (or *swarāj*) from the area which he drained of its resources but did not administer. He treated his own subjects comparatively well, but he was able to do so only because he was in a position to draw a large income from the subjects of neighbouring rulers. The exactions of *chauth* and *sardeshmukhi* in Mogul territory lie outside our period,[5] and it must suffice to say that they came as the proverbial last straw on peasants who were already assessed to the uttermost. There can be no doubt that the system inaugurated by Sivaji contributed materially to hasten the economic collapse of the Mogul Empire, but the evidence which has been adduced shows that the evil was already at work when the Marathas first appeared upon the scene, and to my mind there is no doubt that the national bankruptcy which ensued must be attributed primarily to the enhancement of the land revenue, coupled with the administrative methods by which it was assessed and collected....

SUMMARY AND CONCLUSION

... regarding the economic conditions which prevailed in India during the reigns of Jahangir and Shahjahan. The task remains of estimating the changes which took place during this period, and of attempting a rough balance-sheet, which may go some way towards answering the questions whether the national income was increasing or diminishing, and whether its distribution was approaching to, or receding from, modern standards of equity. At first sight, the outstanding facts are the appearance in India of agents of the great commercial companies formed in Holland and England, and their gradual penetration into all the most productive regions of the country; but on a closer examination the economist, while recognizing the eventual significance of those phenomena, is led to attach greater immediate importance to the administrative changes of the period, which intensified existing defects in the system of distribution, and thereby brought about a marked and cumulative reaction on productive industry. On the one hand, India benefited by an increase in the efficiency of the marketing agencies at her disposal, but on the other she suffered from the intensification of the economic parasitism which was destroying her productive energies: some localities, and some classes of producers, profited by the new external facilities, but the country taken as a whole was being impoverished by the operation of internal forces; and in my judgment there can be no question that the final balance is on the adverse of the account...

... the internal forces in operation were wholly injurious. The demands made by the various governments on producers were so large that there is no exaggeration in the statement that administrative activities were the most important factors in the distribution of the national income. Speaking generally, their effect was to leave to producers very little, if anything, above the minimum required for their subsistence, and to offer the surplus in rewards to energy or ingenuity exerted in unproductive ways. In the south of India, the administrative system operated steadily in this direction throughout our period, and here the changes to be recorded are comparatively slight: pressure on producers tended to intensify, because the local authorities had the strongest motives to discover every possible form of income, and to increase their demand to the utmost on those forms which were already familiar; but the system itself was unchanged, and even at the opening of our period its severity was such that a great increase of pressure could have led only to starvation or rebellion. In the north, on the other hand, there was a definite change in system. Akbar's financial institutions, which judged by modern standards, were severe, but not necessarily inequitable or destructive in their operation, gave way under his successors, and the direct demand on production was largely increased, while the simultaneous deterioration in administrative methods resulted in a steady approximation to the conditions which already prevailed in the south. The effect of these changes is shown by direct contemporary evidence to have been a diversion of energy from productive to unproductive pursuits, a process which was necessarily cumulative in its effects, and which is to my mind the outstanding economic fact of the half century. Almost throughout India, the tendency was to reduce the reward of production to a point where it ceased to offer an adequate incentive, to attract brains and energy to the struggle for a share in what had been produced by others, and thus to lead the way towards the national bankruptcy which eventually occurred....

... The low standard of life, and the small spending power of the people, are, however, facts established by direct evidence...Let us imagine, then, a self-supporting community, consisting of five producers, each securing about the same income, and one non-producing consumer, whom we may describe either as a policeman or as a parasite. A simple sum in arithmetic shows that, in order to secure equality of income in this community, each producer should surrender one-sixth of his income to the parasite or policeman. If now, in place of a rule of equality, we introduce the revenue system as it worked under Shahjahan, so that each producer surrenders one-half instead of one-sixth, then the income of the policeman or parasite will be five times that of each individual producer, and, provided that the conditions of his existence are in other respects tolerable, there will be an exceedingly strong temptation for each producer to secure his place. If we multiply this community by some figure of the order of 4 millions (that is, about 20 to 25 million households, which I take to be about the standard of the population of India at this period), we get something very like the economic skeleton of the India of our period. The bulk of the peasants and artisans of all classes lived on practically the same level, and, while there must have been individual differences due to skill or fortune, we are justified in assuming that they diverged from the norm to about the same extent on either side, so that we can think of the mass as homogeneous. The proportion of 'parasites' to producers cannot, of course, be determined accurately, but the figure I have taken seems to me to be probably an over-statement (the figures of the census of 1911 give a proportion of about one 'parasite' to nine producers, as against the assumed ratio of one to five). Neither cities nor armies had greatly increased during our period, for local advances are offset by retrogression elsewhere, and there is no doubt that peasants formed the bulk of the population, while the proportion of artisans was at any rate substantial; and without attempting to secure numerical exactitude, it is safe to say that a relatively large number of producers contributed half their gross income to the support of a relatively small number of economic parasites. The latter class was not, however, economically homogeneous, for it extended from the greatest noble to the humblest slave; in point of fact, most of the parasites lived on substantially the same plane as the producers, and it was only the small minority which engaged actively in the struggle for the surplus product. There was thus a very large income to be divided between a very small number of competitors, and, since saving resulted only in confiscation at death, the dividend was usually spent as quickly as it accrued. The conditions thus rendered inevitable the extravagant luxury of the nobles which struck foreign observers so strongly, and the dissipation of the surplus income of the country in unproductive channels. The humbler parasites, while living on the same plane as producers, were in some important respects substantially better off. If, for instance, seasons were bad, the peon's wages might buy less food, but the peasant might see his wife and children sold into slavery; and the general result of the administrative changes which occurred during our period was to increase this disparity to a point where the producer's life ceased to be worth living. He bore the brunt of the struggle with natural forces, but he could hope to retain no appreciable portion of the spoils, which were employed in maintaining a few parasites in luxury, and a much greater number in a life of comparative security.

The unproductive population was to be found mainly in towns or camps, while production was carried on chiefly in the villages, so that, from a somewhat different standpoint, the economic system of our period may be regarded as operating to provide the urban population with subsistence below cost... Such was the economic system which at the close of our period was drawing towards collapse. Weavers, naked themselves, toiled to clothe others. Peasants, themselves hungry, toiled to feed the towns and cities. India, taken as a unit, parted with useful commodities in exchange for gold and silver, or in other words gave bread for stones... The only way of escape from that system lay through an increase in production, coupled with a rising standard of life, but this road was barred effectively by the administrative methods in vogue, which penalized production, and regarded every indication of increased consumption as a signal for fresh extortion... the story of the century which followed is the story, first of the eventual collapse, and then of the gradual change, which was in time to render a new economic system possible.

AUTHORITIES FOR CHAPTER VIII

SECTION 1.—This section is mainly a summary of the conclusions reached in *India at the Death of Akbar*, and a forecast of the results to be reached in the sections which follow. Detailed references will be given in these, and it is unnecessary to repeat them here.

SECTION 2.—Much of this section is based on two papers in *Journal RAS*: (1) Akbar's Land Revenue System, January 1918; (2) The Development of the Land Revenue System, January 1922. The original authority for Akbar's system is *Ain*; the changes during the period are deduced from two of Aurangzeb's *farmāns*, of which the text was printed with translations in *Journal ASB*, June 1906. Translations are also available in Sarkar's *Studies*, p. 168 ff. For Akbar's capacities, see Dr Vincent Smith's *Akbar, the Great Mogul, passim*.

References to assignments are *idem*, p. 121, *Akbar-nama* (tr.) ii. p. 95, *Tuzuk, passim*. Hawkins's account is in *Purchas*, I. iii. p. 221, and *Early Travels*, p. 114; Terry's statement is in *Purchas*, II. ix. p. 1480. For the prevalence of the system under Shahjahan, see Mundy, ii *passim*; for frequency of changes, *idem*, ii. p. 85, and van Twist, Vol. XVIII; and for statistics, *Badshahnama*, ii. p. 710 ff.

Ravesteyn's account of farms in Gujarat is in Terpstra's *Surat*, Appendix VI. Roe's observations on the subject are pp. 124, 239: see also *Dagh Register*, 31 October 1636, 28 January, 1642 (Surat); *English Factories*, vi. pp. 100, 276, and vii. pp. 23, 24; and Pelsart, MS. p. 20f. The account of Shahjahan's expenditure is in Elliot, vii. pp. 171, 172. The demand of one-half of the produce is mentioned in van Twist, XLI, Manucci, ii. p. 451, Ovington, p. 197, and other writers. The peasant's position in regard to revenue is discussed at greater length in *India at the Death of Akbar*, p. 295 ff. Flight of peasants can be inferred from Aurangzeb's orders in Sarkar's *Studies*, pp. 172, 189, 191; Bernier's discussion of the subject is p. 205 ff.

For the Deccan administration, see Sarkar's *Aurangzeb*, especially i. p. 179 ff., and *Shivaji*, p. 470; also an article by S. Sen in *Calcutta University Journal* (Department of Letters), 1921, p. 237. The paragraph regarding the rental system is based on Aurangzeb's *farmāns*, quoted above.

NOTES

1. Hawkins's pointed description of the system of assignments will be found in *Purchas*, I. iii. p. 221, and *Early Travels*, p. 114. The prosperity of the peasants under Farid Khan is described in Elliot, iv. p. 313, and Shaista Khan's beneficence in Bengal is recounted in a chronicle translated in Sarkar's *Studies*, p. 155 ff., but both these documents are eulogies, and their language is subject to a rather high rate of discount. In both it is easy to see the extent of the general oppression with which these favoured areas are contrasted.

2. Jahangir's rank as administrator can be judged from his own statements in the *Tuzuk*, as well as from the accounts given by Roe and other contemporary writers; Pelsart, on p. 2 traces the commercial decline of Agra to the time when this Emperor abandoned the drudgery of administration for his pleasures, and justice was replaced by violence. I think there are good grounds for the view that Shahjahan's capacity deteriorated with age, though it would carry us too far to set out the evidence at length: in 1636 we are told that 'every man honours the king, but no man obeys him'; in 1645 we read of daily appointments and removals of high officials; and a year later of 'the king's wavering mind, which like a weathercock turns with the wind' (*English Factories*, v. p. 204, vii. p. 302, viii. p. 51). Manucci's favourable account of this emperor (i. p. 188) is

obviously coloured by time; his caustic descriptions of Aurangzeb's methods (for example, ii. p. 382) are perhaps better evidence of fact.

3. *India at the Death of Akbar*, c. iv.

4. 'Timariot' denotes the holder of a military tenure in the Turkish Empire (*Dictionnaire de l'Academie*, s.v.). The brief descriptions of it which I have seen indicate that the tenure was practically the same as that of an assignee in the Mogul Empire, and the expression in the text may be read as 'assignees, governors, and farmers'.

5. *Chauth* was an old-standing tenure in the Deccan; some sixteenth-century references to it will be found in *Dalgado* (Chouto, s.v.), which suggest that it originally denoted liability to pay one-fourth of the gross produce, but the proportion varied in practice, and under the Marathas the word seems usually to have meant one-fourth of the revenue. *Sardeshmukhi* was a cess, or extra demand, of 10 per cent on the revenue. Manucci, ii. p. 25, asserts that Sivaji had obtained a grant of *chauth* in the Mogul Deccan as early as 1658, but the statement seems to be inconsistent with the careful account of the transaction in question given in Sarkar's *Shivaji*, p. 65.

The Jagirdari Crisis
A Fresh Look*

SATISH CHANDRA

Following my *Parties and Politics at the Mughal Court* (1959), there have
been many studies in which discussion on some of the issues that had been
raised in my book were carried further. Thus, the character, composition,
and role of the Mughal nobility; the structure and composition of the rural
society with special reference to the landed elements; the growth of the
economy including the agrarian economy and its impact on the primary
producer, the peasant; the role of opposition and dissident movements and
elements, such as the Marathas, the Rajputs, the Jats, the Afghans, and the
Sikhs have been subjected to critical and scholarly study by a number of
historians. I have written elsewhere on some of these.[1] It is not my purpose
here to review these various works except insofar as they have a bearing on
the crisis of the *jagirdari* system. In the context of the discussion on the
factors leading to the downfall of the Mughal empire there has been a good
deal of discussion and I have also written on the subject separately.[2]

I had argued that the basic problem facing the Mughals was that
the available social surplus was insufficient to defray the cost of
administration, pay for wars of one type or another, and to give the
ruling class a standard of life in keeping with its expectations.[3] I had
linked the problem to the continuous expansion of the ruling class, price
rise, and the like, on the one hand, and, on the other, to 'a deep seated
social crisis which had resulted in limited expansion of agriculture and
also limited rapid expansion of industry and trade both of which were

* Reproduced from Satish Chandra, *State, Society and Culture in Indian History*,
New Delhi, Oxford University Press, 2012. First published in Satish Chandra,
Parties and Politics at the Mughal Court 1707–1740, New Delhi, Oxford
University Press, 2002, 4th edn, pp. xi–xxi.

based on the introduction of new technology, and the removal of all barriers hindering that expansion'.[4]

In recent studies there has been a tendency to look upon the *jagirdari* crisis as merely a financial-cum-administrative crisis rather than treating it simultaneously as a manifestation of a deep-seated social crisis. Athar Ali has provided a great deal of statistical information on the expansion and composition of the Mughal nobility under Jahangir and Shah Jahan, as also under Aurangzeb. He has shown that between 1595 and 1656–7, the number of *mansabdars* holding ranks of 500 *ẓāt* and above increased 4.2 times. During Aurangzeb's reign the number of *mansabdars* holding rank of 1,000 *ẓāt* and above (figures below that are very hard to get) increased much more slowly—from 486 in 1658–78 to 575 during 1679–1707, that is, an increase of only 16.25 per cent.[5] While Athar Ali notes that these figures are incomplete, he argues plausibly for a slowdown of the increase of ranks under Aurangzeb. However, the *jagirdari* crisis continued to grow during the period. J.F. Richards has argued against it, pointing out that the incorporation of Bijāpur and Golconda increased the resources of the Mughals by 24 per cent, with the *manṣab* ranks increasing only to that extent. In support of his contention that there was no *jagirdari* crisis as such, J.F. Richards cited documents from the Deccan from the Inayat Jung Collection showing large areas under *pāibāqī*, that is, areas yet to be assigned as jāgīr.[6]

J.F. Richards' contention that there was no *jagirdari* crisis has been refuted by a number of scholars and needs hardly to be gone into in detail here. It is clear that the graphic accounts of the suffering of the nobility, especially the *khānazāds*, that is, sons and descendants of old nobles, due to lack of *jāgīrs*, or delays in granting them, cited by contemporary observers such as Khāfi Khān and Bhīmsen cannot be set aside on the basis of *jama* figures or stray documents. A careful study has yet to be made of the Mughal documents of the Deccan, especially the mass of documents in the Inayat Jung Collection. Even a cursory study of these documents shows numerous complaints about lack of *pāibāqī* and that due to *be-jāgīri* (lack of *jāgīrs*) people were dying every day. These complaints seem to be particularly numerous after RY 40, 1696–7.[7] Athar Ali has also drawn attention to a document of the year AH 1117, 1706 relating to Hyderabadi Karnātaka, contained in *Selected Documents of Aurangzeb's Reign* (ed., Yusuf Husain Khan) showing that the area under *khalisa* accounted for only 6 per cent of the *jama*, the *paibāqī* accounted for 20 per cent of which 16 per cent was in the hands of *polygārs*, thus leaving very small areas for assignment.[8]

However, even this does not provide us a clear picture of the situation. A recent study of the 'Ināyat Jung documents shows that there was a large amount of *paibāqī* in the Haiderābādi and Bijāpur areas which were called *mulk-i-jadīd* or new areas.[9] In a statement addressed to Aurangzeb it is stated that 'In the *mulk-i-jadīd* Bijapur and Haiderabad the *paibāqī* is considerable, since owing to its low income the (claimants) representative do not accept (*jāgīrs*) from it in accordance with the *jamā*'....'[10]

The background to this situation is clear from the documents. The *mulk-i-qadīm* or the old country was the area in the Deccan conquered upto the time of Shah Jahan, that is, Khandesh, Ahmadnagar, and Berar while *mulk-i-jadīd* or the new country included the areas conquered by Aurangzeb which comprised Bijapur and Haiderabad including the Karnataka, and parts of Daultabad Bidar provinces.[11] Large parts of the *mulk-i-jadīd* were disturbed and unsettled, and were called *ghair-'amlī*. This was particularly so in the Karnataka where the *polygārs* were very powerful, and no settlement had been made with them so that military force was the only means of compelling them to pay. The position was better in the old Haiderabad state, but the situation in Bijapur had deteriorated due to Maratha depredations.[12]

Faced with the unceasing demands for war, provisioning of forts, cost of artillery and payment for the soldiers, Aurangzeb tried to increase the *khalisa* by incorporating into it the more productive areas, and to assign *jāgīrs* to the nobles serving in the Deccan in the less productive, *ghair-'amlī* areas. This was resisted by the nobles because of the yield being far below the *jamā*—in some cases being even of two months.[13] The *mansabdars* were afraid that in this situation they would not be able to present a sufficient quota for inspection (*dāgh*), and their *jāgīrs* would be confiscated.

This was the reason why large areas remained under *paibāqī*. Far from showing that the existence of large *paibāqī* implied that there was no shortage of *jāgīrs*, it indicated a growing crisis in the functioning of the *jagirdari* system.

How did Aurangzeb himself see this developing crisis? Perhaps the situation was too complex for a uniform approach. Thus, he does reluctantly agree to reduction (*takhfīf*) of *jamā* of the *jāgīrs* in the new areas, but also remarks: 'The disorderly, useless Decannis should be confined to the *mulk-i-jadīd*, and to the (old areas) with reduction (only) and only, thereafter in other areas.'[14]

But in general Aurangzeb does not seem to have been conscious of a growing *jagirdari* crisis. His constant refrain was that there was no shortage of *jāgīrs*—pointing perhaps to the large *pāibāqī* which was unacceptable to the nobles. He ordered that expenditure should match with income, and asked for *khalisa* to be expanded to meet the expenditure—'but not at the expense of (*jāgīrs* assigned for meeting) pay claims of the army'![15] He insisted on old rules and regulations (*zābtah wa dastūr*) being implemented, although the situation was vastly different, with many Marathas (probably a euphemism for Deccanis) continuing, in connivance with revenue officials, to hold their *jāgīrs* even without any contingents.[16]

Thus, it seems that Aurangzīb was living in an unreal world of his own, increasingly losing touch with the harsh reality. That the *jagirdari* system was becoming dysfunctional has been hinted at indirectly by Bhīmsen. He points out that because of the smallness of the forces of the *mansabdars* and the *faujdars*, the *zamindars* had become strong, and that in this situation 'it was difficult for a *dām* or *darham* to reach the *jagirdar*'.[17] Bhīmsen has underlined the social basis of the *jagirdari* system. The *jagirdari* system implied delegating to the *jagirdars* the responsibility of collecting state dues from the *zamindars* who were numerous, armed with their own bastions (*garhis*) and clan/caste followers among the cultivators. The symbiotic and contradictory relationship between the state and the *zamindars* has been brought out by Nurul Hasan and we hardly need to dwell on it here.[18] The *zamindars* in the Deccan might have been reconciled to Mughal rule, and were willing to aid them in the tasks of revenue assessment and collection if the *jagirdari* system had worked reasonably well and Mughal rule had stabilized, for which a settlement with the Marathas was necessary. By the time this had been done under the successors of Aurangzeb, the roving Maratha bands had become too powerful to be contained, and the Imperial authority had been weakened due to factionalism, civil wars, and so on. This led to the further accentuation of the *jagirdari* crisis which, in turn, reacted on the Imperial authority.

It has been argued in the present work that the growing factionalism in the nobility was based on struggle for power, on the one hand, and, on the other, struggle for the possession of productive *jāgīrs*, the ethnic form being, at best, an outer cover which could be departed from at any time according to need and convenience.

The *jagirdari* crisis grew apace during the first half of the eighteenth century. Some of the manifestations were: (i) growing factionalism in the nobility; (ii) distancing of the *khānazāds* from the monarchy; (iii) growth of the *ijāra* system; (iv) growing dysfunctionality of the Mughal military system based on cavalry contingents led by nobles; and (v) modification of the *jāgīr* system, with a tendency of both *jāgīrs* and offices to become hereditary.

The old hierarchical society, and the *jagirdari* system which was based on it, were at odds with the rising social forces. The impact of this on the *jagirdari* crisis during the eighteenth century, and its impact on the rise of a new class of *zamindars* who were more assertive, and not prepared to accept the role assigned to them by Mughal administrators, need to be studied concretely.

Recent studies on the nature of rural society in eastern Rajasthan show that there was process of growing segmentation of rural society, largely in response to a growing market-oriented money economy. Mughal agrarian policies also tended to favour the emergence of a class of rich cultivators who had the necessary physical and monetary resources to expand and improve cultivation.[19] The emergence of this class of cultivators with sizeable human and physical resources, including land, at their disposal, and dominating the village community, often on a caste basis, consisted of what were broadly designated *khud-kāsht* or resident owner-cultivators. These sections formed, for some time, what I have called 'a tripod' with the *zamindars* and the state forming the other two legs. I have argued this was the basis of rural stability in north India during the first half of the seventeenth century. We are still not clear about the factors leading to the break-up of this 'tripod' in the upper Gangetic doab and the Punjab during the second half of the seventeenth century. Thus, some of the *khud-kāsht*, such as the Jats of western Uttar Pradesh and Punjab moved towards opposition to the Mughal state. Maybe the slow pace of development, the unwillingness/inability of the Mughal state to involve these rising elements more closely in the tasks of administration, and reluctance to accord to these non-elite elements a higher status than was normative in an essentially hierarchical society may explain it. We have mentioned elsewhere that the rise of the

Maratha movement in opposition to the Mughals was based not merely on a lure for plunder but also a bid to raise social status.[20] Recent studies show that many of the great Maratha military leaders of the eighteenth century and prominent military figures did not belong to old *deshmukh* families, but came from the lower elements aspiring to raise their social status.[21]

Under different circumstances, these development-oriented rich peasants could have played the same role in India as the squirearchy in England. However, during the eighteenth century, we see some of the rich peasants emerging as *ijāredār*s or *mahajans*.[22]

As far as the 'rich firms' of bankers is concerned, there is little evidence to support the thesis that they turned against the Mughal rulers, and aided in the dissolution of the empire. However, once a regional ruler had emerged and stabilized his position, these 'firms' were prepared to play a role in transmitting money or providing loans, as in the case of the Marwaris who migrated to Poona, or the Marwaris such as Jagat Seth, and the Armenian Khwāja Wājid at Murshidabad in Bengal. Some bankers took lands on *ijāra* as security for the money they had advanced.[23] But by far and large, the traders and bankers did not try to purchase land or become *zamindar*s, the Burdhwan *raj* set up by a *khatri* trader being an exception.

The distancing of the *khānazād*s, which consisted largely of the Īrānī and Tūrānī nobility, from the monarchy was a consequence of the growing crisis of the *jagirdari* system during the eighteenth century. These elements, which considered the Mughal monarchy as a racial institution, were reconciled to the induction of Hindus, Hindustanis, and Afghans into the nobility only as long as it provided stability to the state and gave further opportunities of territorial expansion. There was growing resentment among them at the refusal of Aurangzeb to give *manṣab*s and *jāgīr*s to *khānazād*s following the large-scale induction of Deccanis and Marathas. Under Aurangzeb's successors, their demand was the removal from service of 'ignoble', 'incompetent' people, who were identified as Hindus, Kashmiris, Hindustanis, as also men from the *Dīwānī* and *Khān Sāmānī* offices, where these elements predominated. Failing to get their way, these *khānazād*s were the sections which took the lead in setting up new principalities or *riyāsat*s. Interestingly, in these *riyāsat*s, while the form of the *jāgīrdārī* system was preserved outwardly, the *jāgīr*s ceased to be transferable, and became hereditary de facto.

Thus, *jāgīr-i-watan* became the norm.[24] This put a virtual stop not only
to the induction of competent people from the lower orders, but also a
stoppage of patronage to the stream of immigrants from abroad. One
benefit of this was the closer identification with or absorption of the
existing Īrānīs and Tūrānīs into the Indian social order. However, there
is no evidence to show that the new class of hereditary *jagirdars* looked
after the interests of the cultivators, or acted as improving landlords,
which Bernier would have us believe would have been the result if the
transfer of *jāgīrs* had not existed. (Bernier's remarks were not directed
against frequency of transfers, but transferability as such of *jāgīrs*.)

It has been pointed out that the Mughals became increasingly
more backward during the seventeenth century in the field of military
technology and methods of warfare. Thus, their field artillery remained
poor as compared to the Europeans, and they were very slow to adopt
the quick firing fling-lock gun and the use of infantry. It has been further
suggested that it was in some sense due to the 'rigidity' of the *mansabdari*
system and the vested interests of the *jagirdars* because infantry forces
would have had to be centrally recruited and paid.

It may be readily conceded that growing technological backwardness
had serious consequences for the Indians when later the Marathas, and
successor states, such as Bengal, Awadh, Hyderabad, and others had
to contend with technologically superior forces led by the French and
the British. But this technological backwardness had little to do with
struggle against the Marathas who emerged as the chief challengers of the
Mughals during the first half of the eighteenth century. The Marathas
depended upon lightly armed cavalrymen living on the countryside,
who conducted a mobile mode of warfare. Superior artillery, or infantry
armed with superior, quick-firing guns would hardly have been effective
against them. As it was, even in its weakened condition, Mughal artillery
was powerful enough to deter Baji Rao from attacking the Niẓām's
fortified position as late as 1738 at Bhopal.

The military and technological challenge faced by the Mughals
should, perhaps, be seen in a different perspective. We have during the
eighteenth century the rise of a new class of aggressive, military-minded
zamindars, some belonging to the old Rajput families, a few to lower
class adventurers, and few to the Afghans and Jats etc. Contemporary
writers use various adjectives to describe this new class of aggressive
zamindars, but they emphasize their 'daring' and 'presumptuousness' in

challenging Imperial officials. Thus, in 1722, 'Azamatullah Khān the *faujdar* of Moradabad, was almost defeated by the Afghans who used 'bows and muskets'.[25] Even earlier, the Afghans were said to be in the employ of local *zamindars* of *ṣūbah* Agra and Allahabad and creating disturbances.[26] The Jats with 200 of their musketeers, riding on their horses 'which were swift-moving like the wind' attacked the imperialists at Ḥasanpur while fighting against 'Abdullāh Khān Bāraha.[27] Even more significant was the case of Bhagwant Adārū, the *zamindar* of Kora-Jahānabād, who defeated and killed Jān Nisār Khān, the *faujdar* of the area. The *wazīr*, Qamaruddīn Khān, failed to suppress him and had to call in the *ṣubahdār*, Burhān-ul-Mulk Sāadat Khān, to help.[28]

In all these cases, we are told that the *zamindars*, proud of the size and strength of their armies, attacked with 'bows and muskets', while Bhagwant Adārū used 'cannons and muskets'.[29] In other words, the wide dispersal of muskets and even cannons had resulted in the loss of the military edge against the *zamindars* which the imperialists had enjoyed earlier. Orders to local *faujdars* to prevent locksmiths from manufacturing guns had little effect.

Thus, the struggle between centripetal and centrifugal forces had reached a new phase. Had the *jagirdari* system based on cavalrymen become redundant in this situation? Was a new type of regional centralization needed to cope with this situation? Larger and more efficient forces, that needed more money, were also required. These are problems which had to be faced by the successor states of the Mughals. But they do not concern us here.

Thus, the working of the *jagirdari* system has to be seen in the wider socio-cultural context. The *jagirdari* system was designed to cope with a social-political situation that was rapidly changing during the eighteenth century. While the system worked it was able to keep in check the centrifugal forces represented by the *zamindars*, and promoted a centralized policy.

The linking of the crisis of the *jagirdari* system with a deepening social crisis and increased factionalism in the ruling classes leading to a break-up of central polity still remains at the core of the Mughal crisis of empire. To that extent, the main thesis put forward earlier by the author still remains valid.

NOTES

1. Satish Chandra, *The Eighteenth Century in India: Its Economy and the Role of the Marathas, the Jats, the Sikhs and the Afghans*, Calcutta, 1986, rev. edn, 1991.

2. 'Review of the Crisis of the Jagirdari System', in Satish Chandra, *Medieval Indian Society, Jagirdari Crisis and the Village*, New Delhi, 1982, pp. 61–75.

3. Satish Chandra, *Parties and Politics at the Mughal Court*, Delhi, 1959, p. xlvi.

4. Ibid., p. xlix.

5. Athar Ali, *The Mughal Nobility under Aurangzeb*, 2nd edn, Delhi, 1997, pp. 9–11; *Apparatus of Empire*, 1985, pp. xiii–xvii.

6. J.F. Richards, *Mughal Administration in Golconda*, Oxford, 1975, pp. 158, 306–9.

7. See S.M. Azizuddin Husain, 'Scarcity of *pāibāqī* Lands during Aurangzeb's Reign in the Light of 'Ināyat Jung Collection Documents', *Proceedings of Indian History Congress*, Vol. XXXLX, 1978, pp. 426–30.

8. Ali, *The Mughal Nobility*, pp. xxi–xxii.

9. 'Problems of the Deccan Administration in the Last Decade of Aurangzeb's Reign—Based on Explorations in the 'Ināyat Jung Collection' of the National Archives of India, Delhi, Zakir Husain, Paper presented to the Indian History Congress, Vol. LXI, Calcutta session, 2001, in 'Papers from the Aligarh Historians Society', (ed.), Irfan Habib, pp. 54–66 (mimeo).

10. 'Ināyat Jung Collection, *IJC* 1/0/0(old 1/14/129, not dated).

11. *IJC* 146/12–167 and 178.

12. J.F. Richards, *Mughal Administration in Golconda*, pp. 111–34.

13. C. I/40/10–27 dt. 25 *Sha'bān* 40 R.Y., 19 March 1697; Zakir Husain, loc. cit., pp. 56–60.

14. *IJC* 1/0/0–486. A separate order says '...newly enrolled Decannis, without contingents should receive most of their *zāt* pay claim in the New Territory (*mulk-i-jadīd*)'.

15. Zakir Hussain, loc. cit.

16. *IJC* 1/45/11–12.

17. Bhīmsen, *Nuskha-i-Dilkasha*, ff. 139a–b.

18. S. Nurul Hasan, 'Zamindars under the Mughals', in F.E. Frykenburg (ed.), *Land Control and Social Structure in Indian History*, Madison, 1969, pp. 18–31.

19. See Satish Chandra, 'Role of the Local Community, the Zamindars and the State in Providing Capital Inputs for the Growth and Expansion of Cultivation', in his *Medieval India: Society, the Jagirdari Crisis and the Village*, Delhi, 1982, pp. 166–83. Also, Nurul Hasan *et al.*, 'The Pattern of Agrarian

Production in the Territories of Amber (*c.* 1650–1750)', *Proceedings of Indian History Congress*, Vol. XXVII, 1966, pp. 245–64.

20. See Satish Chandra's 'Social Background to the Rise of the Maratha Movement during the Seventeenth Century', in *Medieval India*, pp. 139–46.

21. Stewart Gordon, *The Marathas*, Cambridge, 1993, p. 108. '(Except for three families) the rest of Shahu's elite consisted leaders of successful, largely independent bands.' Many of them had been village headmen or petty deshmukhs.

22. Dilbagh Singh, *The State, Landlord and Peasants in Rajasthan during the 18th Century*, Delhi, 1990, pp. 130–7; S.P. Gupta, *The Agrarian System of Eastern Rajasthan*, Delhi, 1986, pp. 225–32.

23. Ibid.

24. Muzaffar Alam, *The Crisis of Empire in Mughal North India*, Delhi, 1986, pp. 124–6.

25. *Iqbāl Nāma*, (ed.) S.H. Askari, Patna, 1953, p. 85.

26. *Akhbārāt 8 Rabī' I* R.Y. Ill (1127)/l4.3.1715; 4 *Ziq'ad* R.Y. IV (1128/10.1716).

27. Shiv Das, *Shāhnāma*, (ed.) S.H. Ashkari, Patna, 1980, p. 139; The Ruhelas were the first to use on a large-scale infantry armed with muskets in field battles. Thus, in 1749, the Ruhelas had 5,000 match-lockmen concealed in bushes who defeated the army of the Bangash chief Qā'im Khān, *Khazānah-i Āmrah*,p. 30.

28. W. Irvine, *Later Mughals* II, p. 277; Alam, *Crisis of Empire*, p. 315.

29. *Iqbalnāma*, p. 130.

The Agrarian Causes of the Fall of the Mughal Empire[*]

IRFAN HABIB

INTRODUCTION

The collapse of the Mughal Empire is a subject that has been studied in minute detail so far as political and military events are concerned,[1] but there has hardly been any serious discussion as to the causes that led to it. It has been assumed that a host of factors combined to achieve this result, such as the decay (from largely unexplained causes) in administrative efficiency; the growth of luxury-loving habits among the Mughal aristocracy fostered by the enervating heat of this country; the incompetence of later emperors; the religious policy of Aurangzeb; the rise of the "Hindu Reaction," that exists, perhaps, more in the sentiment of modern writers than in the writings of contemporaries; the still less real "rise of nationalities" (propounded by some Soviet historians), and so on and so forth. Only sometimes is it suggested, by way of adding yet another factor into the melting pot, that peasant uprisings had also had something to do with the break-up of the Empire.[2] It is not the purpose of this article to discuss all the current assumptions in detail. The belief, of the present writer is that the fall of the Mughal Empire proceeded directly from certain basic structural, contradictions of the system on which it was based, and that all the factors that are generally brought forward in our text-book had, if any, only a secondary role to play.

[*] Reproduced from Irfan Habib, 'The Agrarian Causes of the Fall of the Mughal Empire', published in two parts, *Enquiry* 2, September 1958, pp. 81–98 and *Enquiry* 3, April 1960, pp. 68–80.

THE BASIC STRUCTURE OF THE MUGHAL EMPIRE

The peculiar feature of the state in Mughal—and indeed Medieval—India was that it served not merely as the protective arm of the exploiting classes, but was itself the principal instrument of exploitation. It is this basic characteristic of the Mughal system that led contemporary European travellers to declare with one voice, albeit inaccurately, that the King was 'the owner of the soil' in India.[3] The land revenue, or *mal*, demanded on behalf of the state comprehended by far the largest portion of, if not the entire, surplus produce (i.e., produce above that required for the lowest level of subsistence) of the peasant. This is not only implicit in a number of statements made by contemporaries,[4] but is quite obvious from the magnitude of the land revenue demand in terms of the total produce. Akbar's administration fixed the revenue at a third of the normal produce under the so-called *Zabt* system of assessment. But it seems that this proportion had largely only a theoretical significance and the details of the process by which the cash, revenue rates were determined and imposed leave us in little doubt that the revenue amounted in practice to much above a third of the harvest.[5] Under Aurangzeb (1659–1707) it becomes a very common dictum in official documents that the land revenue should amount to just half of the actual produce.[6] In the fertile coastal strip of Gujarat the revenue amounted to as much as three-fourths of the harvest.[7]

It rested with the Emperor's will to dispose of this enormous tribute and this in the main took the form of 'revenue-assignments.'[8] That is to say, the Emperor assigned the right to collect the revenue and taxes due to him, in particular areas, to certain of his subjects. These assignments were known as *jagirs* and the assignees as *jagirdars*. The *jagirdars* were usually *mansabdars*, or officials and commanders who held ranks (*mansabs*), bestowed upon them by the Emperor. These ranks determined their personal pay and the size of their military contingents, for which they were entitled to claim a separate allowance. While some of them were paid in cash, most of them were assigned *jagirs* in lieu of the pay due to them. Areas whose revenues were retained for the imperial treasury were known as *Khalisa*.

The revenue-assignment was by its very nature a temporary alienation of royal right. It was subject to periodic transfers, a *jagirdar* seldom holding a particular area in his *jagir* for more than three or four years.[9]

Throughout the period of the Great Mughals (i.e. down to the death of Aurangzeb in 1707) this practice was rigidly followed. Its one great merit was to make the *jagirdars* completely dependent upon royal favour; they could never establish themselves as local potentates and were compelled to serve at call in the various regions of the Empire. In this, rather than in the discovery of gun-powder,[10] lay the secret of the military power and the immense centralisation of the Mughal Empire.

Mughal power, based on the *jagirdari* system, proved invincible against all the provincial kingdoms. It also cowed into submission all elements of local despotism which it found anywhere. These elements were, however, far from being eliminated. Side by side with the ruling class of the Empire—the *mansabdars* or *jagirdars*—there existed a heterogeneous class, subordinate in its share of power, but also with certain separate interests of its own. This was the class of the *zamindars*. In the usage of contemporaries, the term '*zamindar*' embraced the holders of a wide category of rights to the land—ranging from autonomous chiefs, who paid a fixed tribute to the imperial court, to persons merely claiming a perquisite from a village, or even a small portion of it. Large areas in Rajasthan, Central India, Kathiawar, the sub-Himalayan tracts and elsewhere lay under the tributary chiefs. But these apart, the *zamindar* was a universal phenomenon in the imperial territories proper.[11] Only the nature of his rights varied. Sometimes he held certain villages as his demesne, his *khudkasht, banth* or *nankar,* while the rest of the villages around would be *raiyati,* or purely peasant-held. Sometimes the *zamindars* laid claim simply to a proportion of the revenue collected in his area, generally known as *malikana,* and amounting in Northern India, to about 10 per cent of the revenue. The administration, on its part, recognised these rights in return for certain obligations, such as realising the land revenue on its behalf, from the peasants, duties of watch and ward, etc. The general tendency of the Mughal administration seems, indeed, to have been to depress the position of the *zamindars* and reduce them wherever possible to mere tax-gatherers. Yet for all its variety of form, the *zamindari* right had everywhere certain features in common: its possession was hereditary; it owed its origin not to the bounty of the Emperor, but to independent acquisition: to clan-settlement, usurpation or purchase. It is also noteworthy that possession of armed force was almost an inevitable complement of a *zamindari* right of any consequence. Abu-l Fazl gives us a detailed census, *pargana-*

wise, of the 44 lacs of armed retainers maintained by the *zamindars* of the Empire.[12] This force was the necessary instrument through which the *zamindar* could fulfil his obligations as the bailiff and watchman of the *jagindar*, and it could on occasion also be pressed into imperial service. But it was also his only means of defence against the pressure of the imperial power itself.

The existence of the centralised system, which the Mughal *jagirdar* represented, can be conceived only within the framework of a particular economic order. The *jagir*, i.e., the assignment of revenue in terms of cash was made possible only by the general prevalence of the cash-nexus.[13] This, in turn, meant that trade and commerce should have reached a high level of development, which, indeed, is a characteristic feature of the period.[14] On the other hand, trade could prosper best under an imperial administration, with its uniform methods of tax-collection, single currency and control over the routes. In so far, therefore, as the *jagir* system strengthened imperial power, it also reinforced the economic foundations of its own existence. Unlike the feudal lord of Western Europe, the Mughal *jagirdar* did not need to have, any fear of the "dissolving influence" of money and trade.[15]

OPPRESSION OF THE PEASANTRY

The source of the crisis of the Mughal Empire seems to have lain really in the dual effect of the system of *jagir* transfers. On the one hand, this practice was essential for the very cohesion of the Empire; on the other, it led inexorably to an unrestrained exploitation of the peasantry. A *jagirdar*, who expected his *jagir* to be transferred any moment, would have had the irresistible temptation to kill the goose; that laid the golden eggs: he could hardly have seen any reason in staying his band for the benefit of succeeding assignees. To reproduce an oft-quoted passage from Bernier:

The Timariots (i.e. *jagirdars*), Governors and Revenue-contractors on their part reason in this manner: 'Why should the neglected state of this land create uneasiness in our minds? and why should we expend our own money and time to render it fruitful? We may be deprived of it in a single moment, and our exertions would benefit neither ourselves nor our children. Let us draw from the soil all the money we can though the peasant should starve, or abscond and we should leave it, when commanded to quit, a dreary wilderness'.[16]

Bernier has discussed the matter at the greatest length, but he is by no means the only contemporary observer to make such a statement. He is preceded for example by St. Xavier and Manrique.[17] Among Indian writers, we have Bhimsen, who declares that owing to the constant and unpredictable transfers of *jagirs,* the agents of the *jagirdars* had given up the practice of helping the peasantry (*ra'iyat-parwari*) or making long-term arrangements (*istiqlal*). Moreover, the '*amils*', or revenue-collectors, of the *jagirdars* were not sure of their own tenure of employment and so "proceeding tyranically" were unrelenting in the collection of revenue.[18] When the *jagirdar,* rather than, taking the trouble of appointing his agents to collect the revenue, farmed out the *jagir,* the evil was worse still. The land was being laid waste, says Sadiq Khan, historian, of Shahjahan's reign, through bribery and revenue-farming (*ijara*), to fulfil, the terms of which, the peasantry was being recklessly robbed and plundered.[19]

It will not be true to say that the *jagirdars* could levy as much revenue on the peasants as they pleased. The revenue rates were fixed by the imperial administration, and such local officials as the *qanungos* and *chaudhuries* were appointed from the Court for the purpose of watching over, as well as aiding, the *jagirdars* or their agents in the work of revenue-collection. It is also not possible to accept Moreland's contention that the official revenue demand itself was raised substantially in the course of the 17th century. Both the revenue-rates and the revenue statistics that have come down to us do not in fact show any increase beyond that justified by the rise in prices which took place within this period owing to the great influx of silver from the New World.[20] The only significant increase in authorised taxation was, perhaps, represented by the imposition, in 1679, of the *jizija,* or poll tax, on non-Muslims.[21]

But the land revenue demand, even if it was not really increased, was heavy enough as it stood and, as we have seen, left hardly enough for the peasant to subsist on. And this apart, the avenues of extortion that were available to the *jagirdars,* were actually unnumbered. Many could be shown to be well in conformity with the regulations laid down by the imperial administration itself, but the rules could also be stretched quite a distance or even evaded completely.

The detailed regulations for revenue assessments could, for example, be followed meticulously on paper, but on the basis of purely mythical figures. Thus as an imperial order issued by Aurangzeb recites, the *jagirdars* in Gujarat, who were required to take half the crop as revenue, were in fact demanding more than the produce by the simple process of assuming the yield to be two and a half times the actual harvest.[22] Past arrears could also be added to swell the demand,[23] while no or only inadequate concession might be made to alleviate the effects of natural calamities or famines.[24] Then, on the plea that revenue would be difficult to collect from the peasants once they had removed the harvest, it came to be demanded in advance, when the peasants would be completely destitute.[25] This was presumably done to compel the peasants to agree to the levy of extra (and illegal) impositions.[26]

Thus heavy as the authorised revenue demand itself was, it was further swollen by all these enhancements and extortions. Its collection from a poverty-stricken peasantry, which, as Manrique remarked, had "no possessions or assets from which to pay," was no refined process. When the 'arrayatos' (ra'iyat, peasants) cannot pay the revenue, continues Manrique, they are "beaten unmercifully and maltreated."[27] Another European traveller, Manucci, who, on this occasion, assumes the viewpoint of the riding class declares that "it is the peasants' habit to go on refusing payment, asserting that they have no money, the chastisements and the instruments (of torture) are very severe. They are also made to endure hunger and thirst.... They feign death (as sometimes really happens) .... But this trick secures them no compassion...."[28]

Frequently, therefore, the peasants were compelled to sell their women, children and cattle in order to meet the revenue demand.[29] But the enslavement was not generally even so voluntary as this. 'Villages,' we are told, 'which owing to some shortage of produce, are unable to pay the full amount of the revenue-farm, are made prize, so to speak, by their masters and governors, and wives and children sold on the pretext of a charge of rebellion.'[30] So says Pelsaert, writing in Jahangir's reign. Again, Manrique—'They (the peasants) are carried off, attached to heavy iron chains, to various markets and fairs, with their poor, unhappy wives behind them carrying their small children in their arms, all crying and lamenting their evil plight.'[31]

Defaulting on the payment of revenue was not, however, the only cause for which such punishment was inflicted upon; the peasants. It was the general law in the Mughal Empire that if any robbery occurred within the assignment or jurisdiction, respectively, of a *jagirdar* or *faujdar* (imperial military commandant), he was obliged to either apprehend the culprits and recover the loot or stolen goods, or to make the restitution himself.[32] This was, perhaps, not an unwelcome duty in that it offered the potentates an excuse to sack any village they chose to suspect of the crime. The men were killed in such cases, says Mundy, and "the rest, with weomen and Children, arc carried away and sold for Slaves."[33] Abu-l Fazl says candidly that Akbar's orders prohibiting the seizure and sale of the women and children of combatants were issued because "many evil-hearted avaricious men, either merely from ill-founded suspicion or only a false imputation of disloyalty or because of sheer greed, make their way to the villages and *mahals* (territorial divisions) of the countrymen and put them to sack. On being questioned, they offer a thousand excuses and attempt delay or evasion."[34]

It is almost a constant refrain in the statements of our authorities that the oppression increased with the passage of time, that cultivation fell off and the number of absconding peasants grew. St. J. Xavier declared that in both Gujarat and Kashmir the Mughal conquest under Akbar had greatly increased the misery of the rural population: 'The lands are much spoiled which at an earlier period were taken by the Mogorcs (Mughals): for they destroy everything with their oppressions.'[35] In the central regions of the Empire too, Akbar's reorganisation of the revenue administration, known as the 'Karori Experiment' is said to have brought about such oppression as to have 'dispersed' the peasants in various directions, with a consequent fall in the revenues.[36]

During Jahangir's reign the peasants are said to have been 'so cruelly and pitilessly oppressed' that 'the fields lie unsown and grow into wildernesses.'[37] And so, says another observer, 'the poor labourers desert them (their lands) and run away which is the reason they are poorly peopled.'[38] And yet the historian of the next reign (Shahjahan's) declares that 'owing to natural calamities, the rebellions of seditious *zamindars* and the cruelty of ill-fated potentates' vast lands became depopulated and despite the efforts of the Emperor and his able ministers, 'the land appeared more desolate than during the time of Jannat Makani (Jahangir).'[39] In 1629 a Dutch traveller noted in Gujarat that 'the peasants are more oppressed than formerly (and) frequently abscond' so that the revenue had fallen.[40] In the Dakhin, the period preceding Aurangzeb's second viceroyalty saw desolation stalking the land and the peasants 'scattered' owing to the 'oppression and neglect of the provincial governors.'[41]

What the conditions were during the early years of Aurangzeb's reign may be judged from Bernier's long discourse on the ills of the Mughal Empire. He too declares that "a considerable portion of the good land remains unfilled from the want of labourers," many of whom "perish in consequence of the bad treatment they receive from the Governors" or are left no choice but to "abandon the country."[42]

The main fact that emerges from these statements, is that the flight of the peasants from the land had become a common phenomenon of the time and it was growing in scale with the passage of years. With vast areas still unploughed, peasant migrations were a noticeable feature of the time.[43] Famines and natural calamities also initiated large movements of population. But it was the man-made system, which as the evidence set out above shows, lay at the root of the peasant's 'mobility'. Flight alone might save him if the revenue arrears became impossible to pay.[44] He might settle on new land, for there was no scarcity of land then. But though the imperial administration itself put the greatest emphasis on extending the area of culivation,[45] it could not obviously permit the abandonment of land already cultivated and some official documents specifically stipulate that the peasants to be settled on cultivable wastes were to be *ghair-jam'i*, i.e., those who had not previously, been paying revenue elsewhere.[46] Some peasants abandoned agriculture altogether. Bernier says, for example, that some of them left "the country" to "seek a more tolerable mode of existence either in the towns or in the camps; as bearers of burdens, carriers of water, or servants to horsemen."[47]

Nevertheless, as Manucci says in the context of Southern India, the same oppression prevailed everywhere and the lot of the aimless migrant was not a happy one.[48] Beyond a point there was no choice left to the peasant but that between starvation or slavery and armed resistance.

REVOLT OF THE PEASANTRY

The classic act of defiance on the part of the peasants was the refusal to pay the land revenue. Villages, which thus incurred the charge of rebellion, were technically known as *ma was* as opposed to the revenue-paying villages, called *ra'iyati*.[49] As Mundy observed early in the reign of Shahjahan "of theis kinde of broyles" between the authorities and the peasants "there is perpetuallie, in one part or other of India."[50] Until the reign of Aurangzeb, however, these conflicts generally appeared as local and isolated incidents. The resistance might be confined to the members of a village fraternity and leave the neighbouring villages unaffected. Usually, the villages which were protected in some measure by ravines or forests or hills, were more likely to defy the authorities than those situated in the open plains.[51] The purely peasant uprising of a few villages would, perhaps, have contrasted pitifully with the military efforts of even the smaller *zamindars*, and, faced with the forces at the command of the imperial administration or the *jagirdars*, was foredoomed to failure. Mundy noted that "most commonly the Gawares (*ganwars*, villagers) goe to the worst though they may be able to stand a while."[52] As may be imagined, a terrible fate awaited the villagers when, defeated: "Everyone is killed that is met with and their wives, sons and daughters and cattle are carried off."[53]

But as the oppression grew in intensity, the peasant uprisings gained in frequency. Moreover, two factors particularly helped to extend the scale of these revolts. In the first place, there was the community of caste, which made a village fraternity part of a greater whole. The role of caste-organisations as the precursors of the modern peasant movement in India has been well stressed by one of its most distinguished leaders.[54] Naturally, caste must have enjoyed even a more important place in the life of the peasant of Mughal India. It brought him into contact with his peers in the most distant villages through a thousand ties of blood and rites. If they took to arms, he could hardly stand aloof. In the Jat revolt we have, perhaps, the clearest instance of an essentially peasant revolt proceeding on caste lines. But the influence of caste is visible also in the 'lawless' activities of castes are the Mewatis and the Wattus, and Dogars.

At the same time many peasants in this period were finding a new basis for a community that was not complementary to, but was essentially opposed to, caste-divisions. This new basis was provided by the sects formed as part of the great religious movement that had begun in the latter part of the 15th century. The leading ideas of most of these sects were identical: an uncompromising monotheism, the abandonment of ritualistic forms of worship, the denial of all caste-barriers and of religious differences. As important as the content of their ideas was, perhaps, the mode of their propagation. Their preaching was entirely directed towards the masses, the new teaching was clothed in vernacular dialects, and, the prophets, the preachers and the followers belonged mostly to the lower classes. Kabir (c. 1500), the great prophet of the

Beragis, was a weaver; Dadu (a contemporary of Akbar), the teacher of the Dadu-panthis, was a village cotton-carder; Haridas (d. 1645), teacher of the Niranjis, a Jat slave; and Guru Nanak, a grain merchant.[55] None of these teachers, least of all Kabir and Nanak, preached any other code of conduct than that of humility and resignation, certainly not of militancy and resistance. Most of the devotional sects did not, probably, ever assume the form of social movements. But when radical ideas, such as hostility to caste and the sense of unity under a new and convincing faith, had established themselves in the minds and hearts of the masses, the new sects could not remain confined within their old mystic shell. In the event they provided the inspiration for two of the most powerful revolts against the Mughals, those of the Satnamis and the Sikhs, in which peasants were to play such a prominent part.

As the peasant uprisings grew in scale, however, their class origin tended to be obscured by the very two factors, caste and religion, which had helped in their extension. Nevertheless, the real transformation in their nature was brought about by the intervention of elements belonging to the *zamindar* class, which, had their own objects in opposing the Mughal ruling class. The fact that the peasant rebellions passed under the leadership of the *zamindar*s at a certain stage or that, from the very beginning the desperation of the peasants provided recruits for rebellious *zamindar*s, was of decisive significance in merging the revolts of the oppressed into the conflicts between two oppressing classes.

ROLE OF THE ZAMINDARS

We have said earlier in this article that the *zamindar*s formed a subordinate class within the ruling elite of the Mughal Empire. This subordination, however, was by no means voluntary and there existed a basic contradiction between this class and the Mughal, aristocracy. The main point of conflict between the imperial authorities (and *jagirdar*s) and the *zamindar*s was the size of the latter's share in the land revenue and/ or surplus produce. In the imperial territories, the *zamindar*s' exactions from the peasants were restricted not only by formal regulations,[56] but really much more by the fact that the high pitch of the revenue demand would have left little with the peasant to be taken by anyone else. In such a situation it would become difficult for the *zamindar* to collect the state revenue and pass it on to the *jagirdar* without harming his own interests.

A similar dilemma faced the autonomous chiefs. A heavy tribute was usually levied upon them and their states were never free from the threat of annexation.[57] On the other hand, since the *zamindars* usually had armed force at their disposal, they could not easily be dealt with by the imperial administration and were always a thorn in its side.

Thus the statements of official chroniclers frequently reflect an attitude of hostility on the part of the imperial government towards the *zamindars*, as a class Abul-l Fazl declares that "the custom of most of the *zamindars* of Hindustan is that leaving the path of single mindedness they look to every side and whoever appears more powerful and tumult-raising they join him."[58] Elsewhere he remarks that Raja Bharimal "out of wisdom and good fortune aspired to leave the ranks of *zamindars* and become one of the select of the Court" as if the two positions were mutually incompatible.[59] The court historian of Aurangzeb uses the adverb *zamindarana* in the obvious sense of opportunism or disloyalty.[60]

In the documents written from the official point of view it is assumed as a matter of course that the main danger to law and order came from the *zamindars* who refused to pay the revenue and had to be cowed down or destroyed by force whether by the *faujdar* (imperial military commandant) or the *jagirdar*.[61] The letters of Ra'dandaz Khan, *faujdar* of Beswara (?-1702), are particularly, revealing in this respect for they show this official as constantly leading or sending expeditions against *zamindars* in an area in the. plains so close to the heart of the Empire.[62] It is possible that the appointment of *zamindars* by grant from the Court, a practice which comes into prominence during Aurangzeb's reign, was largely motivated by the desire, to establish new local interests in order to counterbalance the power of the old *zamindars*.[63]

Manucci, writing in or about 1700, seems to sum up the situation accurately, when he says: "Usually the viceroys and governors (of the Mughal Empire) are in a constant state of quarrel with the Hindu princes and *zamindars*—with some because they wish to seize their lands with others, to force them to pay more revenue than is customary."[64] He adds elsewhere that "usually there is some rebellion of the *rajahs* and *zamindars* going on in the Mogul kingdom."[65]

It was, probably, their position in this unequal contest with the imperial power that, more than anything else, compelled the *zamindars* to adopt a conciliatory attitude towards their peasants, whose support would be indispensable to them not only during defence but also in flight. Moreover, being local men, closely acquainted with the conditions and customs of the peasants, they would have been able generally to make more flexible arrangements with the peasants under their control (whether in the lands left to them revenue-free or in the autonomous states) than could the officials of the *Khalisa* (Crownlands) or the *jagirdars*, who were unfamiliar with local practice and were interested only in an immediate increase in assessment.

Accordingly, Bernier noted that the peasants found "less oppression and allowed a greater degree of comfort" in "the territories of a *Raja*."[66] Of much greater significance still is the statement of the official historian of Aurangzeb, who declares that:

"the *zamindars* of the country of Hindustan, for considerations of policy—for winning the hearts of, and conciliating, the peasants, in order that they may not cease to obey or pay revenue to them—conduct themselves gently in exacting the revenue in the *mahals* of their *zamindari* and do not apply the regulations and laws followed in the imperial dominions."[67]

It came about, therefore, that the *zamindars* frequently attracted to their lands peasants absconding from the imperial territories. This phenomenon is noted in general terms by Pelsaert and Bernier,[68] but we have a few specific instances as well. When under A'zam Khan, the governor of Gujarat (1632-42), the peasants suffered great oppression "most of them fled and took refuge with *zamindars* in distant places."[69] A'zam Khan thereupon led an expedition against Navanagar and compelled its *zamindar* to expel the peasants who had fled to his territory so that they might return to their old home.[70] In Malwa a similar campaign was organised against the *zamindar* of Kanwar, who not only did not "pay the revenue in the way he should have paid," but also "the peasants of some of the *mahals* of the *jagir* of the governor, who fled to the territory, of Kanwar also evaded paying the revenue, being backed in this by those infidels" (i.e. the *zamindars* men).[71] In the reign of Aurangzeb, we come across a complaint by the *faujdar* of Talkokan to the effect that, first, a large number of the peasants had fled to the territories of the *zamindars*; and when he had brought them back by force, the Portuguese of Salsette enticed them away.[72]

The peasants and the *zamindars* thus frequently became associated in the struggle against the Mughal authorities. The case of Kuch Bihar may not be typical but it is significant. When the kingdom was annexed in 1661 the Mughal officials introduced there the methods of "revenue assessment and collection according to the regulations followed in *mahals* of the imperial territories." Thereupon the peasants rose in rebellion, expelled the Mughal officials and brought back their deposed *raja,* who had treated them leniently in the general manner of the *zamindars*.[73]

The peasants thus not only added to the *zamindar's* resources, by engaging in cultivation on his lands, but also on occasions filled the ranks of his armed bands. Such primitive troops were probably useless against the professional cavalrymen of the Mughal armies. But numbers and terrain still counted, as the Marathas were to show so strikingly.

The new feature that comes to the fore in the reign of Aurangzeb is that the *zamindars'* struggle against the Mughals is no longer merely defensive. As the number of starving, homeless peasants grew and the peasants took to arms themselves, it became possible for the *zamindars* to organise them into large bands and even armies, take to predatory warfare and expand their areas of domination. It was on these lines that, as we will see below, the two most powerful revolts against the Mughals, those of the Marathas and the Jats, proceeded till they ultimately consumed the whole Empire.

GENESIS AND CHARACTER OF THE PRINCIPAL REVOLTS

Hitherto we have been considering the basic features of the crisis which faced the Mughal Empire in the latter part of the 17th century. Our purpose now, in the following pages, will be to illustrate and substantiate many of the general statements made above by a study of the origins and course of each of the principal revolts which this crisis produced.

I

The Mughal province of Agra comprised the central Doab and a broad belt of territory on the right side of the Jamuna both north and south of the Chambal river. Speaking of this province Abu-l Fazl observes that "owing to the peculiarity of its climate: the peasant masses (*'umum-iri'aya*) of that territory are notorious throughout the vast country of Hindustan, for rebelliousness, bravery and courage."[74] The area on both sides of the Jamuna figures constantly in Mughal records as the scene of military operations against rebellious peasantry. Akbar once personally led an attack on a village;[75] and we read of a *raja* in a *pargana* close to Agra, who used to engage in robbery and defended himself when attacked, with the assistance of *ganwars*, or peasants.[76] During the succeeding reign of Jahangir, it was reported to the Court that "the *ganwars* and cultivators" on the eastern side of the Jamuna, near Mathura, "do not cease to commit highway robbery and, protected by dense jungle and fastnesses, live in rebellion and without fear, and do not pay the revenue to the *jagirdars*." An expedition was organised against them, as a result of which "numbers of them were killed, their women and children taken captive and a great booty acquired by the victorious troops."[77] This happened in the 18th regnal year of Jahangir and yet twelve years later (1634) a campaign on a far more elaborate scale had to be conducted against "the malefactors" on both sides of the Jamuna, who used 'to commit robbery' on the Agra-Delhi route. "Ten thousand of those human-looking beasts" were slaughtered, their women and children and cattle—"beyond computation"—captured.[78] In the 18th regnal year of Shahjahan, the 'rebels' near Mathura were still out of control.[79] When Sa'dullah Khan, the great minister of Shahjahan, died in 1656, "the gamors (*ganwars*) of severall his townes (i.e. villages in his *jagirs*) neare Agra rose in armes. But.... they were suddenly surprized by Abdall Nubby, his fouzdarr, their townes sacked and such as escaped not by flight, either slaine or imprisoned."[80]

Such had been the past history of the area which was to be the cradle of the Jat revolt in the time of Aurangzeb. It will be noticed that our authorities have not so far identified the revolting peasants as Jats. The usual term for them is *ganwar*, or villager, and in one or two cases at least the rebels seem to have been led by Rajput *zamindars*.[81] Nevertheless Manucci, who treats of their revolts in some detail, knows the Jat rebels of Aurangzeb's reign also simply as 'peasants' and assumes then to be the partisans of the same cause as those whom Akbar had oppressed.[82] The Jats are, *par excellence,* a peasant caste[83] and it is not unlikely that they had already participated in many of the previous conflicts with the authorities.

The Jat rebellion, properly speaking, however, dates from the time, when Gokula Jat, the *zamindar* of Talpat near Mathura, "assembled a large army of Jats and other villagers and raised a rebellion."[84] He was killed in 1669, but the leadership passed on to Raja Ram Jat and then his nephew Chauraman Jat. Over wide areas the peasants refused to pay revenue and took to arms. For example, we learn from the grant of a *zamindari* near Mathura to a *jagirdar* that the 25 villages covered by it were all inhabited by "evil-mannered rebels" and the grantee was requir ed to expel them and settle new peasants.[85] In 1681 Multafat Khan, the *faujdar* of the district around Agra, was killed when leading an attack on a village whose peasants had refused to pay the revenue.[86] And later in the same decade we hear a *jagjirdar* complaining that for three years he had not been able to obtain anything from his *jagirs* near Agra "owing to the rebellion."[87]

The Jat revolt ultimately grew into a huge plundering movement. The range of the area devastated spread from the one *pargana* of Sa'dabad plundered by Gokula[88] and the *parganas* around Agra, sacked by Raja Ram,[89] to its highest extent under Chauraman, when "all the *parganas* under Agra and Delhi had been sacked and plundered and from the tumult of that perdition-seeker (i.e. Chauraman) the routes and ways were blocked."[90]

II

So far as we know the Jat rebels (in spite of the religious teacher Haridas, a Jat slave) had no connection with any particular religious movement. In the Satnami and Sikh rebellions, on the other hand, religion replaced caste as the cementing bond of rebel ranks. But their class character, was not any different for that reason.

Thus the Satnamis, who were a sect of the Beragis, are described in the following terms by a contemporary historian:

There is a group of Hindu mendicants, known as Satnamis, who are also called Mundiyas. They consist of some four or five thousand house-holders in the pargana of Narnaul. and Mewat. Although those Mundiyas dress like mendicants, yet their livelihood and profession is usually agriculture and trade in the manner of grain-merhcants with small capital. Living according to the ways of their own community they aspire to reach the status of a good name, which is the meaning of the word *satnam*. But if any one should want to impose tyranny and oppression upon them as a display of courage or authority, they will not tolerate it and most, of them bear arms and weapons.[91]

Another contemporary writer castigates the community for being "by its extreme dirtiness rendered foul, filthy and impure. Thus, says he, "under the rules of their sect they do not differentiate between Muslims and Hindus and eat pig's flesh and other disgusting things."[92]

Even before they went into rebellion, the Satnamis were not apparently very submissive to the authorities. In the early years of Aurangzeb a revenue official claims that though certain "cultivators" in a village in the *pargana* of Bhatnair were "living with their women, children, possessions and cattle in the garb of the Beragis," they were "not free from the thoughts of sedition and robbery."[93] The revolt in fact began (1672) as a rural affray. One of the Satnamis "was working in his fields when he exchanged, hot words with a *piyada* (foot-trooper), who was guarding the corn-heap. The *piyada* broke the Satnami's head by a blow from his stick. Thereupon a crowd of that sect mobbed that *piyada* and beat, him so much, as to reduce him almost to a corpse." The *shiqqdar* (local revenue-collector) sent a contingent of troops, which finally precipitated the rebellion.[94]

The plebian character of the revolt Is perhaps best, brought (mi: by the words of scorn which a chronicler pours upon it:

To the spectators of the wonderful works of Fate the occurrence of this event is a case of amazement, i.e. what came into the head of this rebellious, murderous, destitute gang of goldsmiths (*recte* peasants?),[95] carpenters, sweepers and tanners and other mean and ignoble men of artisan castes that their conceited brains became so overclouded? Rebellious pride having found a place in their brains, their heads became too heavy for their shoulders. By their own legs they were caught in the snare of annihilation. To unveil this tale, this huge horde of mischief-makers of the region of Mewat all of a sudden sprang up from the earth like moths and fell down from the sky like locusts. . . .[96]

Despite their great initial success the repeated defeats they inflicted upon the imperial troops and the occupation of Narnaul and Bairat, the rebels were finally destroyed by a large army sent from the Court. But they went down fighting bravely and the same historian, whose words have been quoted above, admits that despite the lack of all materials of war, they repeated the scenes of the great war of Mahabharat.[97]

III

If from a historical view-point, Islam appears as an urban creed,[98] Sikhism may, with equal justice, be characterised as a peasant religion. The verses of Guru Nanak "are all in the language of the Jats of Panjab. And Jat in the dialect of the Panjab means a villager, a rustic."[99] Thus wrote, in 1650s the author of the *Dabistan-i Mazahib,* who gives us a most intimate account of the Sikhs. He adds that "among them there is no such rule as that, a Brahman should not be a disciple (*Sikh*) of a Khatri, for Nanak was a Khatri. . . Similarly, they have made Khatris subordinate to the Jats, who are the lowliest, of the caste of Bais (Vaishya). Thus of the great *masands* (nobles, agents), of the Guru most are Jats."[100] Guru Arjun Mal (1581–1606) took the first steps in creating a well-knit and disciplined organisation. He appointed his agents in every town. "It has been ordained (by him) that an *udasi* or ascetic is not a good believer. Owing to this some of the Sikhs of the Guru engage in agriculture, others in trade and service; and every one, according to his capacity, pays a *nazar* (gift) each year to the *masand,*" who received it on behalf of the Guru.[101] The Sikhs became a military power only under Guru Hargobind (1606–45), who created an army of his own and, therefore, came into armed collision with the Mughal government.[102] He thus founded a tradition, which was doggedly continued by the last Guru, Gobind Singh (1676–1708), till finally in 1709, Banda was able to lead into the field "an army of innumerable men, like ants and locusts, belonging to the low castes of Hindus and ready to die" at his orders.[103]

IV

The three major revolts dealt with above do not by any means exhaust the list of peasant uprisings which occurred in Mughal times in Northern India. Many of these appear in our authorities merely as passing incidents. We read, for example, that when, in 1575–6, the governor of Bhakkar (Sind) levied the land revenue at a uniform rate per *bigha* and 'the peasants were subjected to oppression,' the Mangcha tribe revolted and killed the tax-gatherers. They were, however, defeated and expelled, from their lands.[104] Again, when Manucci passed by Allahabad in 1662, he found the governor absent "on a campaign against some villagers, who objected to pay their revenue without at least one fight."[105]

Of disorders of a different kind were those perpetrated by the Mewatis in Mewat. They were constantly in rebellion and made plundering raids from their villages lying deep in the hills.[106] Jai Singh led a ferocious campaign against them in 1649–50,[107] but they still survived to give further trouble later on.[108] Similarly, the peasants of the Lakhi jungle—

an extensive waste and forest in the Punjab formed by various branches of the Sutlej river—were "notorious for rebellion and mischief." They belonged to the castes of Wattus, Dogars and Gujars and were so well protected by the various river channels and jungles, that most of the expeditions against them proved ineffectual.[109] In Aurangzeb's later years they are once said to have ravaged the whole region of Dipalpur.[110]

The Bundila rebellion, which began after Shahjahan's annexation of Orchha in 1635 and continued intermittently for the rest of the century and later was essentially a dynastic affair, a war for the rights of a royal house. But two despatches from a Mughal commander deputed against them by Shahjahan show that rebels were, after a successful exploit, able to call over to their side 'zamindars and peasants' from 'both the ra'iyati and mawas areas.' Moreover, the peasants took the opportunity to evade the payment of revenue, whenever, the rebels became active.[111]

V

The Marathas beyond doubt constituted the greatest single force responsible for the downfall of the Mughal Empire. In the year 1700 a Mughal officer, Bhimsen, while writing his memoirs, set himself to explain the causes that had led to the rise and success of the Marathas. Himself a native of Burhanpur and with decades of service in the Dakhin behind him, his views on the subject are of great interest.

He begins with a purely military argument. The Mughal commanders were not maintaining their contingents up to the standards required by the regulations. As a result the "male-factors" did not entertain any fear of the *faujdars* and so "those regions that have been assigned to the *mansabdars* (Mughal officers) cannot be compelled to pay revenue." "The *zamindars* also," he adds, "having obtained power, have allied themselves with the Marathas."

He then turns to the second reason and explicitly finds a connection between the rise of the Maratha power and the oppression of the peasants in the imperial territories:

The agents of the *jagirdars*, having apprehensions concerning the niggardly behaviour of the clerks of the Court, who on every excuse. . . effect a transfer, do not have any hope of the confirmation of the *jagir* for the following year and so abandon the habit of protecting the peasants and of stable management. The *jagirdar* who sends a revenue-collector (*'amil*), owing to his own difficult circumstances, first takes something from him in advance (*qabz*) and the latter, reaching the *jagir*, keeps thinking, perhaps, another *'amil* is coming behind him, who has paid a larger *qabz;* and so proceeding tyrannically, is unrelenting in his exactions. Some peasants are not remiss in paying the authorised revenue, but are made desperate by the evil of this excruciating exploitation. It came to be represented (at the Court) that the Marathas obtain collaboration front the peasants of the imperial dominations. It was, thereupon, ordered that the horses and weapons found in every village were to be confiscated. When this happened in most villages, the peasants, providing themselves with horses and arms, joined the Marathas.

And then again returning to the subject of the oppression of the peasants, Bhimsen speaks of:

the tyranny of the *pattis* (agents) of the *faujdars*, *desmukhs* and *zamindars*, who on every excuse collect money from the peasantry—and besides this the imperial tribute (*peshkash-i padshahi*) was fixed upon the zamindars, persons being appointed to exact it and sent everywhere to obtain supplies. There is no limit to the oppression of these men. The *zamindars* do not give a penny from their own purse, but pay it after extorting: it from the peasants. And the *jiziya* (poll tax) that has been imposed and collectors appointed—of their oppression and cruelty what may one write? For no description can suffice. . .

In addition to this, the conditions of the peasants were also being aggravated beyond endurance by Maratha depredations. For—

As the country has been divided into the *Khalisa* and pay-assignments of the *jagirdars*, so the Marathas too have distributed the very same country among their own 'pseudo-chiefs': On one land, there was two *jagirdars*, Quatrain: "The village is ruined by a measuring rod with two measures, &c." The troops of the (Maratha) leaders who come in for the sake of plundering the country, extort money from every *pargana* and all places, in accordance with their desire and let (their horses) graze on and trample upon the cultivated fields... Order has. disappeared. Now things have gone beyond every limit. The produce of the fields does not reach the granary at all. They (the peasants) are absolutely ruined.

But this desolation, apparently, drove the peasants still further into the arms of the Marathas. Thus, says Bhimsen, "when many of Siva's (*sic!* Maratha) forts came into the possession of His Majesty (Aurangzeb), it became difficult for the Marathas to find a place to live, and keep their dependents. (But) they have affinities with the peasants of the imperial dominations and left their families in their custody in inhabited places...."

Bliimsen's passage closes with these words:

The peasants have abandoned cultivation and neither a *dam* nor *diram* (petty coins) reaches the *jagirdars*. Despairing and perplexed because of (their lack of) strength many of the *mansabdars* of this country have gone over to the Marathas."[112]

As a contemporary appraisal of the causes of Maratha success, Bhimsen's statements are invaluable. Such facts as we possess amply justify the leading lines of his argument. The peasants of the Dakhin had suffered for decades before Shivaji's rise to eminence, from the wars between the Mughals and the Dakhin kingdoms. Vast areas used to be ravaged by the invading armies, the grain seized, the people enslaved.[113] The peasants in the Mughal province of Dakhin were laid under a crippling burden owing to the stationing of large Mughal armies, largely maintained from jagirs in the province.[114] And so, as we have noticed earlier, the country was desolate and the peasants in flight when Aurangzeb came to the Dakhin as its Viceroy for the second time.

The result was that even at that early period some of the peasants had begun to render aid to Shivaji. Before he set out to win his throne in 1658, Aurangzeb was careful to urge his officials to mete out capital punishment to "peasants, *deshmukhs, patels* (village headmen) of the *parganas* of the imperial territories, who have gone over to the enemy (i.e. Shivaji and his associates) and have exerted themselves in guiding or abetting those ill-destined ones."[115]

At the same time there will be no greater mistake than to consider Shivaji and the Maratha chiefs as conscious leaders of a peasant uprising. Shivaji himself was the son of a great noble of Ahmadnagar (and later Bijapur) and he began his own career as any other ambitious *zamindar* or chieftain in the Konkan. The fiscal and political practices of the Marathas bore the deepest imprint of the customs and outlook of *zamindars*. The *chauth,* the customary demand of the Marathas from Shivaji onwards, was really simply a form of the traditional *zamindari* right to one-fourth of the land revenue, known, in Gujarat, as *banth*.[116] Similarly, the demand for *sardeshmukhi* or 10 (or 9) per cent of the revenue, also derived from the rights of *deshmukh* (equivalent to the North Indian *chaudhuri*), who used to be the *zamindar,* entrusted by the Government with the task of collecting revenue from the other *zamindars* and peasants of his area, and took his percentage of revenue as a reward for his work. It was, therefore, typical that when the famous Tarabai sought peace with Aurangzeb, she should have asked for "the *deshmukhi* of the country of Dakhin," the acme of ambition for any *zamindar*.[117]

Nor were the conditions of the peasants in the Maratha kingdom idyllic. How Shivaji treated his peasants is described by Fryer, who visited parts of his kingdom in 1675–6. He demanded the revenue, we are told, at double the rates of former days,[118] leaving to "the Tiller hardly so much as will keep Life and Soul together."[119] And in Kanara "three-quarters of the Land lies unmanured (uncultivated) through the Tyranny of Seva Gi."[120]

Shivaji had use for the peasants in an altogether different sphere. They were the "Naked Starved Rascals" who formed his army.[121] Armed with "only lances and long swords two inches wide,"[122] they were "good at Surprising and Ransacking," but not, "for a pitched Field."[123] They had to live by plunder only, for Shivaji's maxim was: 'No Plunder, no Play.'[124] This was the form of salvation which Shivaji and his successors held out to the destitute peasantry of the Dakhin. As Bhimsen's account shows, the military operations of the Marathas completely devastated the land. So that as the range of operations of the Robber State grew, the peasants' destitution also increased. But this only made a still larger number of "naked starved rascals" available for the Maratha armies; and so the unending circle would go on . . . . [125]

"There is no province or district," confesses Aurangzeb in his last years, "where the infidels have not raised a tumult and since they are not chastised they have established themselves everywhere. Most of the country has been rendered desolate and if any place is inhabited, the peasants there have probably come to terms with the 'robbers' (*ashqiya*, the official Mughal name for the Marathas)."[126]

Thus was the Mughal Empire destroyed. Like most systems of oppression, it was its own grave-digger. But the forces ranged against it were so constituted that they could not create a new order in its place. On the other hand, they dissolved the administrative unity of India which the fallen Empire had represented, devastated the towns, throttled trade and commerce and thus created the ideal conditions for foreign conquest.

LIST OF AUTHORITIES WITH ABBREVIATIONS

The following list is arranged in alphabetical order according to the abbreviations used in the notes and put here in capital letters. Works cited only once, of which full reference is given in the notes, have not been included.

'Br.M.' denotes a manuscript belonging to the British Museum: I.O., the India Office Library, London; and 'Bodl.', the Bodleian Library, Oxford.

ADAB-I 'ALAMGIRI, Collection of letters written on behalf of Aurangzeb, before his accession, by Munshi Qabil Khan and on that of Prince Akbar by Muhammad Sadiq. Br. M. Or. 177.

AHKAM-I 'ALAMGIRI, Letters and orders of Aurangzeb, belonging to his later years, collected by Inayatullah Khan. I.O. 3887.

AIN. Abu-l Fazl, *Ain-i Akbari,* ed. Blochmann (2 vols.), Bibliotheca Indica, Calcutta, 1867–77.

AKBARNAMA. Abu-1 Fazl, *Akbarnama,* Bib. Ind., ed. (3 vols.), Calcutta, 1873–87.

AKHBARAT. Akhbarat-i Darbar-i Mu'alla, Court, news-letters of Aurangzeb's reign. 9 vols, in Case 47 at the Royal Asiatic Society, London.

'ALAMGIRNAMA. Muhammad Kazim, *'Alamgirnama.* Bib. Ind., Calcutta, 1865–73.

BADAUNI. 'Abdu-1 Qadir Badauni, *Muntakhaba-t Tawarikh.* Bib. Ind., Calcutta, 1864–69.

BERNIER. Francois Bernier, *Travels in the Mogul Empire* 1656–68, tr. A. Constable, 2nd ed. revised by V. A. Smith, London, 1916.

DABISTAN-i MAZAHIB, the famous anonymous works at the religions of the World, completed between 1653 & 1656. Nazar Ashraf, Calcutta, 1809

DILKUSHA, Bhimsen, Nuskha-i Dilkusha, Br. M. Or. 23.

DURR-AL 'ULUM, Collection of administrative documents and private papers of Munshi Gopal Rai Surdaj. 1688–9 A.D. Bodl. Walker 104.

FACTORIES. The English Factories in India, 13 Vols. (1618–69), ed. W. Foster. Vols. cited by the years covered by them.

FRYER. John Fryer, *A New Account of East India & Persia* 1672–81, ed. W. Crooke, Hakluyt Society (3 vols.), London, 1909, 1912 & 1915.

INSHA-I ROSHAN KALAM, Letters written on behalf of Ra'dandaz Khan by Bhopat Rai. I.O. 4011.

ISARDAS, Mehta Isardas Nagar, *Futuhat-i 'Alamgiri,* Br.M. Add. 23, 884.

JAHANGIR'S INDIA. Pelsaert's *Remonstrantie,* tr. by Moreland & Geyl, Cambridge, 1925.

JASB. Journal of the Asiatic Society of Bengal, Calcutta.

JIH. Journal of Indian History, Madras.

KHAFI KHAN. Muhammad Hashim Khafi Khan, *Muntakhab-al Lubab,* Bib. Ind., Calcutta, 1860–74, 1909–25.

KHULASATU-S SIYAQ, Administrative Manual, compiled A.D. 1703. Br. M. Add. 6588.

LAHORI. Abdul Hamid Lahori, *Padshahnama,* Bib. Ind., Calcutta, 1866-72.

MA'ASIR-I 'ALAMGIRI. By Saqi Musta'idd Khan. Bib. Ind., Calcutta, 1870-73.

MANRIQUE. Fray Sebastian Manrique, Travels, 1629–43, tr. Luard, Hakluyt Society (2 vols.), London, 1907–8.

MANUCCI. Nicolao Manucci, *Storia do Mogor.* tr. W. Irvine (4 vols.). Indian Texts Series, London, 1907–8.

MIRAT. 'Ali Muhammad Khan, *Mirat-i Ahmadi,* ed. Nawab Ali (2 vols. & Supplement). Baroda, 1927–8.

MUNDY. Peter Mundy, *Travels,* Vol. II: 'Travels in Asia', ed. R.C. Temple, Hakluyt Society, London, 1914

NIGARNAMA-I MUNSHI. By 'Malikzada', A.D. 1684. Br.M. Or. 1735

SADIQ KHAN. Muhammad Sadiq Khan, *Shahjahan-nama,* Br.M. Or. 174.

NOTES

1. The classic series is Sir Jadunath Sarkar's *Aurangzib* (5 vols.), William Irvine's *Later Mughals* (1707-39) edited & continued by Sarkar, and Sarkar's *Fall of the Mughal Empire,* 4 vols. (1739–1803). A recent work is Dr. S. Chandra's *Parties & Politics at the Mughal Court* (1707–39), Aligarh, 1959.

2. The point is made, for example, in Nehru's *Discovery of India,* London, 1956, p. 269.

3. E.g. J. Xavier, tr. Hosten, *JASB,* NS, XXIII, 1927, pp. 121–2; Roe, *The Embassy of Sir Thoma Roe,* ed. W. Foster, p. 105; Bernier, 5, 204, 226, 232, 238;

Fryer, I, p. 137; Manucci, II, p. 46. This claim is, however, not put forward by any of the Indian authorities. There is no hint, of it at all in Abu-l Fazl's *Ain-i Akbari*, where one should have most expected to find it.

4. Owing to the high pitch of the revenue demand, says Geleynssen (A.D. 1629) "the peasants in the country cannot earn more than their subsistence" (*JIH*, IV, pp. 78–9) and, says Pelsaert (1629), "so much is wrung from the peasants, that even dry bread is scarcely left to fill their stomachs." (*Jahangir's India*, 54).

5. The administration determined the standard or normal yield per *bigha* of the various crops for each locality, and it was a third of this, not the actual yield, that was settled as the revenue rate. The rates in kind were then, commuted into cash rates, again at prices sanctioned by the Court. The cash rates thus worked out were applied year after year, being unaffected by the harvests actually gathered. See Moreland, *Agrarian System of Moslem India*, Allahabad reprint, pp. 82–92, for the best available description of this method of assessment.

6. The documents are too numerous to be cited here. But see *Mirat*, I, p. 263; *Farman* to Muhammad Hashim, Arts. 4, 6, 9 & 16: *Nigarnama-i Munshi, passim*.

7. Geleynssen, *JIH*, IV, pp. 78–9; Fryer, I, pp. 300–301.

8. This term is borrowed from Moreland, who in his *Agrarian System of Moslem India* was the first, to appreciate the essential aspects of this system.

9. See Abu-l Fazl's reflections on this in *Akbarnama*, II, pp. 332–3, where he likens it, in virtue, to the transplantation of plants.

10. As suggested by Barthold in his *Iran*, tr. Nariman in the *Posthumous Works of G. K. Nariman*, pp. 142–3.

11. I have discussed this point in my paper on "The Zamindars in the Ain-i Akbari", read before the 1958 session of the Indian History Congress, Trivandrum.

12. This is also discussed in the paper referred to in the preceding note.

13. On this the evidence is too extensive to be cited. Moreland's *Agrarian System of Moslem India*, Allahabad reprint, may be consulted, especially, pp. 11, 114, 136–7.

14. For a description of the trade and commercial organisation of the time, see Moreland, *India at the Death of Akbar*, pp. 196–252. European commerce with India also developed rapidly in the 17th century.

15. Cf. W.C. Smith, 'The Mughal Empire and the Middle Class: A Hypothesis', *Islamic-Culture*, Oct., 1944, pp. 349–63. He suggests that the mercantile classes were an ally of the Mughal Empire, but his detailed views are based on very scanty and, as a rule, secondary material.

16. Bernier, p. 227. 'Timariot' is a harmless piece of Turkicism by Bernier. He explicitly identifies the "jah-ghir" with "timar" on p. 224.

17. St. Xavier noted as early as 1609 that since the assignments were held at the King's pleasure 'during the time that someone holds certain lands he squeezes out of them whatever he can and the poor labourers desert them and run away,' &c. (tr. Hosten, *JASB, N.S.,* XXIII, 1927, p. 121). See also Hawkins, *Early Travels,* ed. Foster, p. 114, and Manrique, II p. 372.

18. *Dilkusha,* f. 139a.

19. Sadiq Khan, f. 10b.

20. See Moreland's analysis of the revenue-statistics in his *From Akbar to Aurangzeb,* pp. 260–6. The revenue-rate on wheat given in an administrative manual, *Khulasatus Siyaq,* ff. 75a–76b, near the close of Aurangzeb's reign, for a *pargana* near Lahore is, allowing for the change in the unit of measurement, about 2.6 times the rate in the *Ain* for the same crop and circle. Despite Moreland's findings to the contrary (op. cit., pp. 160–4, 183–5), there was actually a corresponding increase in prices. Thus the wheat price given in the same manual that has been cited above (f.90a–b) for Lahore is 2.9 times the wheat price in the *Ain* (I, 60) given for the Court, then at Lahore. The same trend can be substantiated from the evidence concerning grain prices in other regions. English records also reflect it pretty clearly in the case of sugar and Bayana indigo. The present writer has studied the copper and gold values of the Mughal rupee (minted of silver) in an article contributed to the *Medieval India Quarterly* (Aligarh) (in the press). Evidence has been brought together to show that the gold price increased in the course of the 17th century by 45 per cent, and copper by about 100 per cent There were, however, many violent fluctuations and the respective prices in the 1660s had gone up to as high as 178 and 260 per cent.

21. The *jiziya* was collected from both towns and villages. It was by nature a very retrogressive tax. From the specimen accounts given in a *'Dastur-al 'Amal'* in British Museum, Or. 2026, f. 52a–b, a manual compiled in the later years of Aurangzeb, it appears that most of the males in an ordinary village were held assessable, the minimum rate being Rs. 3, Rs. 2 per annum—an amount which was then roughly equal to the average monthly wage of an unskilled labourer in the towns.

22. *Mirat,* I, p. 263.

23. Aurangzeb's *farman* to Rasikdas, Art. 5 (Text ed. & tr. Sarkar, *JASB.* N. S. II 1906 pp. 223-55). A *hasbu-l hukm* issued in the 16th year of Aurangzeb's reign sought to check this practice in both the lands of the *Khalisa* and the assignments of the *jagirdars.* It cancelled all arrears except those of the preceding year. It also explicitly forbade the exaction of arrears owned by peasants, who had died or absconded, from their neighbours. (*Nigarnama-i Munshi, ff.* 194b–195a: *Mirat,* I 290–1).

24. See, for example, *Factories,* 1634–6, where it is stated that the recovery

in the villages from the great Gujarat famine of 1630–2 was much retarded by "the excessive tiranny and covetousness of the governors of all sorts" and the writers wished but 'one yeares vacancye from oppression. . . to advance the plenty."

25. *Khulasatus Siyaq,* f. 80a; Mundy, pp. 73–4; Manrique, II, p. 272.

26. See a complaint against a *chaudhuri,* who had taken the revenue of a village in farm, in *Durr-ul Ulum,* f. 65a-b; also Manrique, II, p. 272.

27. Manrique. II, p. 272.

28. Manucci, II, pp. 450–1.

29. Badauni, p. 189; Manucci, II, p. 451.

30. *Jahangir's India,* 47.

31. Manrique, II, p. 272, Cr. also Bernier, p. 205.

32. For such responsibility borne by *jagirdars,* see *Factories* 1646–50, pp. 300–302; *Durr-al'Ulum,* ff. 64b–65a; for the *faujdar,* Manucci, II, p. 421. *Ain,* I, p. 284 imposes a similar duty on the *kotwal* or city commandant and the *Char Chaman-i Barhaman* of Chandrabhan Brahman, Br. M. Add. 18,863, f. 25a–b on the *'amil* or revenue-collector.

33. Mundy, pp. 73–4. He says that the villagers were in most cases unable to prevent the thieves from establishing themselves and that those affected by the authorities' punitive expeditions were "some-times . . . Innocent". These remarks are made in the course of a journey through Doab early in Shahjahan's reign.

Shaista Khan, the governor of Gujarat, is denounced in *Factories,* 1646–50, p. 127, for "his unheard of tiranie in depopulating whole townes (villages) of miserably poor people, under pretence of their harbouring theives and rogues (whilst that are such may walk about untoucht at noone day)." 'Towne' in the 17th century English records, invariably means 'a village.'

34. *Akbarnama,* II, pp. 159–60.

35. This is said in respect of Gujarat in 1615 (Letter tr. Hosten, *JASB,* N. S. XXIII, 1927, p. 125). A similar statement is made in respect of Kashmir, which he visited in 1597. (Ibid, p. 116).

36. Badauni, II, p. 189.

37. *Jahangir's India* p. 47.

38. St. Xavier's letter from Agra, 1609, op. cit., p. 121.

39. Sadiq Khan, Or. 174, f. 10a–b.

40. Geleynssen, tr. Moreland, *JIH,* IV, p. 78.

41. *Adab-i 'Alamgiri,* ff. 26b, 30b–31a, 34a.

42. Bernier p. 205; also pp. 226-7. The word 'labourers' in this translation stands for 'labourers' in the original, which really meant 'peasants'. (See Moreland, *Agrarian System,* p. 147n.)

43. See Babur's remarks on the way in which "in Hindustan hamlete and

villages—even towns—are depopulated and set up in a moment." (*Baburnama,* tr. Beveridge, II, pp. 487–8).

44. On this the best evidence is that of official orders which leave us in no doubt as to the large number of peasants who absconded to escape payment of revenue arrears or *taqavi* (Anglicised 'taccavi') loans. (See *Adab-i 'Alamgiri,* f. 123b; *Nigarnama-i Munshi,* ff. 194b–195a; *Mirat,* I, pp. 290–1).

45. See Akbar's general order (*dastur-al 'amal*) to officials in *Insha-i Abu-l Fazl,* Nawal Kishor lith. Kanpur, 1872, p. 60; *Ain* I, 285–6; Aurangzeb's *farman* to Rasikdas, Preamble & Art. 2 &c.

46. *Nigarnama-i Munshi,* ff. 103b–104a, 187a–188a. In interpreting the term *ghair-jam' i,* it should be remembered that the word *jam'a,* in the terminology of the Mughal administration, signified the revenue assessed.

47. Bernier, p. 205.

48. Manucci, III, pp. 47, 51.

49. The word *mawas* is not to be found in the dictionaries. But the following passage from a letter from a revenue-collector to his *jagirdar* (in the reign of Aurangzeb) best explains its significance. "We reached the *pargana* of . . . . Some of the *chaudhuris* and *qanungos* and the peasants from the *ra'iyati* villages have come, but those who are attached to the *mawas* have not shown any inclination . . . .Sir! This *pargana* is rebellious (*zor-talab*): one part *ra'iyati,* three parts *mawas.* For keeping the peasants and rebels in order (and) collecting the full revenue, one needs a contingent, etc." (Hadiqi, *Collection of Specimen Letters,* 1661 A.D. Br. M. Royal 16, B *XXIII,* f. 15a–b).

50. Mundy, pp. 172–3.

51. 'In many parts of the plains thorny jungle grows, behind the good defence of which the people of the *parganas* become stubbornly rebellious and do not pay the revenue,' (*Baburnama,* tr. Beveridge, II, p. 487).

52. Mundy, p. 173.

53. Manucci, II, p. 451. Abu-l Fazl, while speaking of action against rebellious villages, makes 'no reference to the fate of the combatants or their families. He merely says that everything found in the village should be treated as booty, a fifth whereof being reserved for the *Khalisa,* or the emperor's own income, (*Ain,* I. p. 283). An order issued in 1671 by Aurangzeb apparently tries to modify the sternness of the punishment customarily meted out to the rebels (*Mirat,* I, p. 280), but one may well doubt if it had any great effect.

54. E. M. S. Namboodiripad, *The National Question in Kerala,* pp. 102–3.

55. *Dabistan-i Mazahib,* pp. 246, 267–8, 274.

56. See complaints against the exactions of *zamindars* entertained at the Court, Balkrishan Brahman, f. 52a–b; *Durr-al Ulum,* f. 51a–b.

57. Within four years of Aurangzeb's accession, for instance, three large states were annexed: Kuch Bihar (1661), Palamau (1661) and Navanagar (1683).

58. *Akbar-nama,* II. p. 63.

59. *Akbarnama,* II, p. 156.

60. *'Alamgirnama,* p. 571 (with reference to Raja Karan Bhurtiya's conduct).

61. *Hidayat-al Qawa'id* of Hidayatullah Bihari, I.0.3996A, f. 7a–b (duties of a *faujdar*); *Bayaz-i Izad Bakhsh Rasa,* I.0.4014, f. 2a–b (the exploit of a *jagirdar* in a semi-humourous petition to God.)

62. *Insha-i Roshan Kalam,* passim.

63. Detailed regulations concerning the grant of *zamindari* are prescribed in an administrative manual of Aurangzeb's reign (Bodl-Fraser 86, f. 62a–b). Actual instances of such grants during this reign are too numerous to be cited here. But see *Insha-i Roshan Kalam,* ff. 3b–4a, 8a & passim; and *Ma'asir-i 'Alamgiri,* p. 514. Numerous instances will also be found in the *Akhbarat.*

64. Manucci, II, pp. 431–2.

65. Ibid., p. 462.

66. Bernier, p. 205.

67. *'Alamgirnama,* p. 781.

68. *Jahangir's India,* p. 47; Bernier, p. 205.

69. *Mirat,* I, p. 216.

70. Lahori, II, p. 232; *Mirat,* I, p. 214.

71. Lahori, II, p. 370.

72. *Karnama,* Letters written on behalf of Mu'tabar Khan by Chathmal 'Hindu,' I.0.2007, ff. 243b–244a.

73. *'Alamgirnama,* pp. 781–2; *Fathiya-i Ibriya* of Shihabuddin Talish, Bodl.: Bodl. Or. 587.

74. *Akbarnama,* III, p. 231.

75. Ibid., II, p. 163.

76. Badauni, II, pp. 151–2.

77. *Jahangirnama* (Jahangir's Memoirs), ed. Saiyid Ahmad, 1863–4, pp. 375-6.

78. Qazwini, *Padshahnama,* Br.M.Or. 173, ff. 237b, 239b; Lahori I, pp. ii, 71–2, 76. The latter says that 12,000 troops in all were deployed against the rebels.

79. Lahori, II, p. 425.

80. *Factories,* 1655–60, p. 85.

81. Thus the villagers against whom Akbar personally led an expedition are described as Rajputs in Manucci, I, 132, and this is not improbable since the Chauhans are entered as *zamindars* of the *pargana* (Saketa) in the *Ain.*

82. He declares that the 'villagers' took their revenge upon Akbar when they desecrated his tomb in 1691. Manucci, I, p. 134. It was actually the Jats who desecrated the tomb in 1838.

83. Cf. Crooke, *The Tribes & Castes of North-Western Provinces & Oudh*, Calcutta, 1896, III, p. 40.

84. Isardas. f. 53a.

85. *Nigarnama-Munshi*. ff. 199a-200a.

86. Manucci, II, pp. 223–4; *Ma'asir-i 'Alamgiri*, p. 209.

87. *Riyaz-al Wudad*, Letters of Izad Bakhsh 'Rasa,' Br. M. Or. 1725, f. 16b.

88. *Ma'asir-i 'Alamgiri*, p. 93.

89. Isardas, ff. 98b, 131b.

90. Ibid., f. 135b. This was before a check administered to his power by a concerted campaign in 1690–1. But the Jat rebellion smouldered on, to burst out on a far larger scale after the death of Aurangzeb.

91. Ma'muri, f. 148a–b. See also Khali Khan, II, p. 252.

92. Isardas, f. 61b.

93. Balkrishan Brahman, Letters, Br. M. Add. 16, 859, f. 56a–b.

94. Abu-1 Fazl Ma'muri, Continuation of Sadiq Khan's *Shahjahannama*, Br. M. Or. 1671, f. 148b; Khafi Khan, II, p. 253.

95. *Zargar* (goldsmith) in the printed text may well be a mistake for *barzgar* (peasant). The two words are easily confounded in Persian writing.

96. *Ma'asir-i 'Alamgiri*, pp. 144–5.

97. Ibid., pp. 115–6.

98. Cf. Prof. M. Habib, Introduction to Elliot & Dawson's *History of India*, Vol. II, Aligarh, pp. 2–3.

99. *Dabistan-i Mazahib*, p. 285.

100. *Dabistan-i Mazahib*, p. 286; also p. 214.

101. Ibid., p. 286–7. Cf. also Khafi Khan, II, pp. 651–2.

102. *Dabistan-i Mazahib*, p. 238.

103. *Khafi Khan*, II, p. 672.

104. Mir Ma'sum *Tarikh-i Sind*, ed. V. M. Daudpota, Poena, 1938, pp. 245–6.

105. Manucci, II, p. 83.

106. *Jahangir's India*, p. 15; Manucci, II, p. 459.

107. Salih Kanbu. *'Amal-a Salih*, ed. G. Yazdani, Bib. Ind., Calcutta, III, pp. 110–12.

108. Manucci, II, p. 459.

109. Sujan Rai, *Khulasatu-t Tawarikh*, Br. M. Add. 16,680, ff. 53b–54s; Manucci, II, pp. 457–8.

110. *Ahkam-i 'Alamgiri*, f. 215a.

111. Petitions to the Court of Khan Jahan Saiyid Muzaffar Khan, Br. M. Add.. 16,859, ff. 6a–7a, 115b.

112. *Dilkusha*, ff. 138b–140a.

113. Cf. Lahori, I, pp. 316–17, 416–17.

114. This emerges most clearly from the letter Aurangzeb wrote as Viceroy of the Dakhin. See especially *Adab-i 'Alamgiri,* ff. 38a–b, 40b, 117b–118a.

115. *Adab-i 'Alamgiri,* f. 175a–b.

116. Cf. *Mirat,* I, pp. 173–4, Supp. 228–9. S. N. Sen seems to suggest (*Military System of the Marathas,* pp. 20 et. seq.) that the whole system of *chauth* originated from the precedent of an arrangement between local *raja* and the Portuguese of Daman. This is to say the least, most unlikely. What is probable is that both this arrangement and the Maratha system had a common origin in the *zamindari* right.

117. *Alkhbarat,* 44|73; Khafi Khan, II, p. 267.

118. Fryer, II, p. 5.

119. Fryer, I, pp. 311–2; also II, p. 66.

120. Ibid., II, p. 86.

121. Ibid., II, p. 87.

122. Manucci, II, p. 505.

123. Fryer, II, pp. 67, 68; Manucci, III, p. 505.

124. Fryer, I, p. 341.

125. Writing in 1762–3, Azad Bilgrami characterised the army of Marathas as consisting of "low-born people, like peasants, shepherds, carpenters and cobblers" while "the army of Muslims" consisted largely of "nobles and gentlemen". He attributed the success of the Marathas solely to this cause, for the "low-born" were able to bear all the suffering involved in "guerilla warfare" (*qazzaqi*), while the Muslims were unable to abandon their ease-loving habits. (*Khazana-i 'Amira,* Naval Kishor, Kanpur, 1871, p. 49).

126. *Ahkam-i 'Alamgiri,* f. 61b.

The Imperial Crisis in the Deccan[*]

JOHN F. RICHARDS

INTRODUCTION

In recent years, historians associated with the school of Indo-Muslim history at Aligarh Muslim University have developed a persuasive, now widely accepted, view of imperial decline. Satish Chandra, and M. Athar Ali have argued that a primary cause of the collapse of the Mughal empire in the early eighteenth century was the rise of intense factionalism among the Mughal nobility.[1] Conflict within this imperial elite (i.e., the body of *amir*s or *mansabdar*s holding ranks of 1,000 *zat* or above) resulted from a rapid rise to nearly double the number of nobles during the latter portion of the reign of the Emperor Aurangzeb (1658–1707). This growth in the number of nobles was not matched by a corresponding increase in the resources available to pay them and their followers. Consequently, the system of alienation of the land-tax proceeds for salary payments (the *jagir* system) broke down simply because not enough lands could be found to meet a sharply enhanced demand.

Both Satish Chandra and M. Athar Ali have traced the economic squeeze, which made decline and collapse inevitable, to the results of Aurangzeb's dramatic conquests between 1686–89 of Bijapur, Golconda, and the Maratha kingdom in the south. They both point out that in his eagerness to annex these kingdoms, the Emperor lavishly awarded high positions in the imperial service to all nobles—Muslim or non-Muslim—who were willing to defect. The resulting increased demand

[*] Reproduced from J.F. Richards, 'The Imperial Crisis in the Deccan', *Journal of Asian Studies*, Vol. XXXV, No. 2, February 1976, pp. 237–56. An earlier version of this article was read at the 1973 Annual Meeting of the American Historical Association, San Francisco, California.

for *jagirs* (salary assignments) exhausted the reserve (*paibaqi*) of lands usually available for that purpose; this shortage of *paibaqi* lands meant that many long-established families in the imperial elite who had served the empire faithfully (e.g., the *khanazads*) lost heavily. They naturally blamed the newcomers from the Deccan kingdoms for their troubles. Ensuing widespread conflict and demoralization among the Mughal nobility was thus an unanticipated effect of the Deccan conquests.

This interpretation of Mughal decline is persuasive because it rests on well established facts: A widespread loss of morale, cohesion, and efficiency did occur among the imperial elite during the early years of the eighteenth century. Serious shortages of productive salary assignments began even earlier. That the deficiency in *jagirs* and military pay contributed to factional conflict within the nobility can scarcely be denied. However, certain assumptions that seem to underly this explanation for decline are not as plausible. Implicit in this view is a sense of inevitability, of an irreversible sequence of events despite possible variations in policy; that is, as soon as the Deccan kingdoms were conquered and their elites assimilated as *mansabdars,* the *jagir* shortage began to be followed inevitably by the imperial crisis. Another assumption seems to be that economic concerns were of paramount importance for the Mughal nobility; indeed, the extreme importance placed on the shortage of salary assignments suggests that the principal ties between the empire and its leading servants were economic or monetary in character. Finally, those accepting this interpretation have rightly stressed the continued efficiency of the nobility as a necessity for the existence of the empire. This observation, while certainly accurate, overlooks the equally necessary loyalty and service of other—more numerous—groups within the empire. The Mughal imperial system consisted of more than its official and military elite.

This essay reexamines the descending spiral of imperial authority in the new Mughal provinces of the Deccan during the two decades following the conquests of Bijapur (1686) and Golconda (1687). Based, in part, on Mughal archival sources, it suggests an alternative explanation for the failure of the empire in the south. This admittedly tentative hypothesis can be summarized as follows: despite the sudden growth in the numbers of Mughal nobles, the empire need not have collapsed for lack of funds. Had the Emperor successfully secured and stabilized his new southern frontiers, he could well have exploited the resources of Bijapur and Golconda to meet his additional costs. But Aurangzeb, in his eagerness for further expansion, exposed to incessant raiding districts in the Deccan that were formerly secure from outside attack. He was unable to effectively assimilate into the imperial elite the Maratha, Bedar, Gond, or Telugu warrior chiefs formerly living in areas beyond the reach of direct administration by a Muslim state. Nor did he create effective political ties with these local lords, either as tributary chiefs or as *zamindars*. As a result, these local warrior aristocrats—still armed—turned to predator raiding. The consequent inability of the imperial center to provide minimal security demoralized both Mughal officers and *zamindars* in the Deccan. Eventually, by 1711–12 the latter went into open revolt.

ALLOCATION AND UTILIZATION OF JAGIRS IN THE DECCAN

In theory, at least, the annexation of Bijapur and Golconda could have generated new revenues sufficient to offset the influx of new Deccani nobles into the Mughal elite. Figures from one contemporary revenue manual indicate that land-tax collections should have enhanced annual imperial revenues by as much as 23 percent (53 million rupees over previous empire-wide collections of 232 million rupees).[2] These territories and their revenues could have been used to provide salary assignments to any *mansabdars*, new or old, who required them. But the Emperor chose instead to restrict access to the greater part of the most productive and fertile tracts in Bijapur and Golconda to meet his strategic objectives in the south. Aurangzeb set aside the choicest areas as crown lands (*khalisa*), as *jagirs* for members of the provincial cadres serving in the two new provinces, and as sources of funds to meet wage bills for his field armies operating in the Deccan against the Marathas. The remaining tracts placed in reserve (*paibaqi*), although large in total extent, comprised some of the most inaccessible and otherwise least-promising areas for the extraction of revenues. Thus, the shortage of *jagirs* in the 1690s was partly artificial—the result of decisions made by the Emperor, rather than a condition caused by an absolute shortage of territory.

Revenue figures from the twenty districts of Hyderabad province in the eastern Deccan (i.e., Golconda) support this assertion.[3] Within two years after the conquest, the Hyderabad *diwan*—the chief fiscal officer of the province—had completed a reassessment of the provincial revenues. His revised assessment imposed a selective increase by sub-district (*pargana*) of thirteen percent. This raised the Mughal demand to 15.5 million rupees per year. In the course of this settlement, the *diwan,* under the direction of the Emperor, classified each sub-district as either *khalisa* (i.e., crown lands) or as *paibaqi* lands suitable for salary assignments. This division was as follows:[4]

44% *Khalisa*	6.7 million Rupees Annual Collections
56% *Paibaqi*	8.8 million Rupees Annual Collections
100% Total	15.5 million Rupees Annual Collections

The crown lands brought under the central treasury included the most fertile, accessible, and lucrative *parganas* in the interior of Hyderabad.

The Emperor obviously had no intention of placating *mansabdars* demanding pay at the expense of the central treasury. Nearly seven million rupees in annual revenues from Hyderabad supplied a substantial increment (as much as 26 percent) to the *khalisa* of the entire empire.[5] Collections from Hyderabad also offered easier administration and transmission for military operations in the Deccan than those revenues collected in the northern provinces.

As demands for *jagirs* escalated in the last decade of the seventeenth century, we might expect that this pressure would be reflected in a reduction of the Hyderabad crown lands. But the reverse occurred: the Emperor granted no *jagirs* in crown territories. Moreover, Aurangzeb enlarged the Hyderabad *khalisa* considerably in 1695 and 1697 by transferring two districts from *paibaqi* status to the *khalisa.* This removed from possible assignment as *jagirs* lands with potential revenues of 1.7 million rupees.[6]

A substantial reduction in the Hyderabad *khalisa* took place in 1700, when the Emperor shifted 24 *parganas*—with revenues of 1.2 million rupees—to his youngest son, Prince Muhammad Kam Bakhsh.[7] However, this transfer was clearly not in response to the *jagir* crisis. The Prince acquired these *parganas* (and some in Bijapur as well) to enable him to consolidate a power base in the Deccan. Aurangzeb intended that the Prince use Bijapur and Hyderabad as a refuge in the succession struggle that was sure to break out after the Emperor's death.

Although the Emperor set aside nearly half the Hyderabad revenues for the central treasury in 1689, 8.8 million rupees in *paibaqi* lands remained unallocated. From these the *diwan* of the Deccan selected *jagirs* worth over two million rupees to meet the needs of the provincial governor, the *diwan, faujdars,* and fort commanders and their garrisons as well as for the ongoing expenses of the Hyderabad administration.[8] (Presumably the same arrangement took effect in Bijapur.) But even after these deductions, areas bearing revenues of at least six million rupees annually should have been open for general assignment in 1689. Another unknown amount would also have been accessible in Bijapur. Given the clamour for *jagirs,* these lands should have been rapidly allotted to *mansabdars.* Yet the Emperor further revealed his indifference to the pleas of salary claimants by imposing a significant restriction on the assignment of these tracts. In 1604, he announced a general rule that *jagirs* in the Deccan were only to be given out to *mansabdars* actually serving in that region.[9] This policy met the Emperor's military needs but did little to alleviate the *jagir* shortage for officers serving in the north.

Over a decade after the conquests, in 1698, the second *bakhshi* (inspection and payroll officer) of the empire reported that a scarcity of *jagir* lands existed in the northernmost Deccan provinces. However, in the "new lands," extensive tracts of *paibaqi* lands were not utilized for their proper purpose. In Hyderabad, unassigned lands had revenues totalling 1.8 million rupees; in Bijapur *paibaqi* revenues totalled 7.1 million rupees.[10] Four years later, in 1702, unproductive *paibaqi* land in both provinces had only dwindled slightly. The Emperor conceded that "As of now there is approximately eight million rupees of *paibaqi* under the administration of the *diwans* in Bijapur and Hyderabad, excluding the Karnatik. Little of this has proved useful to the state."[11]

To remedy this situation, the Emperor and his senior advisors tried a number of expedients. In order to meet the problem of overvalued *jagirs* where collections did not come close to the nominal assessment, they granted a standard one-third reduction (*takhfif*) on the nominal valuation of all *jagirs* assigned in Hyderabad. As the second *bakhshi* had pointed out in his 1698 report, *mansabdars* given *jagirs* in Hyderabad and the other Deccan provinces frequently could not collect the full amount of their salary claims; consequently they found it impossible to keep up their cavalry contingents. Inevitably, these officers failed to bring men and horses of sufficient quality and number to muster for the regular inspections; therefore, they lost their *jagirs,* which reverted to *paibaqi.*[12] In these instances, the efficiency of the Mughal military system was self-defeating. Reducing the valuation by a third could have provided some assistance in reasonably productive areas, where the discrepancy between expected and realized collections was not more than a third. But in other more difficult parts of Hyderabad, this remedy did not work. Many *mansabdars*, upon learning that in certain areas *jagirs* were worth very little, simply refused to accept the assignments.

The Emperor also resorted to arbitrary assignments of block grants to large bodies of low-ranking *mansabdars* serving as individual troopers in the Deccan field armies.[13] Finally, in 1702, Aurangzeb tried to induce some of the *mansabdars* who were natives of the Deccan (including Marathas) to take up these ruined lands.[14] In addition to the one-third abatement, he offered relaxation of the inspection and branding rules. This seemingly desperate action strongly suggests that the Emperor was willing to ignore a longstanding principle of Mughal administration: the discouragement of local ties in the operation of the *jagir* system.

None of the remedies tried by the Emperor offered a solution to the real problem. None of these measures was aimed at increasing state support and protection for the *jagirdars*. Most absentee salary claimants in Hyderabad and Bijapur suffered because of inadequate assistance from the provincial administration. Only those powerful members of the provincial administration who had direct access to their *jagirs*, or other powerful nobles with extremely large holdings, could employ and direct forces sufficient to protect their lands. Smaller men, dependent on state protection, could not imitate these grandees; and they suffered accordingly.

THE FAILURE TO ASSIMILATE: PADIYAH NAYAK

Continuing disorder in the Deccan can be attributed directly to Aurangzeb's strategic goals. The Emperor's fixed purpose behind his fiscal policies in Bijapur and Hyderabad was to mobilize, as completely as possible, funds that could be used for further aggressive expansion. Consequently, his general approach in these new provinces inclined heavily toward under-administration and over-exploitation. In his anxiety to pull resources out of the two conquered kingdoms, Aurangzeb skimped on the administrative and military manpower necessary to maintain political stability and order.

Aurangzeb's interests and attention were directed elsewhere, at those regions in the Deccan that—unlike Bijapur and Hyderabad—had been only loosely integrated, by varying forms of tributary relationships, with the Muslim states of the Deccan. The Emperor tried consistently to bring these areas under direct Mughal administration. For example, he aimed at more than simple defensive containment of the Marathas. This limited goal could have been achieved by any of a variety of conciliatory approaches to Shambhaji, Shivaji's son and successor. Ignoring these possibilities, the Emperor captured Shambhaji in 1689, brutally executed him, and occupied Raigarh fort—the capital of the Maratha kingdom.[15]

As it did in other similar refuge areas, imperial intrusion into the Western Ghats of Maharashtra failed. The Emperor was unable to establish workable political links with the Marathas or other Hindu warrior elites dominant in areas beyond the zone of long standing direct Muslim administration. By sending in his armies, Aurangzeb had already rejected the possibility of autonomous tributary status for these rajas. Moving beyond this position to establishment of a regional political and administrative system required conversion of these chiefs into intermediary *zamindars* who were willing to collaborate with the empire. But the hostility aroused by Mughal military and ideological pressure ensured that this would be a laborious and costly process. When confronted with resistance to imperial assimilation, Aurangzeb opted for a third, initially easier alternative: he commissioned large numbers of Marathas, Bedars, and Gonds, and a few Telugu *nayaks* directly into the imperial service as *mansabdars*. This costly policy weakened the nobility of the empire and did very little to assimilate those peripheral areas which were the Emperor's objective.

Despite their nominally high ranks, none of the Maratha, Bedar, Gond, or Telugu warriors recruited into the imperial service after the Deccan conquests was fully reliable or loyal—at least in the Emperor's eyes. Few served as omnicompetent administrators who could be trusted to act with efficiency and discretion as provincial governors, district military commanders (*faujdars*), or fortress commanders.[16] At best, these men were commanders of auxiliary troops serving under the direction of Mughal generals in the Deccan armies. The Emperor never succeeded in binding Marathas to him and the imperial service in the same way that the Rajputs had been assimilated in the previous century by Akbar. Aurangzeb never gained the active loyalties of these chiefs to the extent that he could trust them to perform discretionary missions of great importance at long distances from the court.

Fully assimilated *mansabdars*—such as the *khanazads* (i.e., Muslim nobles with familial traditions of unbroken imperial service) and the Rajputs—seemingly responded emotively to the emperor in a way that the Marathas and other Deccan groups did not.[17] For such fully integrated *mansabdars*, an affective tie bound Emperor and servant, establishment of this personal tie was an apparent precondition for full acceptance and trusted employment of each of the Mughal *amirs* and other higher-ranking *mansabdars*. Thus, cohesion and efficiency in the imperial elite depended heavily on links between the Emperor and each of nearly a thousand provincial governors and *diwans*, field and fortress commanders, *faujdars*, *amins*, and other officers posted throughout the provinces of the empire.

If such bonds between imperial master and imperial servant did exist, how were they made effective? The primary mechanism that established and reinforced the mutual bond between the Emperor and individual *mansabdars* was personal encounters. Face-to-face meetings varied from small, probing occasions (as in the less formal atmosphere of the Emperor's private apartments) to formal encounters at the great ceremonials of the daily open court audiences (in the *Diwan-i Khas o' Am*).[18] At each encounter, the Emperor—if pleased—conferred new titles and honors, uttered verbal praise, and announced new assignments and increases in numerical rank and pay. If displeased, the Emperor rebuked the offender and announced reductions in his rank removal of honors, and penal posting. Most of these encounters were marked by a symbolic exchange of articles: the deferential *mansabdar* offering gold or silver coins; the Emperor usually (save in cases of reprimand) reciprocating with gifts such as jeweled and inlaid weapons, saddles or even elaborately decorated robes of honor.

Neither party to these encounters regarded them lightly or casually. An unarmed *mansabdar* performing the ceremonial full-length prostration before beginning his face-to-face dialogue with the Emperor was obviously prepared to respond acutely and attentively to every possible sign of royal favor or disfavor. The Emperor, on his part, devoted a major portion of his energies to close supervision and assessment of the corps of *mansabdars*. At any audience, the Emperor would be likely to know the record of service; the family, caste, or lineage: the factional and personal affiliation; and the administrative and military qualities of the man standing before him.[19] The process of personal interaction continued at a distance. Those *mansabdars* posted away from the court frequently sent petitions and memorials directly to the Emperor. In an interesting substitute for a personal exchange, these petitions and the Emperor's replies were often read out in public audiences. The Emperor also sent written orders and queries directly to members of his nobility.

Behind the mechanism of individual personal encounters lay certain common values and attitudes. The Emperor and his leading servants (with few exceptions) were members of a military aristocracy. As Muslim and Hindu warriors tracing their descent from warrior lineages, they shared common values: strength, hardihood, loyalty, and courage. The Emperor, as a warrior chief commanding warriors, expected to elicit and reward these virtues among his nobles. Indeed, the predominance of martial values is suggested by Mughal official titles (e.g., Jan Sipar Khan—The "Life-scattering" Khan or Rustam Dil Khan—The "Rustam-hearted" Khan). Emerging from this warrior ethic was another less tangible value: the Emperor and his nobles seem to have further shared a sense of the empire as an epic venture—a structure created and expanded by warriors. Together, they possessed a commitment to sustain and enlarge the imperial domain.[20]

The Emperor's claim to be the recipient of affective ties with the elite rested on his control of Mughal symbols of authority. The yak tails and other devices of Turco-Mongol kingship, and the great throne and other appurtenances of Persian monarchy merged with the dynastic charisma of the Timurids—descendants of Timur, Genghiz Khan, and Babur. The twin symbols of Islamic legitimate authority—the *khutba*, reading of the ruler's name in the Friday prayers; and the *sikka*, right to coin—also resided with the Mughal Emperor. However, mere manipulation of these symbols in the absence of dynamic personal interaction with the nobles could not have sustained the imperial system. Thus, Muhammad Shah (1720–1748) and his successors controlled the symbolic system, but could not sustain active authoritative relationships with those eighteenth-century "*mansabdars*" located beyond the lands adjacent to Delhi.

As the symbolic system anchored the Emperor—noble tie on one side, another grounding lay in the rewards resulting from obedience and service. Enormous wealth, high status, public visibility, and great power were rewards that could be enjoyed in relative security. The Mughal Emperors did not terrorize their nobility as did the Safavids or other contemporary Muslim rulers.[21] Until the closing years of the seventeenth century, the strength of the imperial system ensured that risks far outstripped any possible returns from defiance. But as the empire came under stress, *mansabdars* serving in the Deccan were forced to consider the realities of power. Some nobles chose to honour their ties to the Emperor. Men like Dalpat Rao Bundela, the Rajput chief, continuing to display nearly suicidal bravery in battle, followed Aurangzeb during the difficult campaigns of the Emperor's last years. Some nobles, in a more calculating assessment of the political situation, chose to pursue aggrandizement. Men such as Rustam Dil Khan—the deputy governor of Hyderabad (see below)—tacitly set aside their obligations to the Emperor, in their anxiety for survival.

A number of powerful and capable *rajas* from the Deccan and from Central India flatly rejected imperial ties in this period. Instead of enrolling as Mughal auxiliaries in the corps of *mansabdars,* these men—usually after evidence of considerable indecisions went into open rebellion. The great Maratha leader Shivaji's violent reaction to his first public court audience and meeting with Aurangzeb at Agra in 1666, and his flight back to the Deccan, illustrates this response.[22] Another notable example is that provided twenty years later by Padiyah Nayak, leader of the Bedars, a group of Telugu (or possibly Kannada) speaking warriors in the Deccan.

Prior to the Mughal conquest of Bijapur in 1686, a small but strategic buffer kingdom was located between the fork of the Krishna and Bhima rivers, just north of the Raichur *doab.*[23] Sakar, the heavily fortified capital, was the seat of Pam Nayak, the Bedar ruler. Although formally tributary to the Adil Shah ruler of Bijapur, the Bedar king appears to have kept complete autonomy in the internal administration of his kingdom. However, the political structure, or even the approximate boundaries and population of the kingdom, is not fully described in the contemporary sources. Sakar's internal organization was probably based on kinship structures and idioms similar to that of contemporary Rajput kingdoms. The ruler could call on various lesser Bedar chiefs to supply tribute, in both cash and goods, as well as warriors. Whether ordinary Bedars were actually peasant-cultivators themselves or controlled and dominated other non-Bedar peasantry is unclear.[24] What is certain is that the Bedars were a militant warrior group. Pam Nayak, by a generally accepted estimate, could assemble twelve thousand horsemen and several times that number of infantry, drawn from various segments of the Bedars. Moreover, throughout the seventeenth and eighteenth centuries, Bedar musketeers were conspicuous in the Karnatik infantry, which was widely known and employed for its marksmanship and reliability in battle.

A reputation for vigorous military qualities, and a homeland strategically located between Bijapur and Golconda, seems to have preserved the autonomy of the Bedars until 1687. But the security of the Bedars was shattered by the Mughal conquests. As a loyal tributary, with no great liking for the Mughals, Pam Nayak had sent all his available forces with supplies to assist the king of Bijapur during the siege of that city. Later he sent similar aid to Abul Hasan at Golconda. Aurangzeb delayed retribution until Golconda fell. In early 1688, the Emperor sent an army from Hyderabad to Sakar. As soon as the Mughals arrived, Pam Nayak, negotiating an offer of leniency, surrendered without resistance. The Mughal commander occupied Sakar, renaming it Nasratabad ("place of victory") and placed a Mughal garrison in charge of the fortress. He also constructed a mosque (*masjid*) inside the fort.[25] Pam Nayak, his family, and immediate servants, taken into custody, were brought to the Emperor's camp, which had moved to Bijapur. When the captive *nayak* appeared at court, Aurangzeb enrolled him in the imperial service as an *amir* ranked at 5000 *zat*, 4000 *suwar*. His sons Jugna and Nand became *amirs*, as did several other members of Pam Nayak's suite.

The unfortunate recipient of these honors soon found his high rank a burden rather than an advantage. Both Muslim and Hindu nobles at court derisively rejected Pam Nayak. The open hostility displayed by the nobles derived from a mixture of envy at the Bedar ruler's newly gained rank, aristocratic disdain for his unsophisticated manners, and a sense of ritual pollution and color prejudice. Pam Nayak, formerly a ruler of an isolated kingdom, was suddenly thrust into the midst of an imperial court which, even in the field, retained the sophistication and elaborate etiquette of aristocratic Indo-Persian culture. Even though some of the Bedars were Vaishnavites or Lingayats, they still were regarded as an aboriginal hunting group, ranked as outcastes in the Hindu social system. They were also black-skinned, unlike the brown-skinned Mughal officers from the north. The invective of the chroniclers is revealing: Pam Nayak was "hideous" in appearance, "pot-black" with a deformed shape; he belonged to a tribe of "indiscriminate carrion eaters"; when the nobles at court looked at this "odious" creature and realized the rank that had been given to him, they could not restrain their laughter.[26] Moreover, failure to convert to Islam meant that the Bedar ruler was denied the protection that the Emperor's pleasure at this move would have afforded him.

Within a few weeks of his appearance at court, Pam Nayak died. The cause of his death is not mentioned in the chronicles. Defeated and persecuted, he may have suffered from severe depression. Or he may have been killed by Aurangzeb's order. His two sons, retaining their ranks, served with a force of one thousand Bedar horsemen in the field army under the command of Firuz Jang, at least until the end of the year.[27]

Aurangzeb completed the Mughal occupation of the Bedar territories within a year. He sent Ruhullah Khan, the imperial *bakhshi*, with another army to Raichur fort, still controlled by another Bedar chief. Conquest of this fort required a siege, which was ultimately successful. Ruhullah Khan sent the captured Bedar chief to Hyderabad, where he was executed by the *faujdar* of Hyderabad city.[28]

However, direct Mughal rule did not mean that all the Bedars became loyal servants, of the Emperor. One of the Mughal *mansabdar*s present at the siege of Raichur fort was a Bedar called Padiyah Nayak, nephew and adopted son of the late Pam Nayak. Several years before its fall, Padiyah had left Sakar, travelled to Aurangabad, and enlisted in Mughal service. In the course of the siege, Padiyah requested a week's leave to return to Sakar, his home country, which was nearby, in order to recruit fresh troops and get fresh supplies and equipment. At the end of the week he failed to return.

Avoiding Sakar, which still possessed a Mughal garrison, Padiyah took his family and followers to Wakinkira—a hill village twelve miles to the southwest.[29] He began to fortify the town, to emplace guns, and to collect more troops. He also collected taxes from villages near Wakinkira and blocked the major roads. Bedar troops stopped and plundered all caravans passing through the district. In the course of two years, the Bedar chief had assembled the necessities of autonomous power: a defensible stronghold; an ample treasury; a growing reputation; and a compact but formidable army, consisting of 14,000 to 15,000 Bedar archers and musketeers and 4000 to 5000 cavalry, many of whom were Muslim freebooters.

During the years 1688–1691 Padiyah delayed serious Mughal attention to his growing power by heavily bribing a number of imperial officials. From the official Mughal point of view, Padiyah Nayak was little more than a bandit or robber chief, whose rise was due solely to the illegitimate use of indiscriminate force. The attitude of the Bedars is unknown. As nephew and adopted son of Pam Nayak, the deposed ruler Padiyah might have claimed a legitimate right to rule—a right that predated the Mughal invasion of the country. Thus the extent to which he was really "assailing and plundering" an unwilling population, and the degree to which he was asserting the rights of the king of the Bedars to traditional taxes and tribute, is an open question. Aurangzeb ignored this issue and recognized one of Pam Nayak's natural sons as "legitimate heir to that country."[30] Jagia Nayak, already a Mughal *mansabdar* ranked at 2500/1500, also became *deshmukh* of Sakar, now called Nasratabad.[31]

The first real clash came in May 1691. Once again, Ruhullah Khan led a Mughal army into Bedar country. With him was Jagia Nayak, who carried a *sanad* from the Emperor naming him ruler of the Bedars. An opening assault on Wakinkira fort failed, as did a hard-pressed two-month siege. Finally, Ruhullah Khan opened negotiations with the defenders. The talks, protracted by large bribes given to the Mughal commander by Padiyah, continued through the end of 1691. At this point Aurangzeb, recalling Ruhullah Khan with his army, sent Prince Azam Shah with a new force. The Prince did not bother to besiege Wakinkira again; instead he sent raiding parties to ravage the entire area dominated by Padiyah. The latter was safe in his capital but prevented from any form of raiding or revenue-collection. Padiyah made continual overtures to his new opponent. After a full year of this stand-off, a bargain was struck. The Bedar chief offered to pay 200,000 rupees into Azam's personal treasury and 700,000 rupees to the Emperor, in return for undisturbed possession of Wakinkira. Azam took his army south to the Maratha war in the Karnatik, leaving the Bedar chief poorer but firmly in control of his hard-won territory.

In the ensuing four years, Padiyah Nayak's raids grew more and more damaging, to the east in Hyderabad and to the west in the Gulbarga district of Bijapur. He also developed an alliance and working relationship with the Maratha bands who harried both halves of the Deccan in those years.[32] Eventually, in 1696, the governor of Bijapur, Firuz Jang, organized another expedition to eliminate the troublesome Bedar chief. However, the probable cost of storming Wakinkira was formidable; and the rewards for not doing so were attractive. Once again Padiyah used his considerable diplomatic skills, supported by large bribes, to persuade Firuz Jang not to pursue the campaign. The Mughal general accepted Padiyah's undertaking, never fulfilled, to pay 900,000 rupees tribute to the Emperor and departed with his army for Bijapur.

This was to be the last serious effort for a decade by the Mughals to stop Padiyah Nayak. Between 1696 and 1705 he was free to develop his various enterprises, until Aurangzeb himself directed his last personally led campaign against Wakinkira. The amount of territory controlled by the Bedar leader grew steadily. So did the range and scope of his raiding activities west into Bijapur and east deep into Hyderabad.

In late 1702, for example, Padiyah Nayak executed a long-distance raid on the Andhra coast. Marching two hundred and forty miles due east from Wakinkira, the Bedar forces reached Kondavidu district in January or early February of 1703. The Bedar leader quickly drove off the Mughal commandant at Kondavidu and seized the immense fortress. The raiders occupied Kondavidu for several months, while regularly sending out parties to ravage and plunder the countryside. Neither resident Mughal officials nor the local Telugu aristocracy offered any appreciable resistance. On learning of these events through official news reports, the Emperor sharply reduced the rank of the Kondavidu commandant. Aurangzeb also made a substantial reduction in the rank of Rustam Dil Khan, *faujdar* (as well as provincial governor) of the coastal districts in Hyderabad, on the ground that he had failed to act against the Bedars. Finally, Aurangzeb sent a relief expedition under a special officer (a former commandant of Kondavidu) who managed to drive off the raiders and recover the stronghold.[33]

Sometimes in association with Maratha bands, sometimes alone, Padiyah's forces looted and burned freely in Hyderabad, Bijapur, and Bidar. This type of raiding was difficult to stop. If sustained, it was utterly damaging and corroded the whole structure of empire. Perhaps even more dangerous than purely physical damage was the explicit challenge to imperial authority that Padiyah Nayak's activities posed.

The case of the Bedars affords an interesting and significant illustration of the serious consequences of Aurangzeb's failure to assimilate the most capable and vital Bedar leader into the imperial system at any level— whether as tributary chief, *deshmukh,* or *mansabdar.* Although only a single case, it also suggests two possible barriers to full acceptance into the imperial elite. Clearly, full membership in the elite corps of the empire demanded participation in an aristocratic Indo-Persian culture. Even in the field, the Emperor remained the focus and arbiter for a highly refined system of etiquette, manners, and general lifestyle to which *khanazads,* Rajputs, and other nobles had long ago obtained access. As the difficulties of Pam Nayak indicate, access to this shared courtly culture was open to warriors, but only to those who could quickly adapt to the standards of urbanity and polish required of a Mughal grandee.

Another important problem, growing more serious as Aurangzeb's reign progressed, was that of religion. Undoubtedly, Rajput and other non-Muslim families long socialized to Mughal service could, for a time, withstand and ignore pressures for conversion emanating from the Emperor. However, new entrants such as the Bedar, Maratha, and Gond chiefs of the Deccan seem to have come under considerable pressure to convert. The Emperor's views on this topic were well-known; his actions upon the conquest of Sakar forcefully conveyed the point that the land of the Bedars had been conquered by an essentially Muslim empire. Thus the increasing weight given to Islamic legitimation for Mughal rule seems to have been another, not inconsiderable, hindrance to movement of the regional aristocracies of the Deccan into the imperial system.

DISORDER AND DEMORALIZATION: RUSTAM DIL KHAN

In the late 1690s the Deccan provinces came under steadily increasing military pressure. Marathas, Bedars, Gonds, and others raided deep into the imperial provinces of the south. At the same time, bandits, whose power and numbers had swollen, also raided and looted freely— sometimes in alliance with external invaders, but more frequently alone. Dislocation caused by these events was enhanced by a disastrous drought, famine, and epidemic affecting nearly the entire Deccan between the years 1700 and 1704. Agricultural and industrial production dwindled. In the unfortified cities, the expectation or the actuality of raids disturbed the urban population. In the countryside peasants who lived through starvation and disease frequently lost their livestock, tools, and sometimes their lives to raiders. Peasants who survived often migrated in search of safety, or joined one of the bands of raiders or bandits.

Under conditions such as these, precipitous declines in collections from even the most productive *jagirs* must have contributed to the troubles of Mughal officers serving in the Deccan. But the intensifying economic squeeze was only one of a series of difficulties confronting the *mansabdars*. Even more serious was the increasing helplessness and isolation of beset governors, *faujdars*, and fort commanders, who could no longer look to the imperial center for reassurance and assistance. After 1700, the Emperor sent reinforcements only under the most desperate circumstances—if at all. Inability to keep order, and to resist raiders and bandits, hit the standards and morale of the imperial officers. Mass defections or desertions of *mansabdars* had not yet occurred, but too many examples of profitable defiance of imperial authority had taken place for this to be any longer inconceivable.

By the termination of Aurangzeb's reign in 1707, demoralization of the corps of *mansabdars* in the south was well underway, as Maratha and other bands raided without hindrance. The shaken *mansabdars* saw that the structure that—for over a century— had supplied order, rationality, sustenance, and meaning to their lives was rapidly weakening. Accompanying this perception came, inevitably, a loss of emotional security. The survival of the empire in its existing form might even be questioned. Certainly, for men accustomed to obtaining and wielding power, such doubts arose from a cold, calculating assessment of political probabilities. But perhaps more significant was the threatened loss of meaning for imperial service if the empire faltered. Men who were for the most part warriors and military administrators, whose actions were rooted in a military ethic of service, obedience, and courage, needed a sense of purpose for the collectivity as much as they needed victory in battle or dominance over subordinates.

Demoralization also arose from a sense of frustration and futility. *Mansabdars*, prevented by inadequate support from resisting raiders and bandits, could not press for a change in what appeared to be a thoroughly unsuccessful Deccan strategy. The Emperor confined his process of policy consultation to a tiny group of elderly officials of the highest rank.

Isolation and helplessness prompted several specific reactions. Many of the demoralized Deccan *mansabdars* tacitly refused to obey orders readily or fully after 1700 (and sometimes before that date). Rather than eliciting immediate obedience, orders from the Emperor first occasioned careful assessment of the local political climate before action was undertaken. Another symptom of demoralization was the frequent unwillingness of Mughal governors and *faujdars* to meet raiders and bandits in open battle. Often they preferred to negotiate with and bribe the attackers to withdraw. What appears to have been a heightened incidence of personal and factional clashes between *mansabdars* (over claims to salary assignments or occupancy of positions) also occurred. Hoarding was another response to insecurity. Often *mansabdars* built up their personal fortunes through fraud or by means of extortionate tax demands—practices the Mughal system of fiscal checks was carefully structured to prevent. Perhaps the most damaging sign of demoralization was the tendency of powerful Mughal officers—not transferred by Aurangzeb as frequently as by his predecessors—to start building alliances with locally important chiefs. Obviously, many of these practices existed before 1700; but the prevalence of these symptoms in the Deccan suggests that many officers were anticipating future requirements for survival, should the empire fall.

Many of the indicators of demoralization are illustrated in the activities of the deputy-governor of Hyderabad during this period. Rustam Dil Khan served as deputy-governor of that province from 1700 to the end of 1704 and from 1706 to 1708. During those years, he acted as deputy for and reported to the absentee governor, Prince Muhammad Kam Bakhsh, who took an active interest in the administration of the province. Finally, in 1708, when the Prince tried to use Hyderabad as a refuge and military base in the war of succession that followed Aurangzeb's death, the desperate Prince and his powerful deputy clashed. This encounter resulted in the arrest and execution of Rustam Dil Khan.

Two influences, seemingly conflicting, may be seen in the case of Rustam Dil Khan. On the one hand he was a *khanazad,* whose father and grandfather, both prominent nobles, had also served the Mughal emperors.[34] Rustam Dil Khan was, in other words, a member of a distinguished official family whose members had proved their loyalty and ability for three generations. On the other hand, in what appears to have been a remarkable deviation from standard Mughal practice,

Rustam Dil Khan spent nearly his entire official career in Hyderabad. His father, Jan Sipar Khan, became the first permanent governor of Hyderabad after the Mughal conquest, circa 1689–90. Jan Sipar Khan remained uninterruptedly at this post for twelve years until his death. Throughout this period, Rustam Dil Khan acted as his father's principal assistant and deputy. Thus, by a combination of circumstances, Rustam Dil Khan had built up strong local attachments in the course of over a decade of service in Hyderabad. Appointment as governor in 1700 (i.e., as deputy to the absent Prince Kam Baksh) apparently supplied further inducements for the attenuation of his larger loyalties to the empire.

Certainly Rustam Dil Khan's performance as governor scarcely met the normative requirements of that role.[35] Just over a year after Rustam Dil Khan succeeded his father as chief imperial administrator of Hyderabad, the first of a series of deep Maratha raids into the eastern Deccan occurred. A Maratha force, estimated at 50,000 cavalry and infantry, marched unopposed to Hyderabad City, the provincial capital. Still unresisted, the intruders occupied the city and looted the unfortunate inhabitants for three full days. Throughout this episode, Rustam Dil Khan remained with his army behind the walls of Golconda fort, several miles distant from the city. After negotiations, the "Rustam hearted "Khan" paid the Marathas 700,000 silver rupees to induce them to withdraw without inflicting further, damage on the area. The governor took the cash for this payment from the provincial treasury illegally, without obtaining the assent of the provincial fiscal officer (the *diwan*).[36]

Ten months later, in early 1703, a force led by Padiyah Nayak, the Bedar chief, occupied Kondavidu fortress and plundered the coastal districts for several months. Aurangzeb reacted to Rustam Dil Khan's failure to confront the invaders by making a substantial reduction in the delinquent governor's rank. Once again, during the next winter campaigning season, in February 1704, the Marathas simultaneously attacked the provincial capital in the interior and Machilipatnam—the chief port town on the Krishna delta. On this occasion, Rustam Dil Khan, then at Rajamundry, less than 80 miles to the northeast, also failed to act. He did not order any of his subordinates into action against the raiders, nor did he march to the relief of Machilipatnam himself. The European traders operating on the coast indignantly assumed that Rustam Dil Khan was colluding with the raiders.[37]

Rustam Dil Khan also ignored the increasingly serious plundering of a number of bandits who had emerged in the province. For example, a former Mughal *faujdar* turned brigand (titled Riza Khan) joined the Marathas on their march to Machilipatnam in 1704. After their withdrawal, Riza Khan continued to block the roads from Hyderabad to the coastal ports without meeting any opposition from the Mughal governor.[38]

Upon receiving reports from Hyderabad, Aurangzeb removed Rustam Dil Khan from his post and sent Daud Khan Panni, the *faujdar* of the Hyderabad Karnatik (the southern districts of the former kingdom), to recover the situation. The latter, favored by a respite in Maratha assaults, remained at his new post less than a year before being called to assist the Emperor in his siege of the Bedar fort at Wakinkira (see above). On the departure of Daud Khan Panni, Rustam Dil Khan—possibly assisted by intervention from the imperial *wazir,* Asad Khan—returned to the deputy governorship of Hyderabad. In the ensuing two-year period, from 1706 to 1708, before the events of the war of succession claimed his life, we can see most clearly Rustam Dil Khan's strategy.

The Hyderabad governor intensified his vigorous efforts to amass, by various illicit means, as much wealth as possible. For over a year the governor appears to have withheld the pay of the commander and garrison of Golconda fort, a sum amounting to 800,000 rupees.[39] Rustam Dil Khan also intercepted revenue collections from the *khalisa* (crown territories) in Hyderabad and diverted these revenues to his own coffers.[40] These and other methods adopted by Rustam Dil Khan apparently were highly successful. The governor's personal treasure, seized by agents of Prince Kam Bakhsh after Rustam Dil Khan's execution, reportedly amounted to 3.3 million gold coins, as well as large numbers of precious stones.[41]

At the same time, Rustam Dil Khan assiduously recruited and organized large numbers of soldiers in his personal service. He also consolidated political ties with such figures as Ananda Razu Pusapati of Vizianagaram, the most powerful Telugu *zamindar* in the trans-Godavari coastal region; Krishna Malhar, a Maratha chief operating in the interior on the western border of Hyderabad; and with Riza Khan, the notorious bandit leader. Both Krishna Malhar and Riza Khan were so firmly allied with Rustam Dil Khan that they actually supplied troops to the governor for use in his brief skirmish with Prince Kam Bakhsh.[42]

By the early part of 1708, when Prince Kam Bakhsh arrived in Hyderabad, he had to recover control of the province from his deputy governor. On his part, Rustam Dil Khan was reluctant to relinquish that local dominance carefully constructed over nearly two decades. Only the longstanding habit of obedience to the dynasty and fear of future punishment, seem to have caused him to offer formal submission to the Prince, in return for continuation as governor of Hyderabad. Actual conflict broke out between the forces of the Prince and those of the governor and his allies, when Kam Bakhsh, desperate for funds, tried to confiscate Rustam Dil Khan's personal treasury. Later, after a seeming reconciliation, the Prince called Rustam Dil Khan to an audience on routine business, arrested him, and had him trampled to death by elephants.[43]

In the course of his extended career in Hyderabad, Rustam Dil Khan apparently responded to predominantly political, rather than economic pressures. Thus, with the possible exception of a brief period when he was transferred from Hyderabad in 1705, Rustam Dil Khan consistently held salary assignments within the province appropriate to his rank and responsibilities. Rustam Dil Khan's *jagirs* (held first in conjunction with his father, later alone) were located in the most secure part of the province, within a fifty-to seventy-mile radius of the capital. Moreover, the best available information suggests that the governor's salary holdings in Hyderabad were transferred infrequently, if at all.[44] After 1700, in common with other *jagirdars* in Hyderabad and the other Deccan provinces, Rustam Dil Khan may have been unable to extract full collections from his *jagirs*. But his formidable position in the province, and obvious success at gathering funds, suggest that Rustam Dil Khan's deviation from the norms of Mughal service was not prompted by an obvious need for money.

THE FAILURE OF IMPERIAL GUARANTEES: PAP RAI

In the Deccan provinces, imperial authority rested on the services of other groups whose active loyalties were as essential as those of the *mansabdars*. The regime depended heavily upon the notables and gentry of the cities for political support and assistance. The most influential of the latter group were Muslim *ulama,* i.e., the prominent *qazi*-preachers of the Deccan towns and cities. Outside the cities, Mughal officials relied upon the regional warrior aristocracies, (i.e., *zamindars*) of the countryside for collection of taxes and maintenance of order. Within this group, the key figures were the *deshmukhs*—semi-hereditary, officially recognized, intermediary officers, who held dominant power and high status in each sub-district (*pargana*). Predominantly Hindu, they were generally from Marathi-speaking or Kunbi castes in the western Deccan (Bijapur) and from Telugu-speaking Reddi, Valama, or Razu castes in the east (Hyderabad). Although they were autochthonous lords of the land, most of the *deshmukhs*, after generations of transmitted experience, seem to have viewed Muslim political dominance as legitimate and natural. Therefore, after the assumption of imperial control, most *deshmukhs* (and *zamindars*) in the two provinces readily accepted the Emperor as their new sovereign. The *deshmukhs* apparently perceived that their best interests lay in at least minimal collaboration with the new regime.

Soon after the conquest, the Mughal provincial fiscal officers (*diwans*) began the lengthy task of contacting, interviewing, and negotiating continued terms of service with these intermediaries. Upon satisfactory conclusion of these talks, a formal link was created between the state and the *deshmukh*. The latter received a *sanad,* a patent of office written in Persian, which provided for up to a five percent allowance on taxes collected, retention of tax-free lands, and protection for the *deshmukh's* local position and status. The *deshmukhs* executed bonds in which they agreed to pay—by installments—a fixed appointment fee, to collect taxes in cooperation with the agents of the *jagirdar* (or of the *khalisa*), to submit required periodic reports and to encourage cultivation.[45]

For close to twenty years, until the end of Aurangzeb's reign, the majority of Maratha and Telugu *deshmukhs* abided by their agreements with the empire. Given the troubled state of society in the Deccan, especially after 1700, some *deshmukhs* did not meet their obligations to make full tax collections. Yet cases of outright defiance were not common. An analysis of contemporary Mughal official documents and news reports from both Bijapur and Hyderabad supports the view that the *deshmukhs* did not engage in widespread or sustained revolts.[46] Nor did they supply willing assistance to raiders attacking from outside the provincial boundaries.

The war of succession following the death of Aurangzeb in 1707 virtually suspended effective administration in the Deccan for over a year. During this period, the *deshmukhs*, in common with the *mansabdars,* were pushed by events into a reassessment of their position. Disorder in these regions was no longer simply a matter of Maratha and Bedar raids. In Hyderabad, for example, bandits like Riza Khan (see above), whose forces were augmented by deserted soldiers and uprooted peasants, had begun to challenge the local power of the *deshmukh*s and *zamindar*s and seriously threaten their security.

One of the most notorious of Hyderabad's bandits was a man named Pap Rai. Pap Rai, according to the only extant account, was born into a low caste of toddy or palm wine sellers.[47] In the late 1690s, Pap Rai began his career by organizing a band to engage in highway robbery in one of the interior districts of Hyderabad. When he was threatened with reprisals from the local *faujdar* and *zamindar*s, Pap Rai fled to Kaulas in Elgandel district. There he took service as a military retainer with Venkat Rao, the Telugu *zamindar* of Kaulas. In this role, Pap Rai found opportunities to extort money from the subjects of his new master. Venkat Rao, discovering this, threw Pap Rai into his prison.

Freed accidentally by a general amnesty (carried out for religious propitiation), Pap Rai moved on to Bhongir district. In partnership with another desperate character named Sarva, Pap Rai discovered that political turmoil now made banditry profitable. The two bandit chiefs built a hill fort at Shahpur, only fifty miles from the capital. From this refuge they rode out to plunder travelers and merchants, and to capture wealthy victims to be held for ransom. Outraged complaints from merchants and others led to direct orders from Aurangzeb to Rustam Dil Khan, deputy governor of Hyderabad, to capture and punish Pap Rai. An assault by the local *faujdar* on Pap Rai ended in the death of the Mughal commander and the dispersal of his army. When Rustam Dil Khan personally directed a two-month siege of the bandit stronghold at Shahpur, Pap Rai and Sarva fled. They returned to reoccupy and rebuild the fortress in stone after the departure of the deputy governor. A second three-month siege led by Rustam Dil Khan failed to penetrate the defenses of the strengthened bandit headquarters, and the governor returned to Hyderabad.

The high point of Pap Rai's violent career came during the war of succession. In March 1708, while Prince Muhammad Kam Bakhsh and Rustam Dil Khan confronted one another outside the walls of Hyderabad, a real prize fell into Pap Rai's hands. The populace of nearby

Warangal, the old Kakatiya capital, which had become a rich commercial center famous for its carpets, was at that season busily engaged in the celebration of Muharram. The inhabitants of the town awoke one holiday night to find the fort captured by invaders, and a sack and massacre in progress. Throughout that night and the next day, an estimated twelve to fifteen thousand persons lost their lives, while those who survived— especially the local gentry—had little honor or wealth left. Between two to three thousand foot soldiers and four to five hundred horsemen had mustered under Pap Rai's command for the assault on Warangal. Two months later, the same force failed in a similar night assault on Bhongir fort, located only twenty-eight miles from Hyderabad. Nevertheless, Pap Rai's forces looted the large town at the foot of the hill fort and carried off several thousand captives.

Enriched by these victories, Pap Rai constructed a new stronghold at Tarikonda, a hill within sight of his older fort at Shahpur. Pap Rai used captive labor and stolen cattle to work his extensive lands. To stimulate trade, he established a market town at the foot of Tarikonda fort. By late 1709, Pap Rai was confident enough to begin direct territorial expansion. He mounted an attack on the *zamindar* of Kilpak, who controlled that town and the area adjacent to Shahpur.

By this time, Pap Rai's successes had provoked great hostility and fear on the part of the two most important locally dominant groups: the urban Muslim gentry and the Telugu *zamindars*. Steady pressure from these two groups brought about his downfall. In the course of the sack of Warangal, Pap Rai had abducted the wife and eight-year-old daughter of the *qazi*, the leading Muslim resident of the town. Pap Rai placed the wife in his own harem and enrolled the girl in a troupe of dancers. The father-in-law of the aggrieved *qazi* led a deputation to the imperial court to complain in person to Bahadur Shah, the victor in the war of succession. Bowing to demands that he avenge Muslim honor, the Emperor ordered the new governor of Hyderabad, Yusuf Khan, to assemble a large force and proceed against the bandit chief.

Just at this juncture, frantic pleas for assistance reached the governor from Bhongir district, where the *zamindar* of Kilpak was fighting for his existence against Pap Rai. A relief force sent by Yusuf Khan drove off Pap Rai's forces and pursued them back to Shahpur. Assisted by an escaped group of prisoners in the bandit fort, the Mughal army succeeded in capturing the stronghold. Pap Rai retreated to Tarikonda fort with the remainder of his followers.

With the quarry run to ground, the Mughal commander quickly began siege operations at Tarikonda. After a stalemate lasting several months, the Hyderabad governor himself, leading another large army, arrived to take charge of the siege. He also mobilized, with the assistance of the *zamindars* and *deshmukhs* of the district, ten to twelve thousand cavalry and twenty thousand foot soldiers. Nine months after the siege began, in early 1710, the offer of pardon and employment as soldiers caused many of the defenders of Tarikonda (whose supplies were running low) to desert and surrender. In desperation, Pap Rai escaped alone from the fort. At Hasanabad, a toddy seller from his caste recognized the bandit and reported him to the Mughal *faujdar.* Following a speedy and brutal execution, Yusuf Khan paraded the grisly remains of the once-feared outlaw through the streets of Hyderabad before sending his severed head to the imperial court.

Partly as a result of this triumph, partly because of temporarily restored stability at the imperial center after the accession of Bahadur Shah, a slight recovery in imperial authority in Hyderabad and the other provinces of the Deccan seems to have occurred. But the imperial government's guarantees of secure local power and status for *deshmukhs*, *zamindars,* and urban gentry became less and less credible. Extended plundering by Marathas and bandits continued near the capital. More and more *deshmukhs* in Hyderabad refused to pay the taxes and the fees they collected. As the tax-flow diminished, the provincial administration in Hyderabad went bankrupt. The governor no longer had funds with which to pay his troops. The incidence of plundering by *deshmukhs* intensified dramatically, as did the number of punitive expeditions mounted by Yusuf Khan against recalcitrant *zamindars.* Finally, by 1711–12, many—if not a majority—of the *deshmukhs* and *zamindars* of both Hyderabad and Bijapur, in alliance with raiders and bandits, went into active revolt.[48] At the same time, Mughal troops mutinied for back pay. Hapless *mansabdars* plundered the countryside to find funds to pay their troops. If the harried commanders failed, they were killed by their own soldiers. When the condition of public order reached this point, the imperial structure was almost irreparably damaged.

CONCLUSION

The explanation advanced herein for the descent of imperial authority and power in the south has been offered as an alternative to that now accepted by many historians. Rather than a failure of resources for *jagirs*, incomplete administrative and political consolidation in Bijapur and Golconda after 1686–87 and commitment of the best military and administrative resources of the empire to continued expansion in the south brought about a crisis of public order and public confidence. By the years 1711–1712 in the Deccan provinces, the political crisis had reached the point that it had demoralized the imperial elite in that region, the *mansabdars*. But of equal importance was the precipitous loss of confidence on the part of those groups whose support and cooperation was also essential for the imperial system. Muslim urban notables, Telugu and Maratha *deshmukh*s and *zamindars,* and tributary chiefs of all descriptions, not fully integrated by Aurangzeb into the empire, in effect declared a moratorium on participation in the empire.

Whether a similar explanation holds for the remaining territories of the vast empire is not answerable in the present context. We can only suggest that apparently some of the same indices of decline found in the Deccan provinces also existed in the provinces of the Indo-Gangetic plain. S.N. Sinha's detailed study of Allahabad province demonstrates that, after 1685, failures to support and sustain imperial officers in the province, and to encourage the loyalty and service of *chaudhuri*s (the northern equivalent of *deshmukh*s) resulted in intensified disorder and defiance of imperial authority.[49] Sinha also concludes that Aurangzeb's continued absence from the north encouraged this reaction to imperial authority.

In any analysis of the demise of the Mughal empire, a key point of departure must be consideration of the various regional warrior aristocracies, the *zamindar*s and chiefs of all descriptions. The imperial system relied on the willing cooperation and service of *zamindar*s and especially the *deshmukh*s or *chaudhuri*s for revenue collection and maintenance of Order. From Akbar's time the empire had gradually been converting these local warrior chiefs—largely non-Muslim—into a semi-official, collaborating class in rural society. By fostering a new ethic of administrative service, and supplying rewards and security for that service, the regime was beginning to surmount the older, particularistic warrior ethic. To what extent this conversion of the rural warrior class was possible—given the sharp cultural, religious, and ethnic cleavages between them and the dynasty and the majority of the imperial elite— is an unanswerable but pertinent question. Nonetheless, these local figures, if their expectations were met, could mobilize lineage and caste networks of power and loyalty for state service rather than for revolt. Thus, the failure of the empire of the south (and perhaps in the north) lay in the inability of Aurangzeb to initiate or to continue this process of assimilation of the rural aristocracies. Failure in this endeavor ended all long-term prospects for peace and order in Mughal India.

NOTES

1. See Satish Chandra, *Parties and Politics at the Mughal Court, 1707–1740*, Aligarh, 1959, pp. xlvii–xlix; and M. Athar Al*i*, *The Mughal Nobility under Aurangzeb*, Aligarh, 1966, pp. 92–4. For evidence of recent wide acceptance of this view see P. Hardy, *The Muslims of British India* (Cambridge, 1972), pp. 20–21; S.A.A. Rizvi, "The Mughal Elite in the Sixteenth and Seventeenth Century"*Abr-Nabrain*, Vol. XI, 1971, p. 79; and by the same author, 'The Breakdown of Traditional Society', in *The Cambridge History of Islam*, Cambridge, 2 vols 1970, II, p. 69. Irfan Habib, also of the Aligarh school, agrees that a shortage of *jagirs* did exist but he holds a divergent view of imperial decline. For his views on the *jagir* crisis see *The Agrarian System of Mughal India*, Aligarh, 1963, pp. 269–71. Habib argues that the empire collapsed because of a structural flaw in the system of *jagirs* which allowed and encouraged ever-increasing exploitation and oppression of the producers by the *jagirdars*. The flaw—put simply—is that *jagirs* were transferred so frequently as to preclude any sense of responsibility for the welfare of the peasantry from arising in the mind of the *jagirdar*. The end result was migration or flight, followed by armed resistance by the peasants and their leaders, the *zamindars*. In the end, it was a series of revolts of *zamindars* that brought down the empire. In his evidence for oppression and revolt, Habib leans heavily on descriptive accounts of events in the Deccan for the period 1690–1707. In addition, more recently, M. Athar Ali has published an essay in which he articulates a larger view of the breakup of the Mughal empire within the context of world history at that time. See M. Athar Ali, 'The Passing of Empire: The Mughal Case", in *Modern Asian Studies*, Vol. IX (1975), pp. 385–96.

2. Cf. Habib, "Other *Hasil* Statistics," p. 409. Habib's figures are taken from the *Zawabit-i Alamgiri*, British Museum Persian Mss. Add. 6598 and Or. 1641 dated *c.*1687–91. If the Deccan kingdoms had maintained these nobles on their

payrolls, we might assume a priori that the same lands in Mughal control could also pay their salaries.

3. After the 1687 conquest, the Emperor divided the territories of Golconda into two nearly equivalent territories: Hyderabad province (*suba*), consisting of the twenty districts to the north of the Krishna and Gundlekamma rivers; and the *faujdari* of the Hyderabad Karnatik, the districts to the south of this line. Hyderabad proper, to which all references in this paper apply, was the object of sustained administrative reorganization in the period 1687–1700. Efforts at a similar consolidation in the Hyderabad Karnatik were cut short by the 1689 rebellion of the Telugu *nayak*s and the flight of the Maratha king to Jinji in 1690. Aurangzeb devoted all revenues and men he could obtain from the Karnatik to a continued war with the Marathas until 1698. See my article 'The Hyderabad Karnatik, 1687–1707', *Modern Asian Studies*, Vol. IX (April 1975), pp. 241–60.

4. These figures are taken from a report titled "List of the *parganas* of province *dar-al jebad* Hyderabad with the exception of the Karnatik, to the end of 1100 A.H.(1689–90 A.D.)", Nos. 1/7/72 to 1/7/105 in the Inayat Jang Collection of Mughal documents from the Deccan provinces. This collection, now in the possession of the National Archives of India, New Delhi, will be cited hereafter as I.J. Coll.; the serial number of each document will be given. For simplicity, precise figures given in the sources have been rounded off and converted from *dam*s to rupees, when necessary.

5. According to figures supplied by Habib, p. 273 n., the proceeds (*hasil*) of the imperial *khalisa* prior to the Deccan annexations were approximately 26.1 million rupees. Addition of the Hyderabad *khalisa* revenues would have raised that figure to 32.8 million rupees. Any lands similarly allocated in Bijapur would also have raised the figure.

6. I.J. Coll., I/11/498; I/14/264.

7. I.J. Coll., I/16/143.

8. This figure is an estimate arrived at by a series of calculations using data from *jagir* assignment papers for the governor and other Mughal officers sent to Hyderabad. For further details, see J.F. Richards, *Mughal Administration in Golconda*, Oxford, 1975, pp. 105–107.

9. Athar Ali, p. 78, citing a Mughal newsreport.

10. I.J. Coll., I/14/129–30. Unassigned *paibaqi* revenues in the Bijapur Konkan were an additional 839,000 rupees; in the Bijapur Karnatik 6.9 million rupees; and in the Hyderabad Karnatik, 1.9 million rupees.

11. I.J. Coll., I/18/269.

12. I.J. Coll., I/14/129–30. Numerous documents from Hyderabad, showing return of *jagir*s to *paibaqi* status for failure to meet branding regulations, testify to the accuracy of this analysis.

13. I.J. Coll.,1/16/947–48. This order assigns five *parganas* in Hyderabad to help defray the wage bill of one thousand *mansabdars* (rank 40 to 250 *zat*) serving under Khan Firuz Jang. Another *jagir* worth 3,65,000 rupees was established in Bijapur for the same purpose.

14. I.J. Coll., I/18/269.

15. In 1704, a Dutch merchant reporting on conditions at Hyderabad noted that no caravans had come to the provincial capital (formerly the capital of Golconda) in the past two years because of the depredations of bandits and Marathas. He went on to comment that "Whereas the Emperor Aurangzeb concerns himself more to conquer the far distant territories of the Marathas than to demonstrate scarcely any concern for the affairs of the conquered kingdoms of Golconda and Bijapur, His Majesty's great governors [in those provinces] are not sufficiently empowered to do so. As a result trade everywhere has come to a halt". Koloniaal Archief of the Algemeen Rijksarchief, The Hague, "Inkomend Briefboek" Volume 1584 (2.2.1704), fol. III. Although but one comment, this does suggest that contemporary observers noticed the problems caused in the eastern Deccan by the emperor's expansive policies.

16. Cf. M. Athar Ali, 'Provincial Governors Under Aurangzeb—An Analysis', in *Medieval India A Miscellany*, K.A. Nizami, ed., Aligarh, 1969, pp. 96–133. A complete analysis of the origins of *faujdars* and fortress commanders has not been completed, but no Maratha officers were appointed in that capacity in Hyderabad.

17. My definition of *khanazads*, who numbered close to half the Mughal nobility in the period 1679–1707 is taken from Athar Ali, *Mughal Nobility*, pp. 11–12. However (unlike Athar Ali), I have used the term 'noble' to indicate generally those *mansabdars* with ranks over 500 *zat* (rather than 1,000 *zat),* thus increasing the number of the nobility to well over a thousand. *Mansabdars* holding ranks as low as 500 *zat,* or even lower, frequently held responsible positions as *faujdars* and corresponded directly with the Emperor. See also U.N. Day, *The Mughal Government A.D. 1556–1707*, New Delhi, 1970, p. 184, for a discussion of the classification of *mansabdars.*

18. See Ibn Hasan, *The Central Structure of the Mughal Empire*, Karachi, 1967 (reprint), pp. 65–91 for a detailed description of the Emperor's daily routine and the audiences held by him.

19. For one index to the amount of time and effort expended by the Timurids on *mansabdari* affairs, note the frequent references to such matters in the *Memoirs of Jahangir*, (trs.) A. Rogers and H. Beveridge, Royal Asiatic Society, Calcutta, 1909–14, 2 vols. See also, for Aurangzeb's reign, the *Ma'asir-i Alamgiri* of Saqui Musta'id Khan, (tr.) Jadunath Sarkar Calcutta, 1947.

20. In the absence of well-documented studies of the world view of the Mughal nobility, this assertion is, of course, speculative. That men like the

Rajput general Jai Singh, who served Aurangzeb so well in numerous campaigns, possessed such a view of the empire would be hard to deny. Cf. Jagdish Sarkar, "The Haft Anjuman of Udairaj Alias Tale'gar, Munshi of Mirza Rajah Jai Singh", *Bengal Past and Present*, Vol. LXXXI (1962), pp. 69–75; Vol. LLXXXII (1963), pp. 65–73; Vol. LXXXIII (1964), pp. 43–55; Vol. LXXXIV (1965), pp. 63–76; Vol. LXXXV (1966), pp. 113–22.

21. As Athar Ali points out, one of Akbar's major contributions was the enunciation of an essentially humane approach to the individuals constituting the nobility"(p. 8. Unlike the Safavids or the Uzbeks, the Mughals did not execute members of the nobility for offenses less serious than rebellion. See M. Athar Ali, "The Mughal Empire in History", Presidential Address Section II, Medieval India, India History Congress, 33rd Session, Muzaffarpur, 1972, pp. 8–9.

22. Other important examples include Raja Bakht Buland, the Gond ruler of Deogarh, who, despite his conversion to Islam, fled from Aurangzeb's service in 1696. See Jadunath Sarkar, *History of Aurangzib*, Calcutta, 5 vols, 1912–30, Vol. V, pp. 408–12. The Telugu raja of Venkatagiri, Yachim Na'ir, alternated between rebellion and acceptance of Mughal service before he was finally executed by Aurangzeb. For details, see my article "The Hyderabad Karnatik..." cited above.

23. For the Bedars and their relations with the Mughals, see Jadunath Sarkar, *History of Aurangzib*, Vol. IV, pp. 387–89; Vol. V, pp. 214–34. Also see Muhammad Hashim Khafi Khan, *Muntakhbab-al Lubab* (eds), K.D. Ahmad and Wolseley Haig, *Bibliothecha Indica* No. 60, Calcutta, 3 vols, 1860–74, Vol. II, pp. 369–70 and 524–27.

24. Cf. Sarkar, 'Their tribal organization under the heads of families and the judicial authority of their hereditary headmen ensured discipline and solidarity among them, *History of Aurangzib*, Vol. V, pp. 214–15.

25. Khafi Khan, Vol. II, p. 370.

26. Ibid. Another vivid description appears in the *Ma'asir-i Alamgiri* (tr.), pp. 185–87.

27. See Yusuf Husain Khan, *Selected Documents of Aurangzeb's Reign*, Hyderabad, 1958, pp. 205–206.

28. Bhimsen, 'Nuskha-i Dilkusha', British Museum Persian Ms. Oriental 23, fols. 98a–98b.

29. This detailed account of Padiyah's activities is taken from Khan, Vol. II, pp. 526–8.

30. Ibid.

31. Jagia, *deshmukh* of Nasratabad, was given an increase in his *mansab* in 1706. *Ma'asir-i Alamgiri*, p. 305.

32. In October 1692, the Dutch reported that Padiyah Nayak's bands (*troepen*) in combination with the Marathas of Ram Raja, daily raided the interior districts near Hyderabad city. These raiders levied taxes (*contributien*) and robbed many merchants on the roads. Koloniaal Archief, Vol. 1408 (25 April 1692), fol. 697.

33. Sec J.F. Richards, 'Mughal Rule in Golconda, 1687–1724', unpublished PhD dissertation, Berkeley, 1970, p. 206.

34. Ibid., p. 148 n. Rustam Dil Khan's grandfather migrated from Iraq via Khurasan to serve Jahangir in the early seventeenth century. At one time, under the title Mukhtar Khan, the grandfather held the governorship of Delhi. Rustam Dil Khan's own rank was that of an *amir* at 1500 *zat* and 1000 *suwar.*

35. The obligations of a Mughal governor to sustain peace and order were well established from the founding of the empire. See I.H. Qureshi, *The Administration of the Mughul Empire*, Karachi, 1966, pp. 228–29. For a model patent of office addressed to a Mughal governor see British Museum, Persian ms., Or. 1779, fol. 215b.

36. See Richards, *Mughal Administration in Golconda*, Oxford, 1975, p. 218.

37. Ibid., pp. 227–28.

38. Ibid., pp. 219–20.

39. Ibid., p. 239.

40. Ibid., A Mughal fiscal officer stationed at Machilipatnum tried to report this fact to the imperial *wazir* in 1708 but was prevented from doing so by Rustam Dil Khan.

41. Ibid.

42. Ibid., pp. 240–41.

43. W. Irvine, *Later Mughals*, New Delhi, 1971 (reprint), Jadunath Sarkar, ed., Vol. I, pp. 52–54.

44. See I.J. Coll., I/16/126 for a summary of the combined salary *jagirs* of both Jan Sipar Khan and Rustam Dil Khan in 1700. I.J. Coll., 1/16/143 supplies details of Rustam Dil Khan's *jagirs* in Hyderabad after 1700.

45. For summaries of conditions of appointment of *deshmukh*s in Hyderabad, see I.J. Coll., 1/16/602 to I/16/636. For a similar accommodation in the western Deccan see Muzaffar Alam, 'The Zamindars and Mughal Power in the Deccan, 1685–1712". *The Indian Economic and Social History Review,* Vol. XI (March 1974), pp. 74–91. Dr. Alam, following Nurul Hasan, makes an important and necessary distinction between the intermediary, more powerful *zamindar*s and the primary, or smaller village-level ones. Because, most Mughal documents for Hyderabad do not distinguish between the two levels of *zamindar*s; I have not been able to follow his example. The conclusions reached and generalizations made for the *deshmukh*s in Hyderabad almost certainly apply to the remainder

of the intermediary *zamindars*. The entire question of the possibility of differing responses on the part of primary *zamindars* needs further examination.

46. Richards, *Mughal Administration in Golconda,* pp. 254–63; Alam, pp. 81–84.

47. Khafi Khan, Vol. II, pp. 630–43 provides a detailed narrative of Pap Rai's rise and fall. Official Mughal newsreports from Hyderabad verify and corroborate the essential accuracy of the chronicle in regard to Pap Rai's exploits. See also Richards, *Mughal Administration in Golconda,* pp. 245–52, pp. 224–35.

48. For events in Hyderabad in 1711–12, see Ibid., pp. 252–63. For the increased incidence of revolt by *deshmukh*s in Bijapur at the same time, see Alam, pp. 86–88.

49. S.N. Sinha, *Subah of Allahabad under the Great Mughals,* New Delhi, 1974, pp. 72–82.

Shivaji and the Decline of the Mughal Empire*

Michael N. Pearson

SOME THEORIES OF MUGHAL DECLINE

The decline of the Mughal empire is usually considered to begin late in the reign of the emperor Aurangzib (1658–1707). The favorite explanations consist of circles, or even spirals, usually vicious in nature. One important interpretation sees the decline as originating from an increased taxation burden on the peasantry, who revolted in several areas, ultimately with such success that the empire was weakened. More money was needed to crush more revolts, so there was more oppressive taxation and so more revolts.[1] This is less than convincing, for peasant revolts—whether or not led by *zamindar*s (locally important landholders)—were more or less a constant in Mughal India. They were particularly prevalent in Gujarat and Bengal, but Hindustan was far from exempt. What we really need here is an attempt at a quantitative assessment of the number of revolts, and of participants in them, during the whole seventeenth century.

A second interpretation, associated particularly with the work of M. Athar Ali, finds the consequences of the move south crucial, for this resulted in more nobles chasing an almost static pool of resources. The Mughals were unable to defeat their Maratha enemies in the south, and so resorted to bribery, mostly in the form of high *mansab*s (ranks) in the Mughal nobility. As a result there was an influx of new nobles, and not enough good *jagir*s (land revenue assignments) to support them. They had to be given land in unsubdued or infertile areas, and so were unable to support their *sawar* (military) ranks. Consequently, military

* Reproduced from M.N. Pearson, 'Shivaji and the Decline of the Mughal Empire', *Journal of Asian Studies*, Vol. XXXV, No. 2, February 1976, pp. 221–35. An earlier version of the article was first presented to the 1973 Annual Meeting of the American Historical Association, San Francisco, California.

performance declined further, bribery had to be used more often, and so on.[2] There are some weaknesses in Athar Ali's calculation of the rate of increase in the nobility under Aurangzib, for the two periods into which he divides Aurangzib's reign are of unequal length, and he makes no effort to account for nobles who carried over from the preceding reign or period. Nevertheless, even when his calculations are corrected, there still clearly was a large rise in the numbers of nobles late in the seventeenth century. A more central problem is to work out what resources were available to pay them and their troops.

Finally, a different line of attack tends to see the Mughal empire as still strong and effective to the end of Aurangzib's reign, and even beyond.[3] Among the evidences cited to bolster this is the continued loyal activities of some nobles late in the seventeenth century, and the continuance well into the eighteenth century of the sending of tribute from Bengal and other places to the Mughal emperors. If nothing else, such claims point to the need for more research, for they raise serious questions concerning such matters as the proportion of total provincial revenue sent to the center at different times, and the nature of "loyalty," "legitimacy," and "independence" in eighteenth-century India.

These questions cannot detain us now. Rather, it seems more profitable to return to the explanations of those who believe the empire was in trouble by late in Aurangzib's reign, for we share in this opinion; we simply differ as to the causes. Circles and spirals, especially vicious ones, are certainly pictorially attractive, but they do not start from nothing; something has to happen somewhere to get the empire into the circle. Various theories are put forward here, but they all find the root problem in Aurangzib's move south. This happened in 1681–82, and is variously—or in combination—ascribed to his desire to root out the heretical or semi-infidel rulers of Golconda and Bijapur to the south of his empire; to the "imperatives" of Indian history, which see every strong ruler, of north India as desirous of ruling the whole subcontinent; or to a desire to crush the Maratha revolt.

The "imperatives of Indian history" interpretation requires a brief elaboration. Percival Spear presents a common view when he says that "It [geography] has encouraged aspirations to empire. . . ."[4] At first sight, this is tempting. The subcontinent is clearly a well-defined geographic unit: what could be more natural than for an established empire, usually in the north, to attempt to complete the conquest by moving south? The subcontinent is a graspable area, almost an island, and it seems logical to hold it all. Unlike a strong empire in Eurasia, there is a place to stop.

The difficulty is that this view is based on modern man's knowledge of South Asian geography. Many of us see a relief map of South Asia nearly every day. At the start of our history courses we give a survey of South Asian geography, point out the mountains, and demonstrate the geographical unity of the area. But it is questionable that a Mughal emperor had, in this concrete geographical sense, any such conception. We do know that geography was not an important part of the education likely to have been received by a Mughal prince. Further, maps and globes were rarities at court in the seventeenth century: Europeans found them to be esteemed gifts.[5] At the least, we need to be careful not to transfer our knowledge of South Asian geography to the minds of Mughal emperors.

There is, of course, another aspect to this problem. In the Hindu tradition is the concept of the *chakravartin,* the universal ruler. It is unclear what sort of area a *chakravartin* should fitly rule: it may or may not be coterminous with South Asia. Nor is there any proof that the Muslim emperors had acquired any such perceptual baggage from their Hindu predecessors. The matter is open, but I suspect they thought primarily in terms of Hindustan, and saw the northwest as the logical place for expansion.

It is clear that the circles and spirals are at least implicitly seen as symptoms or consequences, not as causes of the decline, for the circle spins off from the move south. The proximate cause of the decline is thus claimed to be this move south. Our aim in this paper is to show that the move south was itself a symptom of a central weakness in the Mughal empire. Because of the centrality of military concerns in the upper levels of the state, there was no alternative but to respond aggressively to a military challenge. The move south was thus a final desperate attempt to crush a formidable enemy that had already inflicted humiliating defeats on the empire. The move was not expansionist, it was entirely defensive, a product of desperation, not of free Mughal choice.

Once in the south, the Mughals of course failed to defeat decisively the Marathas. The strains of protracted war produced, late in the century, obvious signs of decline: a growing imbalance between the number of *jagirdar*s and the resources made available to pay them; peasant revolts in different areas; a disheartened and increasingly disloyal nobility. But these were all caused by the move south, and the subsequent military failure. The real question is thus: Why the move south? The answers lie in the composition of the Mughal nobility, the nature of their ties to the empire, and the impact on them of Maratha successes up to 1666. In what follows, we make two assumptions about the nature of the Mughal state and its nobility; it is necessary to spell these out clearly.

THE MUGHAL STATE AND NOBILITY

First, we see Mughal rule as very indirect. The subjects of the state should be visualized as constituents of one or more groups based on kin, caste, occupation, locality, religion, or some other determinant. Each group had a head of some sort—a *seth* (merchant head), a *pir* (Muslim saint), a *zamindar*, a street chief, a village headman or council—who was the intermediary with the Mughal administration on the rare occasions when the group or a member of it needed to be connected to this administration. But most of the time, most of the subjects of a Mughal emperor handled their own affairs for themselves, within their own group or groups, and had nothing to do with any official.

The maximum core of the empire, the only people directly connected to the ruler and the only people concerned with his fate—were a small number of men bound to him by patron–client ties. These men can be mechanically defined as those holding any *mansab* (rank) bestowed by the emperor. They numbered at most 8,000 men in an empire of sixty or seventy million people. Radiating out from these people were many others, connected to these *mansabdars* (rank-holders) by their own patron–client ties: the soldiers, the artists, the household officials of the *mansabdars*—all bound only indirectly, through their patrons, to the empire. The 8,000 men were the empire, the only people linked to the emperor by direct patronage ties, the only people in whom it was possible that the concept of the Mughal Empire outweighed other primordial attachments, the people who were Mughal India's "core of more fully integrated members" providing it with a "level of integration or solidarity and a distinctive membership status."[6]

In fact, this figure of 8,000 is very much a maximum number for those bound directly to the empire, for it includes all those holding any rank at all. Athar Ali includes in his category of 'noble' only those *mansabdars* with ranks of 1,000 or more; until late in the seventeenth century these people numbered less than 500 men. This limit of a rank of 1,000 is rather arbitrary, for men with a rank of only 500 could hold responsible positions. Given our lack of knowledge of the lower-ranked *mansabdars*, it is perhaps best to say simply and arbitrarily that the core nobility of Mughal India numbered about 1,000 men.

Our second basic claim is that this small group of 1,000 nobles was connected to the emperor only by patronage, and the continuance of this patronage depended on military success. Neither religion nor racial origin provided any reason for loyalty: in the period 1658–78, of Aurangzib's top *mansabdars* (those with *mansabs* of 5,000 or more), 49 per cent were Hindu or born outside India, while an astounding 82 per cent were Hindu or of foreign extraction.[7] Even within such categories as 'foreign-born', the heterogeneity could be great. At the end of Shah Jahan's reign (reigned 1628–58), his foreign born nobles came not just from Persia or Central Asia but from seventeen different places.[8] There was thus no ethnically based solidarity amongst the nobility vis-à-vis the emperor, nor between the emperor and his nobles. Nor did any sort of abstract loyalty to Aurangzib as ruler of an impersonal ongoing state exist.

Finally, Muslim law was always suspicious of temporal rulers. An association with courts and rulers was, at least in theory, considered to preclude the possibility of leading a good Muslim life.[9] The practical effect of this was probably limited, but it did restrict active support of the state from at least some religious groups. The nobles followed the emperor as a person and nothing more, as a man who at least temporarily was ruler and who—through the fruits of military success—was able to dispense patronage.

The importance of military matters is demonstrated by some interesting evidence from Shah Jahan's reign. A. Jan Qaisar presents figures to show that in 1647, 77.2 per cent of the total salary claim of Shah Jahan's top 445 nobles was from their *sawar* (military) rank, and so-at least in theory—was spent on military matters. Perhaps even more indicative is Qaisar's claim that 47.5 per cent of the total *jama* (standard land revenue assessment) of the empire was allocated to the *sawar* salaries of these top 445 nobles. Qaisar is rightly cautious of this data, but even if they do exaggerate reality they still illustrate an enormous stress on military activities, and a large allocation of available resources to this area.[10]

The primacy of the military ethic found ample expression in the sayings and doings of the emperors and their nobles. Thus Akbar (1556–1605) said that a "monarch should be ever intent on conquest." Aurangzib allegedly told his deposed father that "although the greatest conquerors are not always the greatest Kings," "I am indeed far from denying that conquests ought to distinguish the reign of a great Monarch, and that I should disgrace the blood of the great Timur, our honoured progenitor, if I did not seek to extend the bounds of my present territories."[11] Acting on the latter belief, he attempted to bolster the shaky legitimacy of his early reign by a period of furious military activity. In this, he was simply following established Mughal practice: as has recently been noted, the Mughal empire "was created by conquest and attuned to constant military activity."[12] Similarly, P. Hardy says that "at no time did Muslim rulers [in medieval India] preside over a demilitarised, society."[13]

The nobles were thus bound to a person, and this person had to be a winner. As to the first point, it was demonstrated by the requirement that all nobles at court attend on the emperor twice daily. The converse of this requirement was that the nobles could thus constantly check that the emperor was indeed still alive and well. Shah Jahan's deposition was the ultimate proof that a Mughal emperor had to be functioning and active; even a suspicion of his death or incapacity led to a breaking of loyalty. This lesson Aurangzib learnt: even when critically ill, he would drag himself out once a day so all could see the empire still existed.

Not just a personal appearance but an aura of success was needed; and this martial mandate of heaven could be extremely cruel. In 1658, Aurangzib and his brother Murad Bakhsh, temporary allies in the war of succession to the ailing Shah Jahan, defeated Dara Shukoh. For the nobles, this was enough: their decision was clear. With only two exceptions, they deserted Dara Shukoh and his father Shah Jahan, and rallied unhesitatingly to Aurangzib. "The high grandees and other imperial officers came in troops to the Court of Aurangzib in hope [of his patronage] and each received favours suited to his rank." A year later, at Aurangzib's formal coronation, and with Shah Jahan still alive, indeed destined to live seven more years, "The courtiers bowed to do honour, and sang the praises of and prayed for the Emperor."[14] The bulk of Delhi's population may have supported Dara Shukoh, but as Bernier noted, "It is certain that the close confinement of Chah-Jehan [in June 1658] seemed the signal for nearly the whole body of Omrahs to pay their court to Aurang-Zebe and Morad Bakche. I can indeed scarcely repress my indignation when I reflect that there was not a single movement nor even a voice heard in behalf of the aged and injured Monarch: although the Omrahs who bowed the knee to his oppressors were indebted to him for their rank and riches."[15]

This martial orientation dictated that nearly all nobles, regardless of their talents, had *sawar* (military), as well as *zat* (personal), ranks. A noble's position could be based on artistic ability, scholarship, or on his ability to entertain the emperor; but no matter—they still had military ranks. Bernier's patron, Danishmand Khan, was primarily a scholar and diplomat: indeed, his scholarship and achievements were so highly valued by Aurangzib that he was exempted from twice daily attendance at court, the better for him to be able to pursue his studies. Yet he was also a commander of 2,500 troops.[16] Frequently such non-martial nobles were required to live up to the implications of their military ranks; Abul Fazl and Raja Birbal both died on military expeditions. Nor apparently did the nobles object to this, for advancement and controls of greater resource usually came from military success. More than routine promotion came most often after victories.

Given these two attributes of the Mughal system, an important corollary follows: in such a system only the *mansabdar*s were loyal to the empire, for only they were part of it. The dependents of a *mansabdar*, his family, employees, and troops, were perhaps loyal at one remove, through the mediation of the *mansabdar*; but for all other subjects of the empire, loyalty went to the social group to which they belonged, not to the empire or the emperor. This in turn meant that the only way a man could be made loyal to the emperor was by making him a *mansabdar*. Thus, the emperor could not negotiate with a rebel; the choice was to bond him to the emperor by incorporation in the nobility, or to crush him. With this background, we can now consider the nature and impact of the defeats suffered by this small, militarily oriented group of nobles.

THE MARATHA REVOLT

Our main interest is in the effects of the revolt of the Marathas, not in the causes of their revolt nor in the reasons for their early successes, for both of these are obvious enough. There were always *zamindar*s ready to revolt in India, as Dr. Naqvi's tabulation of 144 revolts against Akbar shows.[17] Most often they first reduced the amount of revenue they handed over to imperial authorities. If the latter retaliated in strength, the *zamindar* acquiesced, knowing that he had misread the situation. If no punishment was forthcoming, the *zamindar* used his extra money to acquire men and then territory continuing to do this until the imperial power was awakened and responded. As Abul Fazl noted, "The custom of the majority of the *zamindar*s of Hindustan is to leave the path of single-mindedness and to look to every side and to join anyone who is powerful or who is making an increasing stir."[18] More specifically, in 1663–4, a man claiming to be Aurangzib's late elder brother, Dara Shukoh, appeared in Gujarat. "The *Kolis*, who always have the wind of revolt and passion of rebellion in their heads, made that base person a handle of revolt, and created disorder."[19] Similarly, Shah Jahan, in revolt against his father, reached Bengal in 1624, and "The suppressed unruly elements once more raised their heads."[20]

The Maratha success became self-sustaining after the mid-1660s, and went on and on in a self-generating fashion. The initial successes were a result of several well-known factors: the terrain of the Maratha *swaraj* (homeland), so difficult for a cumbersome Bijapuri or Mughal army; Shivaji's tactical expertise, especially the use of light fast horses and the strong yet inexpensive hill forts; the existence of happy hunting grounds in the weakened sultanate of Bijapur; Aurangzib's involvement in the war of succession just when it seemed that he could and would turn on Shivaji and nip him in the bud.

With this fortuitous start, Shivaji was able to build on strength. By his death in 1680, he was very much more than just another rebel. He controlled an area of about 50,000 square miles, or 4.1 per cent of the area of the whole subcontinent.[21] His revenue was between one-fifth and one-sixth of that of Aurangzib.[22] In his territory he had set up a comparatively elaborate administrative apparatus.[23] None of the other contemporary rebels—the Satnamis, the Sikhs, the Yusufzais, the Jats, the Afridis—achieved anything remotely comparable to this. Indeed, Shivaji had moved beyond being a rebel to a position as head of a rival state. The effect of Shivaji's successes is more difficult to define, but our basic contention is that by 1666 he had had such success that the Mughals had no alternative but to respond massively by a move south to Shivaji's homeland. The decline followed from this. Thus it is as early as 1666 that we can find the entrance to the circle, the beginning of the decline.

Until he called himself away for the war of succession, Aurangzib had apparently planned to crush Bijapur and then deal with Shivaji. But the Marathas remained in the forefront of his mind, for one of his first acts after he had defeated his brothers was, in July 1659, to send Shaista Khan south as viceroy of the Deccan, his main task being to oppose Shivaji. Shaista Khan was no mere troop commander. He ranked third in the noble hierarchy; bearing the prestigious title of *Amir-ul-umara*, he was a son of the great Asaf Khan, and the maternal uncle of Aurangzib. Typically, Shaista Khan did little. He remained in camp in and around Poona for more than two-and-a-half years, until Shivaji carried out an audacious attack in April 1663. Shaista Khan lost a son, a thumb, several attendants, and much prestige. The attack on such an eminent and well-connected noble caused consternation at court and dismay for Aurangzib. Shaista Khan was sent off in disgrace to the penal province of Bengal without even being allowed the usual interview with Aurangzib.

THE SACK OF SURAT

Shivaji's second, and most astounding, exploit was his first seizure and sack of Surat in January 1664. The importance of this raid has not been generally appreciated. During the whole of the seventeenth century, Surat was far and away the greatest port of Mughal India, or in Tavernier's words "the sole port of the whole empire of the Great Mogul."[24] In 1644, the value of goods passing through the customs house was around Rs 1,00,00,000. By comparison, the total capital available on 165 ships sent to the east by the English East India Company between 1601 and 1640 amounted to about Rs. 3,00,00,000. In 1646–47, the standard assessment of the land revenue of the fertile province of Gujarat was Rs. 1,32,50,000; with a rate of one-third, we can value agricultural production in all Gujarat at about Rs. 4,00,00,000.[25] Clearly, Surat and its trade were of considerable economic importance in Gujarat, and also in the whole empire.

Politically, and militarily, the seizure of Surat was a bombshell. The new viceroy of the Deccan Prince Muazzam, sat in Aurangabad with a large army and did nothing to prevent the raid or to intercept Shivaji as he moved back to the Deccan. In the town itself, the officials fled to the impregnable castle and undertook no offensive action at all, although they commanded a force of over 20,000 men[26] and Shivaji had only 10,000.[27] In fact, the Mughals performed ingloriously. Yet the true political impact of this raid can be appreciated only when it is considered that Shivaji was the first rebel ever to capture and plunder an important Mughal town and not be punished immediately. His action was unprecedented, both in scope and success. The only parallel seems to have been an occurrence in 1610, when a man claiming to be the Mughal prince Khusrau was, by luck, able to seize Patna and hold it for one week; he then was attacked and killed.[28]

For a pious emperor, Surat had more than economic and political importance; it was the port from which the (pilgrimage) ships left Mughal India for the Red Sea. The port was variously known as the Bab-al-Makkah, the Bah-ul-Hajj, the Dar-ul-Hajj, and the Bandar-i Mubarak. Aurangzib himself sent two large ships to the Red Sea each year from Surat, carrying pilgrims free of charge. The principal persons of his harem and his nobles joined him in sending considerable contributions via Surat to Mecca. More quantitatively, the importance of the *hajj*, of Mecca, and thus of Surat as the gateway to the Red Sea is revealed by the gifts Aurangzib sent after his coronation. In 1662, the Shah of Persia sent Aurangzib presents worth Rs. 422,000, and Aurangzib reciprocated with Rs 535,000; but to the *sharifs* of Mecca and Medina, in 1659 he sent articles worth Rs. 630,000.[29] The sacking of the "blessed port" was a more-than-routine affront to Aurangzib, and was aggravated by Shivaji's navy, from the early 1660s, beginning regular program of plundering Aurangzib's pilgrim ships.[30]

The first sack of Surat thus had an enormous impact on Mughal prestige, an impact of much greater significance than the more-than-a-crore (10,000,000) of rupees Shivaji took away in plunder. The memory lingered on, unsettling to the inhabitants of Surat and derogatory to the prestige of the empire. Even in 1695, a European traveller found recollections of this raid still alive in Surat.[31] The remembrance was encouraged by Shivaji, who—in 1664 and later—audaciously demanded annual *chauth* (protection money) from the town, on pain of a return visit. Surat was subject to almost annual panics, as rumors spread of Shivaji's return. An assumption of inevitable Mughal victory had in a few years swung completely around to an assumption of inevitable

Maratha victory, and this in the most important and prestigious port of the empire.

The rich merchants fled to the castle or left town each time these rumours spread; in this, they were wise. The Mughals had responded to Shivaji's first raid, but, despite their concern, not very effectively. Immediately after the raid, the governor of Gujarat came to the town with a considerable force and stayed three months. Aurangzib sacked the delinquent officials, and the town was walled; but to no avail. The defense opposed to Shivaji's second raid, in October 1670, was even more feeble than that to the first; and by 1677, things had reached such a pass that Maratha leaders would nonchalantly walk into the town accompanied only by a handful of troopers, and insolently demand food and money from the governor.[32]

MUGHAL RESPONSE

These two coups, the attack on Shaista Khan and the first raid on Surat, left Aurangzib with no choice but to respond massively. As Manucci said, "He could no longer endure the insults of ShivaJi."[33] In 1665, Jai Singh, the top general and top noble in the empire, was sent south with a large and well supported army and full diplomatic powers. The result was an impressive victory: Shivaji was defeated, and signed a treaty with Jai Singh in June 1665. By this treaty of Purandar, Shivaji was forced to cede twenty-three of his thirty-five forts and 80 per cent of his revenue from forts. Yet this was only a partial victory: Shivaji kept some of his forts, and the Mughals made other concessions. Shivaji's son was given a high *mansab;* Shivaji himself was invited to join in the spoliation of Bijapur, and he was not at this time compelled to come to court and pay homage to Aurangzib. It was clearly far from complete eradication, yet such as it was it was greeted with slightly hysterical joy at court. Jai Singh and his family and retainers were lavishly rewarded.

What went wrong at court in 1666? For the Mughals, the prognosis must have appeared good. Shivaji had, after all, been defeated by Jai Singh, and since then had achieved little fighting with the Mughals against Bijapur. In May 1666, his fortunes were at a low ebb; the time seemed ripe to pursue Akbar's Rajput policy: to beat enemies and then buy them. This was indeed the crucial moment, for this was the time when perhaps Shivaji could be incorporated in the *mansabdari* system and thus bonded to the empire.

Several factors dictated failure. Unlike the Rajputs, Shivaji was something of a barbarian in the refined atmosphere of the Mughal court; his unruly conduct may have stemmed from a reflex action designed to cover his embarrassment at his lack of ability to fit in with Mughal courtly etiquette. More important, he was not completely beaten; and he knew it. Had Aurangzib offered a really large bribe, perhaps a very high *mansab* combined with some freedom of action for Shivaji in the Deccan, an accommodation might have been reached. But Aurangzib did not offer this; he could not. Neither he nor his nobles were prepared to offer Shivaji a position he could accept. How, for example would the top Rajputs or the courtly Persians feel if a low-caste brigand, a "mountain rat," was raised above them? Aurangzib knew this, and presumably also knew that too lavish rewards to a successful brigand would set a most dangerous precedent. But it is unlikely that Aurangzib personally was disposed to treat Shivaji too gently. Even by receiving him at court and giving him a robe of honor, he was going further than he wanted to and also further than certain influential people around him thought he should go.

These people—opposed to Shivaji for diverse reasons—included Jafar Khan; Ra'd Khan; Jaswant Singh, who was simply jealous of Jai Singh, and several of the women of his harem. Two influential women had particular grievances: The wife of the *wazir*, Jafar Khan, was a sister of Shaista Khan. Jahanara, Aurangzib's favorite sister, had been receiving the customs duties from Surat; and Shivaji's raid was thus a direct affront to her. All these people opposed Aurangzib's half-hearted attempt to befriend the attacker of Shaista Khan and the plunderer of the Gate of the *Hajj*. They were able to play on Aurangzib's latent hostility and get Shivaji imprisoned while they continued to debate his fate. Even by 1666, Shivaji had been too successful, had made too much of an impact on the very highest levels of the Mughal court, for Aurangzib to be able to buy him.[34]

Shivaji's escape in August was thus merely the final straw. It completely nullified Jai Singh's victory of the previous year, and further decreased the prestige of an emperor who apparently could neither win over nor kill a rebel at his court. It also bore out again how feared Shivaji had by this time become. The English at Surat knew of the escape within a month, and anxiously noted that the "feares of the countryes hereabouts begin againe to be great." Two months later they reported that "now all waite some cruell" revenge upon the country and people. We were lately hotly allarum'd upon a reported that he was come neere with a flyeing army, that all the people began to flye again: but the report proved false. Yet, let him come when he will, the whole towne will be dispeopled: for none will face him or abide the place."[35] Modern authors agree on the decisiveness of the failure at reconciliation and the later flight,[36] as indeed did Aurangzib both at the time[37] and later. His will included these retrospective reflections on the events of 1666: "Negligence for a single moment becomes the cause of disgrace for long years. The escape of the wretch Shiva took place through carelessness, and I have to labour hard [against the Marathas] to the end of my life [as the result of it]."[38]

ANALYSIS OF THE MUGHAL RESPONSE

Where exactly lay the damage from these three feats, and other, less spectacular Maratha raids in the Deccan? Certainly there was almost no threat to the immediate economic interests of the nobility, or to the heartland of the empire. Hindustan was not visited by Maratha bands until the eighteenth century. Plunder in Malwa was of little concern to the home base of the state. Nor were most nobles affected directly in any economic sense, except for a few minor officials in Surat. Shaista Khan went on to a long and personally profitable stay as governor of Bengal; and there is no sign that Jahanara was ever short of funds. Surat survived the raids, and remained India's greatest port into the eighteenth century.

Today we know that the empire probably could have moved inward to Hindustan remaining there secure and inviolate. But for the Mughal nobility, the sociology of their knowledge of Shivaji's activities to 1666 dictated a very different response. In Robert Berkhofer's stimulating terms, the problem for Aurangzib—and for the empire—was that "Behaviour is not a direct reaction to the stimuli, but a response made in accordance with ideational mediation."[39] Given the open challenge, and the orientation of the nobility, there was no alternative to a military response; and this meant a move to the south.

One crucial element here was who had initiated the combat. Defeat was not new to the Mughals, but previously it had been defeat in a war started by them, and in peripheral areas of slight concern to them. In two centuries, Qandahar was besieged fifteen times and transferred twelve times; but the "real significance of Qandahar was as a testing point, a limited arena, where each side [the Mughals and Safavid Persia] could probe the strength of the other."[40] Qandahar could be lost, unsuccessfully besieged, regained or whatever; success and failure here were relatively unimportant economically, politically, and in terms of prestige. Similarly, the Mughals could operate with rather modest success in the northern Deccan for sixty years, and not suffer deleterious consequences. But Maratha raids on Surat, and into Khandesh and Malwa, objectively also unimportant, had far more serious consequences, for they demanded retaliation.

The many challenges to Akbar had no long-term effects, for, as Dr. Naqvi documents, they were all crushed quickly; if anything, they helped him to build up an aura of invincibility. In Aurangzib's move south, doubtless the usual motive for the expansion of an empire was present, the need for ever more resources to maintain the allegiance of the nobles. This, however, was not an imperative, at least not for a move south, for expansion could have gone elsewhere. Nor was Aurangzib's religious opposition to the heterodox rulers of Bijapur and Golconda an imperative. Expansion on either of these grounds implies at least an element of free choice. But Shivaji's success ended the freedom; thanks to him, the involvement was unavoidable.

By 1666 Shivaji had humiliated the Mughals three times. Sarkar sums up the significance of this: "A hundred victories since the second Panipat had taught the Indian world to believe that Mughal arms were invincible and Mughal territory inviolable. Shivaji broke the spell."[41] Aurangzib acquired the pall of a loser. The empire had been challenged, and had to strike back decisively. Given the obvious tensions for a Hindu noble serving an orthodox Muslim emperor, and for a Shia Persian serving a strict Sunni emperor both religiously and politically at loggerheads with Persia, the fact becomes clear. With no bond for the empire except precarious military success, the whole military ethic, the image of a noble as fitly engaged when he galloped over the plain leading his troops, dictated that this small group were forced south. The ideational mediation of Aurangzib and his nobles left them with no alternative.

How can we demonstrate more clearly the fatal impact of Shivaji's early successes and of the crucial failure to bond him in 1666? We should first perhaps show that most— or at least many—nobles were acutely aware of Shivaji and his challenge, for Sarkar stresses the unimportance of the Deccan and the Maratha revolt until Aurangzib himself moved south in 1681.[42] Using Athar Ali's list of the top nobility for 1658–78, and adding one—Abul Muhammad, whom he seems to have missed— we have counted the number of the top nobles of this period who had extensive contact with Shivaji. For this purpose we have included all those engaged in military operations against Shivaji, all those who took central roles in the discussions at court in 1666, and all Maratha and Deccan additions to the Mughal nobility. The results are startling. Even though our figures for those involved with Shivaji are certainly low, at Shivaji's death in 1680, thirty-one out of the top fifty, and fifty-seven out of the top one hundred had been directly involved with him. Even more important, the figures as of Shivaji's flight from Agra in 1666 are nineteen out of fifty, and thirty-two out of one hundred. As early as 1666, about 35 percent of the top nobility had been closely involved with the problem of the Marathas. He and his successes were very much alive in the minds of the nobility by 1666.

Less quantitative evidence also demonstrates how widely known and feared Shivaji had become during the 1660s. Bernier, who left India in 1667, wrote that Shivaji "is exercising all the powers of an independent sovereign; laughs at the threats both of the Mogol and of the King of Visapour. ... He distracts the attention of Aurang-Zebe by his bold and never-ceasing enterprises. . . . How to put down Seva-Gi is become the object of chief importance."[43] Aurangzib clearly agreed with this opinion, not just in 1682 when he moved south himself, but much earlier. "A significant statement is made in a newsletter of his Court in 1670 that the Emperor read a despatch from the Deccan, recounting some raids of Shiva, and then 'remained silent'. In the inner council of the Court he often anxiously asked whom he should next send against Shivaji, seeing that nearly all his great generals had failed in the Deccan." As early as 1666 he was taunted by his great rival, Shah Abbas II of Persia: "You call yourself a Padishah, but cannot subdue a mere *zamindar* like Shiva. I am going to India with an army to teach you your business."[44] Conversely, those nobles who did succeed against the Marathas were lavishly rewarded, such as Jai Singh and his associates in 1665, or Khan

Jahan Bahadur in 1675.[45] Even the officially sanctioned abuse of Shivaji as the "wild animal," the "mountain rat," the "knave," is indicative more of fear than of confidence. The courtly chronogram for the date of Shivaji's death was a pungent "The infidel went to hell."

Two other groups of figures, those for immigration to India and those for revenue collections, bear out the impact of Shivaji's early successes. There is no doubt that Mughal India's neighbors kept a close eye on what was happening in the empire. Embassies, which doubled as information gatherers, were numerous: no less than seven in the early 1660s—from places as diverse as Ethiopia, Mecca, and the Uzbegs. Shah Abbas II of Persia taunted Aurangzib with his losses to Shivaji as early as 1666.[46] Given this foreign knowledge of events in Mughal India, we would expect the conspicuous losses suffered by Aurangzib to lead to a less rosy view of India as a place to which to emigrate. Such is indeed the case. All the indicators bear this out when we follow Athar Ali's comparisons of 1658—78 and 1679–1707. The percentage of nobles born outside India fell from 11.3 per cent to 8 per cent. Iranis and Turanis among the nobility fell from 41.3 per cent to 34.4 per cent. Iranis alone fell from 28 per cent to 22 per cent.[47]

Two standard explanations for this decline need to be considered. Athar Ali claims that the Uzbeg and Safavid empires weakened late in the seventeenth century; and this explains the drop in emigration.[48] But surely a declining native empire would foster emigration if a more attractive empire were available. Second, Aurangzib's religious policies are sometimes blamed for the drop in Shia Persian immigration. This also is unconvincing. Aurangzib was always ready to use capable Shias; indeed, Sarkar considers him to have been especially eager to have Persians and Turks enter his service.[49] Furthermore, Athar Ali finds Aurangzib using Persians at the highest levels, as governors, much more often than did Shah Jahan.[50] In any case, not just the Persian percentage but the percentage of all born outside India fell in the latter period. The true explanation has to be that Mughal India was no longer seen as the El Dorado it once had been. Even foreigners suspected its star was waning, and voted with their feet, by not moving them in that direction.

Mughal revenue statistics are notoriously unreliable, and the only runs we have are for the *jama*, or standard assessment; actual collections frequently had little relation to the sums done in the offices of remote Delhi or Agra. With the *Ain* taken as a base, Habib finds the *jama* of

the empire (excluding the Deccan so that the area is roughly constant)
going as follows:

1595	100
1633–8	142
1646–7	162
c. 1656	168
1667	145
1687–1709	169[51]

In Bengal, Chatterjee's figures seem to show a small fall in the *jama* of
Bengal in 1667 as compared with 1658, and a large fall in the amount
sent to the center from the province: Rs. 87,00,000 in 1658, Rs.
55,00,000 in 1665.[52] These large falls in the mid-1660s are enormously
suggestive. I at least suspect that they derived from *zamindars* taking
advantage of the apparent weakness of the empire in the face of Shivaji.
The traditional action of *zamindars* in such circumstances was to keep
back some extra revenue and wait to see how weak the empire really was.

THE RESPONSE OF THE NOBLES

Finally, the serious impact of Shivaji's successes seems to be reflected
in the actions of the Mughal nobility. Some of them had apparently
lost heart during the 1660s; this was revealed when war resumed in the
1670s. Again we are in difficult terrain, for we are trying to describe
how a Mughal noble thought; in the absence of contemporary diaries
and letters, such an undertaking must be hazardous, the results only
tentative. Before Shivaji ever appeared, it was notorious that the Mughal
nobility did not always fight as hard as they could. They had very
practical reasons for not winning too quickly. Power in India consisted
of control over resources, most notably land and people. For a noble,
power was maximized when he was campaigning for his troops, and so
the number of people he controlled expanded as also did the amount
of land used to pay these extra people. In a noncritical situation, it was
thus best to appear to be laboring heroically against a formidable enemy,
with victory always just around the corner but never quite definitively
attained. Shaista Khan put it best. When urged to attack Shivaji directly,
"the shrewd noble replied that if the Deccan campaign was so quickly
concluded, an attack on Qandahar would be ordered, and if that too

succeeded the contingents would be disbanded."[53]

On this point, the distinction made earlier about who started the war is important, as also is the progress of the particular war. Thus for Mughal nobles to jog easily along, procrastinate, take bribes from the enemy and generally display less than total martial valor was understandable when they were engaged against a non-essential outpost such as Qandahar. Similarly, to hasten slowly against the Deccanis of Ahmadnagar in the first third of the seventeenth century was simply to preserve one's own interests. But the last time this could be done against Shivaji was up to 1663. Shaista Khan, sitting at ease in Poona for thirty-two months, was simply following the old standard; it is clear that he never expected to have any difficulty in crushing Shivaji if Aurangzib forced him to do so, or if he wanted to himself. It appeared to be in his interests not to do so.

The situation was reversed by Shivaji's attack on this same Shaista Khan, and by the plunder of Surat only nine months later. Now the Mughals were being challenged. Until now they had always responded decisively to such a challenge: Akbar's second conquest of Gujarat in 1573; his defeat of the rebellions of 1580–1; the crushing of the mock Khusrau in 1610; the effective responses when Malik Ambar came too far out of Ahmadnagar; and a host of other Mughal victories. Jai Singh's victory in 1665 was in the same line of descent; again the Mughals were showing that they could deal quickly and decisively with any challenge. The problem was that the victory and the treaty were nullified very promptly by Shivaji's escape from Agra. This situation was quite new for the nobles; and when active war resumed in 1670 (significantly, again initiated by Shivaji, not by the Mughals), some responded by less than valorous activities.

Clearly, some nobles were not so much despairing as victims of mixed motives. After all, it was not their empire that was failing; it was Aurangzib's. So why worry if Shivaji rampaged? Those opposing him were rewarded by large contingents, and thus greater power. Nevertheless, some nobles apparently were not being expedient; they had simply given up. In the twenty-three years from 1658, Shivaji was subjected to intensive opposition for only eight years. There are recurrent reports of nobles taking bribes reaching accommodations, and displaying simple cowardice in the face of Maratha attacks.[54] The dispiritment of many nobles was perhaps most clearly revealed a little later, in the mid-1680s, in the sieges of Bijapur and Golconda. Aurangzib, two princes and a huge Mughal army besieged Bijapur city for eighteen months. At the end of the siege the garrison numbered only 2,000 men, yet finally the city was not taken; it surrendered at discretion. The Mughals then moved on to Golconda, and after an inglorious siege of seven months managed to take the fort by treachery.[55] Athar Ali finds these lackadaisical noble performances "peculiar,"[56] but indeed they were not. Given Shivaji's unprecedented successes, they were only to be expected.

Finally, when was the last chance for salvation lost? By the mid1660s, two chances to end Shivaji's threat had been missed. In 1657, it looked likely that Aurangzib, then viceroy of the Deccan, would soon crush Bijapur and then turn on Bijapur's revolted vassal. He was distracted; ironically his victory in the war of succession was pyrrhic, for it was predicated on giving Shivaji the opportunity—which he ably seized—to expand dramatically. Thus one chance had been lost through, ultimately, the Mughal failure to evolve a systematic method of succession to the throne. It is true that the Mughal wars of succession were routinized, the battles often mock battles, and the nobility free to support their princely patrons—secure in the knowledge that a bad guess would not be held against them by the ultimate victor. Nevertheless, these wars did have serious consequences elsewhere. The mice on the borders played while the cat was away in 1600–05 and 1627–8, but most notably and fatally in 1657–8.

The second and last chance came and was lost in 1666 in Agra. It was clear that Shivaji was, in 1666, as humiliated and down as he was ever to be. He was open to an offer, provided it was a very generous one. We have already argued that Aurangzib by this time was unable, for both personal and political reasons, to offer a bribe high enough to buy off Shivaji. Thus, the only way Aurangzib could have succeeded was to kill Shivaji, or at the least imprison him. This would probably have been effective; the Maratha challenge at this time, though demonstrably not later, could have been crushed if it were first beheaded. But this chance also was lost when Shivaji escaped.

Why did Shivaji survive? Possibly Aurangzib intended to kill him. But first felt it necessary to win complete support for this move from his nobles—especially Jai Singh, who had guaranteed Shivaji's safety. But it is more likely that Aurangzib was genuinely at a loss about what to do. The Mughals, at least at this time, had no tradition of murdering people who were loosely or potentially members of the nobility.[57] Rebels against the empire were despatched with alacrity, often with barbarity, such as two of the Sikh *gurus* (Arjun in 1606, Tegh Bahdur in 1675), and a host of others. But as of 1666, Shivaji was not an active rebel. Aurangzib had made a treaty with him, his son was a *mansabdar*, and Shivaji himself was still potentially open to cooptation. Mughal emperors did not kill people in this position.

What little hope there was of winning Shivaji over disappeared when he escaped. The Mughals, disheartened by the escape of their arch-enemy and distracted by other revolts, were glad to let Shivaji lie quiet until 1670. No doubt they hoped his narrow escape had so impressed him that he would subside. But Shivaji did not. The attacks of the 1670s revealed how well he had used his respite. Aurangzib and his nobility were forced to respond. The disastrous consequences of his escape, and of the impact of his attacks on Shaista Khan and Surat, were thus revealed; and the true "Tragedy of Aurangzebe" (pace Dryden), tragic because inevitable, began to be played out in the Deccan.

In conclusion, it is worthwhile to stress that the defeats dictated such a response only because of the nature of the tie between emperor and noble. The military orientation of the tie, and the consequent need for victory to produce more pickings, meant that such an empire had to respond to every military challenge. To avoid decline, it had to achieve the improbable feat of never being humiliated militarily. Thus at a more abstract—and perhaps tautological—level, the empire declined because it failed to evolve to a more impersonal level, where criteria other than personal military ones could be allowed to have more influence.[58] Had such an evolution occurred, it is at least arguable that the empire would have been able to cut its losses in the mid-1660s or a little later and retire to Hindustan. But the empire, because of its fundamental character, could react to a military challenge only by a military response.

NOTES

1. Irfan Habib, *The Agrarian System of Mughal India* (Bombay, 1963), pp. 317–51. The following frequently cited works will be abbreviated as follows: M. Athar Ali, *The Mughal Nobility under Aurangzeb* (Bombay, 1966) as *Mughal Nobility,* Jadunath Sarkar, *Shivaji and his Times* (Calcutta, 1961, 6th ed.) as *Shivaji;* Jadunath Sarkar, *A Short History of Aurangzib, 1618–1707* (Calcutta, 1962, 3rd ed.) as *Aurangzib.*

2. *Mughal Nobility*, pp. 9, 11, 89–94, 171–4.

3. Most recently Percival Spear, *A History of India*, vol. II (Baltimore, 1965), p. 60.

4. Percival Spear, *India, Pakistan, and the West* (London, 1967, 4th ed.), p. 19.

5. Pran Nath Chopra, *Some Aspects of Society and Culture during the Mughal Age* (1526–1707)(Agra, 1963, 2nd ed.), pp. 158–9.

6. Talcott Parsons, *Societies: Evolutionary and Comparative Perspectives* (Englewood Cliffs, N.J., 1966), p. 17, referring to any society. Figures: *Mughal Nobility*, pp. 7–9. There is a growing body of literature on the characteristics of Islamic states. Marshall G.S. Hodgson in his recent monumental *The Venture of Islam* (Chicago, 1975, 3 vols) is typically provocative and acute; see, for example, I, pp. 241–7, 280–4, 292–4, 320–22; II, pp. 62–151, 404; III, pp. 3–5, 25–7. Nevertheless, I feel that his description of the powers of Muslim rulers, especially the Ottoman Turks (III, pp. 26, 99–133), greatly exaggerates the real influence of these rulers. To my mind, the analysis by H.A.R. Gibb and Harold Bowen in *Islamic Society and the West*, (London, 1950–7, 2 vols) gives a much better impression, for it stresses the importance of local ties and norms rather than state control in governing the lives of most people most of the time; see I, i, pp. 158–60, 208–16, 276–81.

7. *Mughal Nobility*, pp. 33–5.

8. S.A.A. Rizvi, "The Mughal Elite in the Sixteenth and Seventeenth Century," *Abr-Nahrain*, v ol. II (1971), p. 78.

9. Muhammad Mujeeb, *Islamic Influence on Indian Society* (Delhi, 1972), pp. 68–71; H.A.R. Gibb, "Religion and Politics in Christianity and Islam," *Islam and International Relations*, (ed.) J. Harris Proctor (London, 1965), pp. 3–23.

10. A. Jan Qaisar, "Distribution of the Revenue Resources of the Mughal Empire among the Nobility," *Proceedings of the Indian History Congress* 27(1965), pp. 239–40. Habib thinks perhaps two-thirds rather than three-quarters of a noble's salary went into military expenditure; Irfan Habib, "Potentialities for Capitalistic Development in the Economy of Mughal India," *Journal of Economic History*, 29 (March 1969), pp. 35–60.

11. Francois Bernier, *Travels in the Mogul Empire, A.D. 1656–1668*, trans. A. Constable, (ed.) Vincent A. Smith (London, 1914, 2nd ed.), p. 168.

12. John F. Richards, review of Riazul Islam, *"Indo-Persian Relations: A Study of the Political and Diplomatic Relations between the Mughal Empire and Iran,"* in the *Journal of Asian Studies*, XXXII (November 1972), pp. 198–9.

13. P. Hardy, *The Muslims of British India* (Cambridge, U.K., 1972), p. 13.

14. Saqi Must'ad Khan, *Maasir-i-Alamgiri*, trans. Jadunath Sarkar (Calcutta, 1947), pp. 3, 13; Niccolao Manucci, *Storia do Mogor or Mogul India, 1653–1708*, trans.William Irvine, (Calcutta, 1965, 2nd ed., 3 vols to date), I, p. 279.

15. Bernier, pp. 65, 98–100.

16. Ibid., p. 186; *Mughal Nobility*, p. 179.

17. H.K. Naqvi, *Urbanization and Urban Centres under the Great Mughals*, Simla, 1971, pp. 160–86.

18. Rizvi, p. 74.

19. Ali Muhammad Khan, *Mirat-i Ahmadi*, trans. M. F. Lokhandwalla (Baroda, 1965), p. 227.

20. P.C. Roy, *History of Bengal: Mughal Period, 1526–1765*, (Calcutta, 1968). p. 135, see also pp. 130–1, 136–7, 257–60.

21. Personal letter from Dr. Joseph Schwartzberg, Director South Asia Historical Atlas Project, 14 July 1973. Schwartzberg considers that this figure is probably low, for it encompasses only the disparate areas Shivaji controlled. It must be assumed that, at least for most of the time, he also had some sort of "rule" over the communicating lines linking his scattered areas.

22. *Aurangzib*, p. 452; *Shivaji*, p. 358.

23. See references to Shivaji's administration in A.R. Kulkarni, *Maharashtra in the Age of Shivaji* (Poona, 1969), *passim*.

24. Jean Baptiste Tavernier, *Travels in India*, trans. V. Ball, ed. William Crooke (London, 1925 2nd ed, 2 vols), I, p. 5.

25. Ali Muhammad Khan, p. 193; K.N. Chaudhuri, *The English East India Company: The Study of an Early Joint Stock Company, 1600–1640* (London, 1965), pp. 22, 226–30; Habib, *Agrarian System*, p. 406.

26. William Foster (ed.), *The English Factories in India.1661–64* (Oxford, 1923), pp. 296, 305.

27. *Shivaji*, p. 95.

28. Beni Prasad, *History of Jahangir* (Allahabad, 1962, 5th ed), pp. 153–4.

29. *Maasir-i-Alamgiri*, pp. 17, 22.

30. *Shivaji*, p. 260.

31. Surendranath Sen (ed.), *Indian Travels of Thevenot and Careri* (New Delhi, 1949) p. 163.

32. *Shivaji*, pp. 311–12.

33. Manucci, *Storia do Mogor*, II, p. 112.

34. For the dealings at Agra, see Francois Bernier, *Travels*, p. 191; *Shivaji*, pp. 134–59; Jadunath Sarkar, *House of Shivaji* (Calcutta, 1955, 3rd edn), pp. 151–67.

35. William Foster (ed.), *The English Factories in India, 1665–67* (Oxford, 1925), pp. 165, 171.

36. *Mughal Nobility*, p. 98; P. Hardy, *Muslims of British India*, p. 20.

37. *Shivaji*, pp. 151, 153.

38. Jadunath Sarkar, *Anecdotes of Aurangzib* (Calcutta, 1963, 4th edn), p. 49.

39. Robert F. Berkhofer, Jr, *A Behavioral Approach to Historical Analysis*, New York, 1971, p. 46.

40. Richards, p. 198.

41. *Aurangzib*, pp. 419–20.

42. Ibid., pp. 3, 94.

43. Bernier, *Travels*, p. 198.

44. *Shivaji*, p. 370.

45. *Maasir-i-Alamgiri*, pp. 33, 88.

46. *Aurangzib*, pp. 107–8.

47. *Mughal Nobility*, pp. 33–35.

48. Ibid., p. 17. Athar Ali also claims that because Aurangzib was seldom involved in wars in the northwest, he felt no need to bribe or recruit nobles attached to Mughal opponents in this area.

49. Jadunath Sarkar, *Mughal Administration* (Calcutta, 1952, 4th edn), pp. 159–160.

50. Athar Ali, 'Provincial Governors under Shah Jahan: An Analysis', *Proceedings of the Indian History Congress,* 32 (1970), p. 291.

51. Habib, *Agrarian System*, p. 328.

52. Anjali Chatterjee, *Bengal in the Reign of Aurangzib, 1658–1707* (Calcutta, 1967), pp. 72–74.

53. *Mughal Nobility*, p. 102.

54. *Aurangzib*, p. 178; *Shivaji*, pp. 178–80, 184–5, 195.

55. *Aurangzib*, pp. 247–52, 262–8.

56. *Mughal Nobility*, p. 102.

57. See M. Athar Ali, "The Mughal Empire in History," Presidential Address, Section II, Medieval India, Indian History Congress, 33rd Session, Muzaffarpur, 1972, pp. 8–9 of off-print.

58. An important paper by M. Athar Ali (ibid.) presents a rather different view of the nature of noble ties to the emperor. He also stresses a great advance in centralization and systematization under the Mughals (pp. 3–5), but significantly this does not appear to have been an advance towards a more impersonal regime, towards a Weberian bureaucracy rather than a pre-modern administration. Rather, it was a refinement of an existing structure.

The 'Great Firm' Theory of the Decline of the Mughal Empire[*]

KAREN LEONARD

Most historians of the Mughal empire currently emphasize economic factors in their attempts to locate and measure the causes of imperial decline in seventeenth- and eighteenth-century India. Recent articles reiterate a standard set of tensions: those between monarch, military and service nobles (*mansabdars*), landholders (*zamindars*), and peasants.[1] Existing theories attribute the Mughal decline to the nature of the monarchy, the breakdown of the *mansabdari* administrative system, and the challenges from newly established regional rulers. One influential analysis points to the increasing burden of taxation and consequent *zamindar*–peasant rebellions throughout the empire as the fundamental cause of decline.[2] The nobility and the *mansabdari* system have received most attention, however. Historians have emphasized the strains caused by numerical expansion, inflation of noble ranks, and the 'aristocratization' of the *mansabdars* through conspicuous consumption and hereditary control of positions.[3] Analyses of the availability and distribution of economic resources neglect one group whose relationship to the Mughal state and whose roles in the political system were crucial: the bankers— *sahukars*, *shroffs*, *mahajans*—particularly those in the 'great firms.' It will

* Reproduced from Karen Leonard, 'The "Great Firm" Theory of the Decline of the Mughal Empire,' *Comparative Studies in Society and History*, Vol. 21, No. 2, April 1979. pp. 151–67, © 1979 Society for Comparative Study of Society and History. A preliminary version of this article was presented at the Seminar on 'Decline of the Mughals' at the University of Pennsylvania, May 1974; criticism from the other participants, but even more from Dr. John G. Leonard, has helped improve that version.

be argued here that the great banking firms of Mughal India played a key role in the decline of the empire.

The 'great firm' theory of Mughal decline, which relies on secondary sources for its comprehensive data base, clarifies and extends existing economic theories of imperial decline. Indigenous banking firms were indispensable allies of the Mughal state, and the great firms' diversion of resources, both credit and trade, from the Mughals to other political powers in the Indian subcontinent contributed to the downfall of the empire. The period of imperial decline coincided with the increasing involvement of banking firms in revenue collection at regional and local levels, in preference to their continued provision of credit to the central Mughal government. This involvement increased from 1650 to 1750, and it brought bankers, more directly than before, into positions of political power all over India. This period of 'great firm' partnership with regional powers, among them the East India Company, was followed by political losses for the great banking firms. When in the 1750s the Company began to achieve political dominance throughout India, it turned against indigenous bankers and systematically displaced them, usurping their functions as bankers to the Company and to other political rulers and downgrading their roles in the collection of land revenue. One consequence was the relegation of indigenous bankers to less crucial roles in the political system. A second effect was the diminished historical awareness of the bankers' earlier importance in Mughal India.

The theoretical literature on historical bureaucratic empire points to the importance of the banking firms to the state. Imperial authority derived from a mixture of charismatic, legal-rational, and traditional religions and cultural factors.[4] A ruler's authority was strongest where the political order was closely interwoven with the cosmic, religious, and cultural order, that is, where political legitimacy was based on the maintenance of that traditional order. In Mughal India, with a ruling class which was largely Muslim and initially drawn from outside, economic and political alliances were extremely important to maintenance of the state.[5]

The establishment of the Mughal empire required the conquerors to co-opt indigenous groups and institutions and to counter the opposition of various indigenous elites menaced by the imperial trend towards political centralization. Moreover, the Mughal emperors had to achieve some measure of legitimacy in traditional terms through political accommodation with traditional elites. And they had to form alliances with groups in the population which could benefit from the establishment of a more unified polity. Such allies theoretically could come from one of two categories: those (largely urban) economic, cultural, and professional groups who were by origin or interest opposed to the nobility and landholder; and the larger, lower-class groups (for example, peasants) who could at least indirectly benefit from the weakening of aristocratic forces and the establishment of greater order. The Mughals had to find and utilize such new economic and political resources.[6]

The creation of the *mansabdari* system, a new organ of centralized administration directly supervised and staffed by new personnel, was important in establishing the empire. But just as clearly, the Mughals depended upon urban merchants and bankers for the provision of goods and commodities and cash, the latter for direct spending and payment for services. Given the geographic scope of the Mughal empire, the decentralized military forces and their employment in expansionist ventures, these financial resources had to be accessible and flexible. Since there was a monetized market economy and a highly developed system of credit in Mughal India, conditions of political stability encouraged the alliance of the Mughals and indigenous bankers and ensured a continuous flow of trade goods and notes of credit.

Yet the interests of the Mughal state and of the great banking firms sometimes came into conflict. The rulers had a constant need to mobilize extensive resources for military expansion. Such mobilization could either exhaust the available resources or strengthen the groups which produced and controlled those resources, making the bankers less dependent on the rulers and ultimately threatening the basis of the political system. For the banking firms, the conflict of interests was intensified by the practice of short-term loans, increasing the dependence of the rulers on them but possibly undermining the availability of resources in the long run.[7]

The ruler's relationships with diverse groups and institutions had to be carefully balanced, and any disruption could set off a chain of events weakening the empire. External pressures combined with internal tensions could intensify problems of imperial control. When other powers competed with the Mughals for the credit and other services offered by Indian bankers, the imperial bureaucracy was threatened. It became more dependent upon the banking firms and it had to develop better working methods or offer additional services to maintain the relationship.[8] The later Mughals, in policy and in practice, do not appear to have placed enough importance upon retaining the confidence of the great banking firms, and this was a critical error.

Most writers have treated bankers and other financial and merchant groups in India as 'segmental' rather than 'strategic' elites, viewing them as outside the governmental structure and not instrumental in decisions affecting society at large.[9] They have been analyzed as 'hinge' groups, largely autonomous and apolitical,[10] or, even more negatively, as passive and parasitic beneficiaries of the conditions established by a strong imperial government.[11] Certainly they do not fit comfortably into the usual contemporary definitions of a strategic elite, seldom being included in the ruling class of nobles and officials; yet they played a very large political role in Mughal India, as has been remarked in the cases of particular individuals. In fact, so little analysis of bankers and banking firms has been attempted that there is considerable confusion about the unit with which historians should be concerned. Should we be examining those famous individual bankers, or caste and merchant guilds in urban centers, or, rather more vaguely, 'banking castes,' assumed to be following traditional occupations wherever they were?[12]

The 'great firm' has already been proposed here as the appropriate unit for historical analysis. This term has been used to describe a business firm engaged in a wide variety of enterprises, with several branches, often based on one 'household.'[13] For our purposes, a basic functional distinction is essential: moneylenders were those individuals or firms habitually making loans, while bankers were those individuals or firms which not only made loans but received deposits and/or dealt in *hundis*, the written orders for payment transmitted throughout India.[14] A further distinction in terms of customers proves useful: moneylenders dealt customarily with agriculturalists; bankers very seldom dealt with agriculturalists.[15] The last distinction directs us away from questions of the degree of monetization of the Mughal agrarian economy and brings us back to the extensive development of credit facilities, not those oriented towards the production of agricultural or other goods, but those oriented towards investment and profit through transactions with the Mughal government and its functionaries. A good working definition of the 'great firms' allied to the Mughal government should specify a certain magnitude of the firm's operations, both in volume of credit and in geographic range through the firm's branches: such specifications must await more empirical data.

'GREAT FIRMS' AND THE MUGHAL STATE: TO 1750

Historians have found scattered evidence of the transactions between the great firms and the Mughal state. Irfan Habib's two articles on bankers and moneylenders in seventeenth-century India include many useful facts, although he places no emphasis on the political aspects of the transactions. Bankers performed important, but, in his view, limited services: they validated and minted money, maintained exchange ratios between different currencies, and issued *hundis*.[16] D. R. Gadgil has also discussed bankers at length, delineating their functions as money-changers and dealers in *hundis* and adding a major role in government finance. Here he mentions bankers serving as lenders of cash and credit, as receivers and remitters of land revenue, and as financiers of tax farmers.[17]

Particularly crucial were the bankers' roles as state treasurers. Specific banking firms were frequently appointed by a ruler to provide cash and credit for the payment of salaries and other expenses on a regular basis. Thus the delays and irregularities consequent upon sole dependence on the seasonally delivered land revenues to the capital could be avoided. There are many examples of such appointments.

The Jagat Seth firm gained fame in this treasurer role in mid-eighteenth century Bengal. The Jain family firm had moved from Rajputana to Patna, and from there to Dacca and Murshidabad with the Mughal governors of Bengal. In the seventeenth century, the Mughal Emperor Aurangzeb had personally honored the firm's head, Manek Chand, for his large loans to the government. Manek Chand's nephew was appointed 'imperial Treasurer' and awarded the title, Jagat Seth, by the Emperor Farukhsiyar. Jagat Seth was accorded mint privileges by 1717, and after 1728 the imperial tribute from Bengal was sent to Delhi by draft on this banking house. The house of Jagat Seth had personal access to the Mughal emperor in the 1720s and 1730s, and it could allegedly obtain *farmans* of appointment for high officials.[18]

Other great firms served as treasurers to rulers throughout India. Kallidaikurichy Brahmin firms were bankers to the Rajas of Cochin and Travancore.[19] Branches of a single Marwari firm served as bankers to the Nawab of Fatehpur, the Pindari Nawabs, and Ranjit Singh.[20] Particular firms were named as bankers to the Nawab of Arcot and to the Nizam of Hyderabad.[21] Many other examples can be cited and the practice has been generally recognized; its significance, however, has been understated by historians.[22]

Other strong connections between great firms and the Mughal state came through the loans and credit extended to individual nobles and officials. Successive attempts by the state to regulate or prohibit these transactions testify to their persistence and to the state's perception of them as weakening imperial control. Nobles borrowed money frequently, using their *jagirs* ('land assignments') as security and giving claims upon the anticipated land revenues to bankers. High interest rates prevailed, but nobles allegedly preferred *jagirs* to payment of a cash salary, since *jagirs* were acceptable security for bankers.[23] The Emperor Akbar tried to establish a royal treasury and avoid reliance on 'moneylenders,' and he tried to advance loans from the treasury at an interest below that asked by bankers.[24] In the time of Aurangzeb, state officials served as intermediaries to recover debts for bankers from nobles: officials usually claimed one-fourth of the debt for this service, a practice Aurangzeb tried to stop.[25]

Both the central administration and its individual officials often had to transfer large amounts of money from one place to another, and this was done through banking firms. Habib's impression from the authorities he has seen is that the total amounts transferred on behalf of the Mughal government and individual officials 'rivalled if not exceeded' money remitted for purposes of trade.[26] In a similar attempt to estimate the volume and kind of various business transactions, Gadgil contradicts himself on whether the larger banking firms were more likely to be engaged in government financing or in trade.[27] These are questions of major historical importance, and while further empirical data are obviously needed, the impressions of both of these scholars emphasize the political potential of the functions banking firms performed in Mughal India.

In addition to investment through the extension of credit to the central administration and its officials, three other types of profitable activities linked bankers to the Mughal state. These activities are often dismissed as examples of wasteful extravagance and dissipation of capital,[28] but that assessment must be reconsidered. First, there were the organized units of production and supply to the court, the *karkhanahs*, which Gadgil suggests were the major banking firms' most direct connection with 'industry' at the time.[29] Second, contracting for the construction of public edifices in the sixteenth and seventeenth centuries—mosques, tombs, pleasure gardens and so forth—must have been extremely profitable. It was a major type of capital expenditure by the Mughal state.[30] Third, dealers in bullion and jewelry played major roles in economic life, and they were often involved in the great banking firms. Habib was surprised to find that *shroffs* rather than jewelers and goldsmiths were the chief buyers of foreign silver in Mughal India,[31] but in fact most banking firms were engaged in several enterprises and jewelry was a common sideline.[32] These court-related economic activities can no longer be viewed as superficial. Attempts must be made to measure them, ascertain who was engaged in them, and relate them to other areas of the Mughal economy.

Finally, there is the increasingly important role of banking firms in revenue collection. It is abundantly clear that by 1750 it was bankers who controlled access to the actual collection of land revenue, through provision of credit or cash. They, rather than officials of the Mughal or any other ruler, were the people to deal with. The amount of interest set and the securities demanded by bankers were more critical economic conditions than the revenue demand fixed by a territorial ruler. Most of the evidence for this state of affairs is from the eighteenth century and seemingly linked to the practice of revenue farming. Bankers provided the funds which enabled *talukdars* ('contractors') to gain their positions as tax farmers, and bankers sent their own agents into the countryside to collect from the land given to them as security or mortgage.[33]

Historical instances of bankers involved in the land revenue system are numerous. In Bengal, the Jagat Seths presided over annual negotiations with leading *zamindars* at their Murshidabad residence, settling accounts and allocating fresh supplies of funds.[34] Other bankers in Bengal in the eighteenth century stood surety for landowners and paid the revenue on their behalf. They turned over to the East India Company sealed bags which were not opened, because the bankers were 'averse to the opening and inspection of them, declaring it contrary to established custom of the country and destructive of credit.'[35] Shah, discussing the revenue system of eighteenth-century Gujarat, terms moneylenders and bankers 'part of the entire system of state finance.' He notes that urban bankers made loans to rulers for military and other purposes and were in return authorized to collect the revenues.[36] Cohn shows many such instances in the Benares region in the eighteenth century, and he traces several bankers into official positions in the political system.[37] Lengthy descriptions of the Madras hinterland in the eighteenth century testify to the bankers' control of the land revenue; some of these bankers were based in Hyderabad and sent their agents out to collect revenue on lands ceded as security by *zamindars* in the Circars.[38] It was in the Madras area also where 'customary arrangement' found a rural official collecting funds on the first of the month and then loaning the amount at interest to a banker, who used it as working capital until the official turned it over to the government on the twenty-eighth of the month.[39]

The banker's assumption of key positions in eighteenth-century systems of revenue collection has usually been attributed to the increasing weakness of the central government, leading to revenue contracting and emphasizing the need for capital to secure initial contracts. But so little is actually known about the operation of the Mughal land revenue system that it is hard to say where and when salaried officials were used, or whether there may have been an intermediate stage when collection was entrusted to private individuals working on commission.[40] Whether it is a symptom or a cause of imperial decline, the bankers' powerful role in regional and local land revenue system developed during the same period that bankers were redirecting their financial investments from the central Mughal administration to regional and local political powers.

From 1650 to 1750, several historical developments indicate why and how bankers were shifting their support and investment from the Mughals to other political rulers. First, the Mughals failed to protect bankers adequately in the second half of the seventeenth century. Shivaji's famous raids on Surat from 1664 on were far more significant for their impact upon the commercial interests there than upon the loyalties of the nobility.[41] This was the wealthiest port of Mughal India, and it has been shown that the sea trade here and in other Gujarati ports, and the customs revenue going to the Mughals, was far more considerable than has been generally recognized.[42] Leading officials and relatives of the Mughal emperor were involved in trading ventures.[43] Heads of the Gujarati great firms had access to the emperor in the seventeenth century, and successive emperors responded favorably to requests made by the Surat business community.[44] Yet Aurangzeb proved unable to protect Surat and other ports from raiders, and merchants and bankers left Surat for other cities.[45] Many eventually settled at Poona, capital of the Peshwas.[46]

Policies and actions of the later emperors Aurangzeb and Farukhsiyar indicate tensions between bankers and the Mughal state. By 1702, when Aurangzeb attempted to secure interest-free loans to pay troop arrears in the Deccan, he was turned down by banking firms.[47] Aurangzeb's expectation of financial support must have been perceived as contrary to the bankers' interests at this time, towards the end of the Deccan campaigns. Another indication of conflicting political and economic interests for the state and the banking firms was the emperor Farukhsiyar's need for money in 1712 and his plan to levy contributions on the rich merchants of Patna, including the Dutch and English merchants. His plan was thwarted by the governor of Bihar, who had his own dealings with the Europeans.[48] It has been suggested that Mughal officials at all levels were increasing their own commercial activities and actively competing with indigenous bankers and merchants at this time,[49] though without a comparison with the past commercial networks and activities the evidence shows only commercial involvement.

Two other developments from 1650 to 1750 show the changing economic and political orientation of the great banking firms: the migration of bankers from Mughal urban centers to those of other powers, and the banker's extension of trade and credit transactions to newcomers, the Dutch and the English, in contrast to their earlier policies. Where the new commercial relationships have been noted, there has usually been no attempt to reconstruct the commercial networks of the banking firms prior to their connection with the European traders.[50]

Historical research on migration elsewhere has used empirical data to measure the opportunities available according to distance from the source of migration. Lack of systematic data on the movements of great firms in Mughal India prevents such an analysis here, but the information available supports the hypothesis that after 1650 banking firms moved to regional kingdoms and the commercial centers being established by European trading companies.[51] The emigrations from Surat have been mentioned; some of those bankers settled in Poona, where they gained mint privileges and became bankers to the Peshwa.[52] A Surat Brahmin firm moved to Calcutta through transactions with the East India Company in the eighteenth century, later on opening a Bombay branch.[53] The Jagat Seth firm's move to Dacca and Murshidabad was due to its tie to Murshid Quli Khan, governor of Bengal, in the early eighteenth century.[54] Firms based in the Nizam's capital city of Hyderabad moved into the northern Circars, where they encountered the East India Company agents operating out of Madras. One Marwari firm gave up banking for Indian princes and moved to Calcutta, dealing in opium with the East India Company.[55]

These migrations have generally been attributed to negative factors, such as the Mughal inability to protect commerce or the raids of Marathas, Jats, and Afghans. No doubt the political instability and wars of the eighteenth century were destructive of some trade and commercial activities, but wars also offered positive inducements to many financiers and contractors.[56] The eighteenth century might better be viewed as a period of expansion and diversification for many banking firms and merchants.

The historical evidence for the process of realignment of leading banking firms with the East India Company during this century before 1750 is plentiful and unambiguous. Detailed evidence from Surat and from the Jagat Seth firm in Bengal documents an early and strong transition to doing business with the Company. While early seventeenth century Dutch records from Surat show that the Mughals failed to protect Indian traders from Dutch and English competition from the sea trade then,[57] other records show at least eight leading Gujarati firms providing extensive credit to the English at Surat from 1634 to 1677.[58] Pearson shows that Gujarati merchants at Surat strongly opposed English traders in the 1620s, but by the 1660s they considered European traders to be among their best customers.[59] One Gujarati firm originally from Surat moved to Murshidabad, then to Calcutta and Benares, proudly claiming to be 'bankers to the Company' by the late eighteenth century. This firm showed a marked preference for the English throughout the second half of the eighteenth century. Its historian asks why that should have been the case and what the wealth of that firm and others like it actually was, when that firm alone lent one lakh of rupees a month to the English Company.[60]

The history of the Jagat Seth firm, already discussed in its Mughal context, is perhaps more fascinating in relation to the East India Company. Most accounts first link the firm to the English in mid-eighteenth-century Bengal, but in fact it had loaned funds to the English factory in Patna as early as 1652. An even stronger tie to the Company existed through the 'real' family of Jagat Seth—for Jagat Seth was the son of Manek Chand's sister, adopted by Manek Chand to continue his firm. Jagat Seth's natal family operated a great banking firm in Patna and Agra in the seventeenth century, the very firm which in 1714 extended credit to the English trade embassy from Calcutta when other leading Delhi bankers refused it credit. Mitra Sen of this firm, real brother to Jagat Seth, represented the East India Company in Delhi from 1712 to 1739, allegedly supervising its interests in all three presidencies.[61] The firm's prominent political role in the 1750s, when it helped the East India Company overthrow Nawab Sirajuddaula, is well known and caused Gadgil to term it 'exceptional.'[62] The argument here is that it was closer to the rule, as further research on banking firms' connections with political rulers will demonstrate.

'GREAT FIRMS' AND THE EAST INDIA COMPANY: AFTER 1750

After 1750, the East India Company brought about major changes which were detrimental to the economic and political interests of the indigenous banking firms. The Company had relied upon Indian bankers as sources of credit, and often as agents for the collection of revenue, as it gained territory. Now the Company displaced them, not only as the Company bankers but as bankers to Indian rulers as well. The Company also displaced bankers as the key intermediaries in the land revenue collection.

Thus, Clive's agreement with the Nawab of Bengal in 1765 specified that all revenues would go to the Company through a newly created board of ministers. This board consisted of the Nawab, the Diwan, and a Seth, the latter from the Jagat Seth firm. The Seth was still termed Company banker, but Clive insisted that all three men keep keys to the treasury, and that the Company be paid before repayment to back debts to the Seths. In 1770, Clive stopped the allowance which the Seths received as ministers of the Nawab. In 1772, the Company treasury was transferred from Murshidabad to Calcutta and the Seths ceased to be Company bankers. A later representative of the firm petitioned Hastings for reinstatement in the hereditary office of 'receiver and treasurer of government revenue,' but he got robes of honor instead.[63] In the 1770s, an inquiry began into the whole system of revenue collection in Bengal, with the aim of 'placing the Company as nearly as can be in the stead of the Shroffs.' It was stated that revenue was being lost to the bankers, upon whom the Company was in any case too dependent.[64]

Similarly, the Company in Madras began to investigate *zamindars* indebtedness and the bankers' role in revenue collection in the 1770s. At first, the recommendation was to continue the 'agency of soucars' as 'innovations might be dangerous'.[65] In the 1780s, however, the Company tried to change the system, arguing that it 'gives the soucar very unreasonable advantage....'[66] But the reforms attempted encountered difficulties. The provision of security by *zamindars* themselves proved unworkable, and when the Company's inquiries appeared threatening, the principal bankers got together and refused to furnish security.[67] Noting that the prevalent system helped conceal information from the Company and kept the *zamindars* indebted to the bankers (who were always paid before the Company's current demand was met), a circuit committee in 1785 proposed drastic remedies. Reforms of the 'vicious system' succeeded in 'suppressing the private interests' and replaced 'commercial ideas by administrative ideas' in the collection of revenue in the Circars.[68] At this time, of course, the Company itself was still a private and Commercial concern.

Not only were indigenous banking firms displaced in Company territories, the Company acted against them in princely states. It did not enforce payment of debts to bankers when Company agents took over from or dealt with ruling princes. This happened in Benares in 1773, in Oudh in 1798, and in the case of the Nawab of Arcot in 1805.[69] The East India Company's view of bankers was much in evidence in the notorious case of Palmer and Company in Hyderabad State in the 1820s. Here, too, the ruler's debts to the banking firm were overlooked by the Company, and the Resident strongly disapproved of the political power exercised by the Palmers in Hyderabad. He said: '... it tends to draw them quite out of their sphere of merchants. ... I lament the power which they exercise ... in an authoritative manner not becoming their mercantile character....'[70]

By the nineteenth century, if one compares the functions of indigenous banking firms before and after the advent of foreign traders, a reversal has occurred. Before, bankers had been state treasurers and were often directly involved in the collection of revenue. The financing of external trade before the seventeenth century had been chiefly in the hands of Indian trading firms; then it was taken over by European firms; and, in the nineteenth century, by European banking institutions. With the 1835 imposition of uniform currency throughout British India, bankers lost much of their money-changing business as well as their mint privileges. In the nineteenth century, bankers and moneylenders were most noted for the financing of internal trade and the extension of agricultural credit; the British created government treasuries and a system of European banking institutions in India.[71] But we have come very far from Mughal India, and part of the reason for doing so is to demonstrate how historians have lost sight of the great Indian banking firms of those days.

ADVANTAGES OF THE 'GREAT FIRM' THEORY

The theory proposes that it was the redirection of economic and political support by the great banking firms of Mughal India from 1650 to 1750 which proved the decisive factor in the decline of the empire. The banking firms had been crucial to the functioning of the central government and to the functioning of many of its employees' households. It is not being argued that the great firms were directly incorporated into the governmental structure, or that a centrally-directed economic policy was being implemented through them, for the Mughal state did not exercise tight control over these firms and their activities. Not only the state 'treasury,' however, but individual *mansabdars*, *jagirdars*, *zamindars*, and *talukdars* were more than likely to be directly dependent upon these banking firms.

The situation of the bankers in Mughal India contrasts strongly with that of bankers in imperial China, and the contrast is an instructive one.[72] Most historians agree that the Chinese bureaucracy tightly regulated the merchant classes. For example, when Chinese bankers invented 'flying money' (the equivalent of *hundi*s in India), the government took over the system as a bureaucratic monopoly. The Chinese imperial bureaucracy was also able to establish control over promissory notes or paper currency, developed somewhat later. But in Mughal India, while there were attempts to regulate some aspects of banking activities, the regulation of *hundi*s was never proposed, and other attempted regulations appear to have failed more often than not. The position of the bankers in

India was that of an allied support group, one which provided essential resources to the state and had a good bargaining position with respect to it. Contrast their position with that of the *co-hong* merchants at the Chinese treaty ports, closely regulated and acting for their government as they carried out commercial transactions with foreigners.

Banking firms in Mughal India had greater power and autonomy than their Chinese counterparts. The tensions between short-term and long-term aims of the Mughal state and its creditors needed careful and constant attention. This was particularly true when military expansion or defense efforts impelled the state to call for more resources, or when banking firms were presented with alternative patrons or clients. From all indications, the later Mughal emperors did not give sufficient consideration to their relationships with the great banking firms, and many firms relocated and redirected their transaction after 1650.

While further research is admittedly necessary to test and fully substantiate this theory, it offers certain immediate advantages over other theories of Mughal decline. It brings together the economic factors associated with the decline in a way that emphasizes their interrelationships. It also reorders the causative factors in significance, pointing to the economic decisions made by the great banking firms as the most important cause of irreversible decline, because so many of the other groups and institutions were dependent upon the banking firms. Virtually all government units of income and expenditure required the extension of credit or cash to continue operations. The refusal or diversion of resources by bankers contributed to the dissension among *mansabdars* and *jagirdars*, the impact of a real or artificially produced *jagir* shortage, the flagging zeal of the military, and so on.

Another advantage of the theory is its potential for measurement and testing. The systematic reconstruction of seventeenth- and eighteenth-century networks of great firms and their connections with Mughal institutions and functionaries, with each other, and with lower level firms and moneylenders should be possible. These were urban-based, well-organized and conspicuous institutions, limited in numbers at the level of operation in which we are interested. Changing patterns of trade and investment, relocation of firms and their branches, should provide yet other measures of loyalty, as well as the movements of individual nobles and themes in poetry and prose.[73] And there should be fewer units to analyze than in the cases of the *mansabdars*, *zamindars*, and other categories of individuals.

A great advantage of this theory is that it relates the rise of the East India Company to the decline of the Mughal empire in a concrete and cumulative manner emphasizing processes rather than events or individuals. It lends continuity to revenue history, linking territorial conquest with the collection of the land revenue through the agency of indigenous banking firms. It emphasizes the development by the Company of partnerships with the great firms, followed by Company displacement of them. The local and regional participants in that process of economic partnership and displacement can be discovered and compared throughout India.

Like any good theory, this one seems fairly obvious, and the puzzle is that it has gone unperceived and un-researched. There may have been a problem of sources,[74] but historians are now utilizing new sources and methods. Determined collection of data can result in the reconstruction of a grid of great firms and their relationships with the political powers of the time. New analytical perspectives will also be useful. Many who have theorized about merchants and bankers in Mughal India have done so from a Marxist perspective, forcing the data into a fairly rigid framework. Other researchers have seldom ventured beyond description, collecting detailed data on specific individuals, firms, or caste groups, following the traditional emphasis upon the diverse and specialized nature of financial communities in India. But now an attempt must be made to describe and analyze this heterogeneous category according to the organization and volume of their economic activities, focusing on the great indigenous banking firms of Mughal and early British India and their decisive participation in politics.

NOTES

1. Peter Hardy has referred to this standard 'diagram of tensions' in his commentary upon two of the most recent articles: P. Hardy, 'Commentary and Critique,' *Journal of Asian Studies*, XXXV, 2 (Feb. 1976), 257. The articles upon which he is commenting are M. N. Pearson, 'Shivaji and the Decline of the Mughal empire,' 221–35, and J.F. Richards, 'The Imperial Crisis in the Deccan,' 237–56, both in the same issue.

2. Irfan Habib, *The Agrarian System of Mughal India* (Bombay, 1963), argues for oppression and revolt. Two often-cited views focusing upon factions among the nobility are Satish Chandra, *Parties and Politics at the Mughal Court, 1707–1740* (Aligarh, 1959), and M. Athar Ali, *The Mughal Nobility under Aurangzeb* (Aligarh, 1966). Two regional perspectives are given by Philip Calkins, 'The Formation of a Regionally Oriented Ruling Group in Bengal, 1700–1740,' *Journal of Asian Studies,* XXIX: 4 (Aug. 1970), and Karen Leonard, 'The Hyderabad Political System and Its Participants,' *Journal of Asian Studies,* XX: 3 (May, 1971), 569–82.

3. See the two articles cited in footnote 1; Pearson argues that military efforts in the south and the defeats inflicted by Shivaji decisively affected the loyalty of the nobles, and Richards argues that policy miscalculations led to artificial *jagir* shortages and inattention to newly incorporated warrior elites in the south.

4. Useful discussions are by S.N. Eisenstadt, *The Political Systems of Empires* (New York, 1963), and *The Decline of Empires* (New Jersey, 1967).

5. The generalization has interesting implications for scholars of cultural and intellectual movements in medieval and early modern India, such as the *bhakti* movements, the development of vernacular poetry, the shifts of artistic patronage to regional courts, and those political movements led by Shivaji or the Sikh gurus.

6. The analysis draws upon Eisenstadt, *Political Systems,* particularly ch. 12.

7. *Ibid.,* and his *Decline of Empires,* pp. 3–5; and A.L. Udovitch, 'Credit as a Means of Investment in Medieval Islamic Trade,' in *Journal of the American Oriental Society,* 87: 3 (July–September, 1967), 60–64.

8. S.N. Eisenstadt, *Essays on Comparative Institutions* (New York, 1965), 203, suggests this line of reasoning, which is clearly relevant to the Mughal empire.

9. For an introductory discussion of 'Elites,' see Suzanne Keller's article in the *International Encyclopedia of the Social Sciences,* vol. 5 (New York, 1968), p. 28.

10. This is Michael Pearson's view, particularly in his unpublished dissertation, 'Commerce and Compulsion: Gujarati Merchants and the Portuguese System in Western India, 1500–1600', University of Michigan, 1971. He has modified his view of their role in politics to some extent in his article, 'Political Participation in Mughal India,' *Indian Economic and Social History Review* IX:2 (April–June 1972), 113–31.

11. See Irfan Habib's three articles: 'Banking in Mughal India,' *Contributions to Indian Economic History,* I (Calcutta, 1960), 1–20; 'Potentialities of Capitalistic Development in the Economy of Mughal India,' *Journal of Economic History,* XXIX (March 1969), 32–78; and 'Usury in Medieval India,' *Comparative Studies in Society and History,* VI:4 (July 1964), 393–423. Also, W.C. Smith,

'The Mughal Empire and the Middle Class—A Hypothesis,' *Islamic Culture*, XVIII: 4 (October 1944), 349–63.

12. For examples of such treatments, see Pearson, 'Political Participation,' op. cit., p. 119–23; D.R. Gadgil, *Origins of the Modern Indian Business Class* (New York, 1959), especially pp. 23–28, and the same author's tentative conclusion that 'mahajans' in Poona were socio-religious organizations for immigrants, 'Immigrant Traders in Poona in the 18th Century,' *Artha Vijnana* I (March 1959), 16; and K.L. Gillion, *Ahmedabad* (Berkeley, 1968), pp. 16–24.

13. T.A. Timberg, 'A Study of a "Great" Marwari Firm: 1860–1914,' *Indian Economic and Social History Review* VIII: 3 (July–Sept. 1971), 267–68. Gadgil, in *Origins*, speaks of firms based on kinship units: p. 34. Neither defines the unit further.

14. L.C. Jain, *Indigenous Banking in India* (London, 1929), makes this distinction on p. 3. He also gives the best explanation of the *hundi* system which was extremely complex.

15. V. Krishnan, *Indigenous Banking in South India* (Bombay, 1959), p. 9. In a twentieth-century survey, he found that 80 percent of moneylenders dealt with agriculturalists, while only 3 percent of the bankers did so.

16. Habib, 'Banking,' pp. 3–8.

17. Gadgil, *Origins*, pp. 32–34. Hameeda Khatoon Naqvi, *Urban Centres and Industries in Upper India, 1556–1603* (New York, 1968), gives specific instances: pp. 62–63, 127–28, 286.

18. J.H. Little, 'The House of Jagatseth,' in *Bengal Past & Present* XX (January–June, 1920), 111–200, and XXII (January–June, 1921), 1–119, is a fascinating history of this firm. The material used here comes from XX, 112–32. Brijen K. Gupta, *Sirajuddallah and the East India Company, 1756–1757* (Leiden, 1962), also documents this firm's closeness to the Mughals, especially pp. 30–31 and 96–97.

19. Krishnan, *Indigenous Banking*, p. 3.

20. Timberg, 'A "Great" Marwari Firm,' in the footnotes, pp. 272–74.

21. For the Nawab of Arcot, Bavany Doss Nanasa Soucar and Dave Boocunji Cashee Dass Soukar were the largest creditors in 1805: Jain, *Indigenous Banking*, p. 21. For Hyderabad, there were the 'Panch Bhai' bankers, which in the early nineteenth century certainly included Seth Kishen Das (now a famous jewellery firm), Makhdum Seth, Mahanand Ram Puran Mal, probably Surat Ram Govind Ram, and perhaps Palmer and Company.

22. Writers on later systems of finance and banking often referred to this prior function of indigenous banking firms, for example, P. Datta, 'Rise of the Calcutta Money Market in Relation to Public Borrowing and Public Credit (1772–1833),' *Calcutta Review* 46 (February 1933), 171–203, and N. Das, 'The Old Agency Houses of Calcutta,' *Calcutta Review*, 46 (March, 1933), 317–26.

But these and other authors completely fail to deal with the historical transition which the indigenous bankers have undergone, even at a descriptive level.

23. Habib, 'Usury,' pp. 408–09.

24. Habib, 'Banking,' p. 6, and 'Usury,' p. 409.

25. Habib, 'Usury,' pp. 414–15.

26. Habib, 'Banking,' pp. 10–11.

27. Gadgil, *Origins*, p. 34.

28. Habib falls into this category most of the time. See his article 'Potentialities of Capitalistic Development', p. 69, where he sees the *karkhanahs* as engaged in the 'production of luxury articles.... This naturally set limits to their economic significance,' and similar remarks on pp. 57–60.

29. Significantly, Gadgil remarks that by 1750 such *karkhanahs* had diminished in importance: *Origins*, pp. 34–35.

30. Gadgil, *Origins*, pp. 35.

31. Ibid., 35; Habib, 'Banking,' p. 4.

32. In Hyderabad, a leading early banking firm is now noted as the leading jewelry firm, a business in which it had always engaged as well: Kishen Das, now Vithal Das. See also Qeyamuddin Ahmad, 'An Historical Account of the Banaras Mint in the Later Mughal Period, 1732–1776,' in *Numismatic Society of India,* 23 (1961), 198–215, where 'precious stones' pass through the mint: pp. 209.

33. Habib, 'Usury,' p. 398.

34. Little, 'House of Jagatseth,' XX, 133, citing Hunter's *Statistical Account,* IX, 256.

35. Jain, *Indigenous Banking,* pp. 18–19, citing Bengal District Records of the eighteenth century.

36. A. M. Shah, 'Political Systems in 18th Century Gujarat,' *Enquiry,* I: 1 (Spring, 1964), 83–95, 92.

37. See specific instances in the following articles by Bernard S. Cohn: 'The Initial British Impact on India, A Case Study of the Benares Region,' *Journal of Asian Studies,* XIX: 4 (August, 1960), 422–23; 'Recruitment of Elites in British India,' in L. Plotnicov and A. Tuden (eds), *Essays in Comparative Social Stratification* (Pittsburgh, 1970), 128–29: 'Structural Change in Indian Rural Society, 1596–1885,' in R. Frykenberg (ed.), *Land Control & Social Structure in Indian History* (Wisconsin, 1969), 80–81; and 'Political Systems in Eighteenth Century India: The Banares Region,' *Journal of the American Oriental Society,* 82: 3 (July–September 1962), 319.

38. See L. Sundaram, 'Revenue Administration of the Northern Circars,' *Journal of the Andhra Historical Research Society,* XIV (1943–44), 22–58, and XV (1944–45), 1–118, for details. The reference to Hyderabad firms: XV, 12.

39. Krishnan, *Indigenous Banking*, pp. 19–20, notes that this was still done in the twentieth century; despite the failure to date its origin, it indicates the complex possibilities the revenue system offered for intermediary profits.

40. Even for this commission method, an initial large *nazr* or payment seems to have been necessary.

41. Pearson argues that the impact upon the nobility was crucial, 'Shivaji and the Decline', op. cit.

42. Pearson, 'Shivaji and the Decline,' pp. 227–28, and his 'Political Participation,' op. cit., 118–19.

43. Ibid., particularly the latter article, pp. 124, 129–30. See also Satish Chandra, 'Commercial Activities of the Mughal Emperors During the Seventeenth Century,' in *Bengal Past & Present*, 78: 146 (July–December 1959), 92–97, where he argues that the *jagir* crisis may have induced nobles to turn to commerce, and his 'Some Aspects of the Growth of A Money Economy in India during the Seventeenth Century,' *Indian Economic and Social History Review*, III: 4 (December 1966), 321–36.

44. Pearson, 'Political Participation,' op. cit., pp. 122–27; Gillion, *Ahmedabad*, 17–18, 21.

45. Pearson, both articles cited above, and particularly 'Political Participation,' p. 128, for emigration.

46. Gadgil, 'Immigrant Traders in Poona,' op. cit., p. 16.

47. Habib, 'Usury,' pp. 408–09.

48. Satish Chandra, 'Early Relations of Farrukh Siyar and the Saiyid Brothers,' *Medieval India Quarterly*, 2: 1 & 2 (1957), 142, for Husain Ali Khan's action (the governor of Bihar).

49. Satish Chandra, in his articles cited in footnote 43, suggests that Mughal commercial activities were increasing in the seventeenth century and persisted right through the eighteenth century. I suspect that their activities were characteristic earlier as well, and that his evidence supports the line of argument here for interdependence.

50. For example, S. Arasaratnam, 'Aspects of the Role and Activities of South Indian Merchants *c.* 1650–1750,' in *Proceedings of the First International Conference Seminar of Tamil Studies* (University of Malaya, 1968), vol. I, pp. 582–96. He prefaces his material on merchants dealing with Europeans after 1650 with these sentences (p. 582): 'After the decline of the great medieval collective enterprises, the mercantile tradition seems to have lived on among certain families with commercial roots in the past. When the European traders … came to Southern India they … soon established firm relations with them.' See also, Sushil Chandhuri, *Trade and Commercial Organization in Bengal, 1650–1720: With Special Reference to the English East India Company*, (Calcutta, 1975).

51. B.G. Gokhale starts his 'Ahmadabad in the XVIIth Century' with the statement, 'The history of India in the seventeenth century is characterized by the emergence of various regions as distinct economic units,' *Journal of Economic and Social History of the Orient*, XII: 2 (April 1969), 187; see also B. Ramachandra Rau, 'Some Specific Services of the Indigenous Bankers of Bombay,' in *Indian Historical Records Commission*, Vol. 12 (1929), 54–59.

52. See footnote 46; also P. K. Gode, 'Keshavbhat Karve, a Poona Banker of the Peshwa Period and His Relations with the Peshwa and Damaji Gaikwad,' in *Journal of the University of Bombay*, Vol. 6 (July, 1937), 87–91.

53. B.A. Saletore, 'A Forgotten Gujarati Brahman Banker,' *Indian Historical Records Commission*, XXX (1954), 155–60.

54. See Philip Calkin's article (cited in footnote 2) and his unpublished paper, 'The Role of Murshidabad as a Regional and Sub-regional Center in Bengal,' which suggests that the city's importance derived more from its commercial orientation towards European factories even in the seventeenth century than from its administrative orientation to the Mughals (8–14).

55. For the Hyderabad firms, Sundaram, 'Revenue Administration,' p. 12; for the Marwari firm, Timberg, 'A "Great" Marwari Firm,' 264–65, 283.

56. This has been stated by Jain, *Indigenous Bankers*, p. 17, and Gadgil, *Origins*, p. 32, where he notes that de Bussy in the Deccan and Karnatak obtained a loan from 'a great banker.' Instances of Kanara Saraswat merchants who allied themselves with the British are given in V.N. Kudra, *History of the Dakshinatya Saraswats* (Madras, 1972), 117–18.

57. Karl Fischer, 'The Beginning of Dutch Trade with Gujarat,' unpublished paper, pp. 16–18.

58. Saletore, 'A Forgotten Gujarati Brahman Banker,' p. 155, citing early East India Company records which he lists in his footnote; see also Habib's charts in 'Usury,' pp. 402-03, and H. Q. Naqvi, *Urban Centres and Industries*, pp. 63–64.

59. Pearson, 'Political Participation,' pp. 125–27. This is also clear in Ashin Das Gupta, 'The Merchants of Surat, *c.* 1700–50,' in Edmund Leach and S.N. Mukherjee (eds), *Elites in South Asia* (Cambridge, 1970), pp. 201–22.

60. Saletore, 'A Forgotten Gujarati Brahman Banker,' pp. 158–60.

61. Little, 'The House of Jagatseth,' (Vol. XX), 115–16, for the 1652 loan, and 126–29, 136–45 for the Mitra Sen firm.

62. Gadgil, *Origins*, p. 32, Little's article, continued in Vol. XXII, and Gupta, *Sirajuddallah and the East India Company*, p. 132, both document the Hindu bankers' new alliance with the East India Company in Bengal by 1760. M. Panikkar, in *Asia and Western Dominance* (New York, 1953), carelessly generalizes that the powerful Indian merchant class worked with European traders because of its 'inherited hatred of Muslim rule' (p. 99).

63. Little, 'The House of Jagatseth, Vol. XXII, 97–103.

64. Jain, *Indigenous Banking*, pp. 19–20, citing the Governor General's letter to the Collector of Rangpur, in Vol. 1. p. 33 of the Bengal District Records.

65. Sundaram, 'Revenue Administration,' Vol. XV, 10–14.

66. Ibid., p. 33, citing Macartney.

67. Ibid., pp. 15 and 34.

68. Ibid., pp. 77–78.

69. Jain, *Indigenous Banking*, pp. 20–22.

70. This was Charles Metcalfe, in a letter to the Governor General, September, 1821: E. J. Thompson, *Life of Lord Metcalfe* (London, 1937), pp. 210–11.

71. Jain, *Indigenous Banking*, pp. 23–25, makes this comparison. The best coverage of this transition period from the point of view of the Company is by B. Ramachandra Rau, 'Organized Banking in the Days of John Company,' in *Bengal Past and Present* Vol. 37 (January–June 1929), 145–57, and Vol. 38 (July–December 1929), 60–80.

72. Both Panikkar (*Asia and Western Dominance,* p. 99) and Gupta (*Siraj ud dau lah and the East India Company,* p. 32) compare the Indian mercantile class to 'Shanghai compradors,' but they do not investigate this comparison further. For China, see the following: E. Balazs, 'The Birth of Capitalism in China,' in Eisenstadt (ed.), *Decline of Empires,* p. 109; Lien-sheng Yang, *Money and Credit in China, A Short History* (Cambridge, 1952); 'Economic Aspects of Public Works in Imperial China,' in *Excursions in Sinology* (Cambridge, 1969); and 'Government Control of Urban Merchants in Traditional China,' in the *Tsing Hua Journal of Chinese Studies,* new series (2nd) 8, August 1970, 186–206. See also Mark Elvin, *The Pattern of the Chinese Past* (London, 1973), particularly pp. 155, 161–62, 215–25, and 285–97.

73. For example, F. Lehmann, 'Shah Ayat Allah "Jauhri" and his Shahr Ashob,' in *Abdul Karim Sahitya-Visarad Commemoration Volume* (Dacca, 1972), and other writing on the eighteenth-century cultural laments.

74. Timberg discusses the problem of sources in 'A "Great" Marwari Firm.' In an unpublished paper, 'Speculative Gains and Primitive Accumulation' which deals only with the nineteenth and twentieth centuries, Timberg's problem is the theoretical one of entrepreneurial values; he had no problems with sources. Morris D. Morris, in a recent unpublished paper, 'South Asian Entrepreneurship and the Rashomon Effect,' also deals with the nineteenth and twentieth centuries and emphasizes the significance of indigenous banking and entrepreneurial activities and how little we still know about them (Paper presented at a Conference on Colonial Port Cities in Berkeley, June 1976).

The Passing of the Empire
The Mughal Case*

M. ATHAR ALI

I

There have been numerous attempts to explain the fall of the Mughal Empire; and I truly feel great hesitation in adding myself to the long list of its exponents. To historians like Irvine and Sarkar, the decline could be explained in terms of a personal deterioration in the quality of the kings and their nobles. The harem influence grew—and women, for some strange unscientific reason, are always supposed to be a bad influence. The kings and nobles became more luxury-loving, though no-one has yet established that the Mughals during the sixteenth and seventeenth centuries enjoyed a less luxurious mode of living than their eighteenth-century successors.[1]

Sarkar, in his monumental *History of Aurangzeb*, also elaborated upon the traditionally recognized factor, namely, Hindu–Muslim differences; Aurangzeb's religious policy is thought to have provoked a Hindu reaction that undid the unity that had been so laboriously built up by his predecessors.[2]

Recently, there has been an attempt at a more fundamental examination. Satish Chandra sought to find the critical factor in the Mughals' failure to maintain the *mansab* and *jagir* system whose efficient working was essential for the survival of the Empire as a centralized polity.[3] Irfan Habib, on the other hand, has sought to explain the fall of the Mughal Empire as an effect of the working of this very system. The *jagir* transfers led to intensified exploitation; and such exploitation led to

* Reproduced from M. Athar Ali, *Mughal India: Studies in Polity, Ideas, Societies and Culture*, New Delhi, Oxford University Press, 2006, pp. 337–49.

rebellion by *zamindars* (rural superior right-holders) and the peasantry.[4] With all these factors is sometimes compounded yet another—the rise of 'nationalities', subverting and shattering the unified empire. The thesis, developed by Soviet scholars like Reisner and maintained by a school of popular Indian Marxist writers, has received strange corroboration from 'young and youngish' American scholars who have found new regional power groups in the states that arose during the eighteenth century.[5]

It is easy to be lost in the welter of these 'factors'. It is also perhaps possible to reconcile contradictions by propounding a complex-cause-sequence-cause chain and by simply disowning the search for the single ultimate cause. Such a synthesis is yet to be attempted; I do not profess any ambition to make the attempt here. I should like simply to relate the entire text to what I conceive to be the proper context.

In following the scholarly discussions over the break-up of the Mughal Empire, I have been struck by the fact that the discussions should have been conducted in such insular terms. The first part of the eighteenth century did not see the collapse of only the Mughal Empire: The Safavid Empire also collapsed; the Uzbek Khanate broke up into fragments; and the Ottoman Empire began its career of slow, but inexorable decline. Are all these phenomena mere coincidences? It seems to me straining one's sense of the plausible to assert that the same fate overcame all the large empires of the Indic and Islamic world at precisely the same time, but owing to quite different (and rather miscellaneous) factors operating in the case of each of them. Even if the search should ultimately prove futile, one must see whether it is possible to discover some common factor that caused more or less stable empires to disintegrate and created conditions in which new political structures which look large enough on the map, like Nadir Shah's empire, the Afghan (Durrani) empire or the Maratha confederacy, emerged and then almost immediately splintered into fragments.

There is one remarkable point too, which may serve as the guide-post in our search. The break-up of the empires distinctly precedes the impact from the armed attack of the western colonial powers, notably Britain and Russia. But it precedes the impact with such a short interval that the question must arise whether the rise of the West was not in some ways, not yet properly understood, subverting the polity and society of the East even before Europe actually confronted the eastern states with its superior military power.

It is a regrettable gap in our study of the economic history of the Middle East and India, that no general analysis has been attempted of the changes in the pattern of trade and markets of these countries, as a result of the new commerce between Europe and Asia. There is a tendency to belittle the significance of the great commercial developments of the sixteenth and seventeenth centuries for eastern economies, owing to the small volume of goods that entered international, or long-distance, trade at that time. But the real question is not of volume, but value. In terms of value, long-distance trade must have accounted for a sizeable portion of the gross product in all the economics with which we are concerned.

The major event between 1500 and 1700 was certainly the rise of Europe as the centre of world commerce, with its dominance over the New World and the high seas, and its total monopoly of the Cape of Good Hope. Recent estimates suggest an increase in the population of Europe from about 50 million in 1450 to 120 million in 1700.[6] An outstanding achievement particularly when we bear in mind the demographic debacle of the Thirty Years War in Germany and the slow decline of population in Spain. No similar estimates exist for Asia. But it would seem that the Indian population remained largely stable between 1600 and 1800. Moreland's estimate of 100 million for 1600 has been properly questioned, and the figure of 150 million probably is nearer the truth.[7] The Census of 1868–72 disclosed a population of less than 230 million. India thus saw an increase of barely 66 per cent in 270 years, whereas Europe enhanced its population by some 240 per cent in a period of 250 years. This contrast in population growth suggests that a real shift in the economic balance between Europe and Asia had already occurred by the end of the seventeenth century.

This shift found its true repercussions in international trade. The discovery of the Cape of Good Hope was certainly an important event, and in giving a direct, unhampered route to India, it had important military consequences in the eighteenth century. But the major economic change was not represented only by the new route (indeed, it is likely that the older, Red Sea route remained as important a channel as the Cape until well after 1700). It was, above all, represented by the emergence of Europe as the principal market for the luxuries and craft-manufactures of the world. Economic historians have so far remained immersed mainly in Europe's problem of payments, a preoccupation inherited from the mercantilist controversies of the period. The other complementary aspects, that is the increase in demand for the products of the world and the effect of this on *other* markets of these products, appear either to have escaped notice or to have not received the attention due to them.

In other words, we have to consider not only the export of large quantities of gold and silver (especially the latter) from Europe to the East, but also the fact that a large part of the luxury manufactures and high-value products of the East were diverted from their other, hitherto 'traditional' markets, and carried to Europe. Unfortunately, owing to the lack of fuller investigations, and partly to the limitations in our sources, it is difficult to set this shift in quantitative terms. But wherever we look in Asia near the end of the seventeenth century, the European demand was exercising its pull, strong or feeble, direct or indirect.

The fact that Iran no longer remained the principal market for a whole range of Indian commodities (indigo, pepper, chintz), and India and Iran, together, no longer for a number of Chinese exports (silk, porcelain), speaks volumes for the relative economic decline of these countries. This decline, was, however, not only relative; it could not but be absolute as well. One-third of the Bengal silk was already exported, through the Dutch and the English, before 1667, and one third through Persian and Armenian merchants (much of it presumably for overland transport to Mediterranean port), and only a third remained for Indian markets.[8] The European companies obtained a virtual monopoly of the pepper of the western coast, and they became the principal buyers of India's finest chintz, that of Masulipatam. It is not very likely that production expanded sufficiently to meet the European demand without reducing the share of the other markets. Indeed, if the production did expand to some extent, in conditions of stationary technology, costs and prices must have gone up, relatively to the general price level.

My suggestion is that these developments caused a serious disturbance in the economics of the eastern countries, and intensified the financial difficulties of the ruling classes. The Great Silk Road no longer carried the great caravans; and this must have distinctly impoverished Central Asia (the Uzbek Khanate). In India and Iran, too, the costs of luxury articles rose—and, after all, for members of the ruling class it was these luxuries that life was all about. The income previously obtained no longer sufficed. Here was a factor for an attempt at greater agrarian exploitation; and when that failed, or proved counter-productive, for reckless factional activities for individual gain, leading to interminable civil wars. Such conditions would, of course, spell the end of the great empires.

While, obviously, what I have suggested is replete with speculation, and requires much detailed investigation for its substantiation, I should like to consider another important historical factor that emerges from a consideration of the Europe–Asia relationship. The European imports of eastern goods were paid for mainly in gold and silver: and these, especially the latter, came from Latin America in hitherto unprecedented quantities. But the European demand for these commodities was generated, not so much by the possession of the specie, as by a distinct qualitative and quantitative development of craft production, leading to the enrichment of the entire economy and a notable expansion of its urban sector. At the beginning of the seventeenth century, towns like Lahore or Agra dwarfed the European cities of the period. By 1700, European towns like London and Paris had populations (at over half a million) exceeding those of all Indian cities, except perhaps Agra. According to Deane and Cole's estimate, 13 per cent of the people of England and Wales were living in towns of 5,000 and above, in 1701.[9] This percentage had not been reached in India even by 1901.

This spurt in European urban growth was the first product of the new science and technology that was generating small advances in a number of sectors, the cumulative effect of which was phenomenal. A completely different picture was presented by Asia, especially India. One need not be a follower of Marx's theory of the unchangeableness of traditional Indian society to accept the fact that there was no conscious spirit of technological innovation (and scientific enquiry) here and in the Islamic East to match the spirit already motivating a large part of European society in the seventeenth century. This does not mean that no mechanical innovation was propagated or spread in the East during the sixteenth and seventeenth centuries. It has been shown that such 'generalization' did take place.[10] But what we are concerned with is its pace and scope. The pace was certainly slow, and the scope severely limited. This is manifested, above all, by the utter absence in the literature of India of any satisfactory descriptions of even the most important products of Europe's new technology, e.g. the clock, the telescope, and the flint-lock.

Whether the source lay in some structural fault of Indian and Islamic society, which perpetuated the divorce between intellect and manual labour, or whether it lay in some peculiar inhibition against science in Islamic (and Hindu) ideology is difficult to decide. The intellectual aridity is manifest; its causes are obscure.

The aridity is relevant to us because of its economic and political consequences. If technological growth resulted in urbanization, this meant that the expansion of towns could provide a safety-value at times of agrarian crises. Since a similar process did not occur in India and other countries of the East, this safety-valve was missing. As has been pointed out, the Indian urban population was parasitical, based upon the expropriation of agrarian surplus.[11] A corollary of this is that if the expropriation of that surplus was affected, the scope of urban employment also declined. This means that, so long as craft production did not obtain an independent base, as it did increasingly in Europe from the sixteenth century, there was no possibility of the absorption of the shock of an agrarian upheaval. In that sense, the Mughal Empire, in spite of its splendid professional army, was peculiarly vulnerable to the ill-armed but million-headed *zamindar* and peasant rebels.[12]

Here, another point suggests itself. If there was anything that was affected most speedily by technological changes throughout the world it was the army. Artillery-making was the 'heavy industry' of the time. In Europe it attracted the ingenuity of scientists and mathematicians from the sixteenth century onwards. But, as one moved eastward from Europe, the pace of its development in each country would have appeared to be slower and slower. India saw no conscious attempt to design new artillery weapons; the making of muskets and guns remained a mere craft, with no touch of science; and accordingly by 1700 these were almost completely out-dated. The Mughals continued to rely upon bow and sword-wielding cavalry when its days were long over. It is, perhaps, this that led to their major debacle at Karnal in 1739, when they had to face Nadir Shah, who had better artillery, copied from the Europeans and the Ottomans.[13]

To me, then, the failure of the Mughal Empire would seem to derive essentially from a *cultural* failure, shared with the entire Islamic world. It was this failure that tilted the economic balance in favour of Europe, well before European armies reduced India and other parts of Asia to colonial possessions, protectorates and spheres of influence. It was this cultural failure again that deprived the empires of the capacity to grapple with their agrarian crises. These twin economic consequences were themselves the causes of the political and military debacles; but as we have just seen, even military weaknesses flowed from the intellectual stagnation that seems to have gripped the eastern world.

Of course, the word stagnation is relative. It is quite possible that if we were not in the compelling necessity to have to be looking over our shoulders at what was being thought and written in Europe at the same time, we might have regarded the Islamic East and India during the sixteenth and seventeenth centuries as fairly productive in the matter of literature and rational sciences. But while we may admire the poetry of Hafiz, the rationalism of Abul Fazl, the religious eclecticism of Dara Shukoh, the astronomical observations of Raja Jai Singh, the fact remains that of modern science there is hardly a trace. This is so very clear in the *Zij-i Muhammad Shahi* (1732), the celebrated work of Jai Singh. Here the entire theoretical text is virtually borrowed verbatim from the *Zij-i Ulugh-khani,* composed nearly 300 years earlier. Only the tables are changed. Jai Singh is interested in European astronomical observations, and he refers to them in his preface. But Newton might not have lived, so far as he is concerned. Thus the entire framework of reasoning and thought, and, indeed, the limits and scope of reflection, remained the same as had been defined by the great Arabic writers before the twelfth century. The stirrings were there and were important; but, unluckily, they brought out only ripples, where a flood, a breakthrough, was needed in order to put men's minds into new moulds.

II

The polities that emerged upon the collapse of the Mughal Empire were of demonstrably two kinds. In one class were the 'succession states' like Hyderabad, Bengal and Awadh, which were really fragments of the Empire, that had to stand upon their own feet as the central government decayed and became powerless to assist or assert. They inherited more or less the entire Mughal machinery of administration in a working order. In the second category were the Maratha confederacy, the Jats, the Sikhs, and the Afghans. Their origins as polities were independent of the Mughal Empire, though they might occasionally come to terms with it, or, indeed, in the case of the first two, even acknowledge the nominal supremacy of the Mughal emperor. They were clearly the products of the crisis that we have touched upon. While they might use certain Mughal administrative institutions for their own purposes, their mode of government was by and large antithetical to that of the Empire, and could not be reconciled with it. Mughal professional cavalry could indeed survive within the Maratha confederacy, but only as Pindaris, that is as real historical Draculas, who drank up the blood of their new masters. The entire contradiction is summed up in the protest expressed by Azad Bilgrami in 1761 that the Maratha leaders, in spite of their conquests, were not behaving as rulers, but as *zamindars*.[14]

Mysore under Haidar Ali and Tipu Sultan stood outside these two categories, and was in some ways the most remarkable. On the one hand, it represented a conscious attempt at implanting Mughal administrative institutions in an area that had only been nominally a part of the Mughal Empire. This was most clearly to be seen in the organization of land-revenue administration, as well as the army (notably under Haidar Ali). On the other hand, it was the first state in India to make a beginning towards modernization, first and foremost in the realm of the army and arms manufacture, but also in commerce, where the English East India Company's practices were sought to be imitated.[15]

This preliminary classification of eighteenth-century polities is important, because some writers tend to speak as if, irrespective of these large differences in their essential natures, we could still find some common basis for them. The theory that these polities were reflections of the emergence of 'regional élites', or gave opportunities to certain groups previously enjoying only limited prominence, to become co-sharers in power, are either statements of the obvious in sociological terms, or are based upon rather untenable assumptions about the Mughal Empire.

Thus, if the Mughal Empire broke into certain fragments, with each fragment an autonomous or independent state, its ruling class must, of course, ipso factor have been regionalized. No longer could an officer serving in Awadh be sent to the Deccan in course of time. But this is an effect, not a cause; and it is an enforced regionalization, if anything. The case of Bengal that is often cited,[16] is rather peculiar. Here the *nazim*s, or governors, first carried out what in an earlier period would have appeared as an act of extreme centralization. Murshid Quli Khan obtained imperial sanction for the conversion of *jagir*s into *khalisa*, and thus secured the withdrawal of all Mughal *jagirdar*s or commanders from Bengal. Then, because he combined his office of *nazim* with that of *diwan*, or provincial revenue minister, he henceforth managed the *khalisa*; and he and his successors remitted enormous amounts to the Mughal Emperor.[17] By 1740 this practice ceased. Thus, the Bengal *nawab*s became masters of the entire revenues of Bengal without having to share them with the *jagirdar*s, that is, without there being any true remnant of Mughal nobility continuing in Bengal except for the *nazim*s themselves. For managing the *khalisa*, the *nawab*s recruited revenue-farmers and officials from amongst the local *zamindar*s and merchant-bankers. This phenomenon has given rise to much misunderstanding about the emergence of a new élite. No such emergence is discernible in Hyderabad or in Awadh, where the *jagir* system continued to be in vogue.

Information about the merchants' role in administration is rather too readily seized upon as evidence of their increased political participation. In fact, their role in the Mughal Empire was equally important.[18] Quite obviously the Gujarat merchants in the seventeenth century exercised a degree of influence at the Mughal court that even the *nagarseth*s of Bengal in the eighteenth century might have envied.

The Maratha confederacy, as I have said, cannot be grouped with the succession states for any political analysis. That it was a failure as an attempt at Empire building is admitted by all serious historians. While succeeding so brilliantly in the field, at least until 1761, the Marathas failed to evolve even those minimum conventions—or fictions, if you like—that are essential for building an empire. The slogan of *Hindu-Pad-Pad-Shahi* died an abortive death, possibly because the Peshwas were not too keen to give undue weight to their titular sovereign, the raja of Satara. In their attempt to make themselves independent of their own nominal masters, the Peshwas seemed always prepared to accept the nominal sovereignty of the Mughal emperor, so long as the actual gains were theirs. But just as they had reduced their raja to a titular status, the Peshwas, too, were subsequently to be reduced to a titular status by Nana Phadnis (Fardnawis). Thus there was a simple failure to establish even a stable repository of sovereign power.

The second difficulty faced in the working of the Maratha polity arose out of the fact that plunder remained an essential element for its continued functioning. It too often seemed that *chauth* and *sardeshmukhi*, and in lieu thereof, a general devastation of a country, rather than its direct conquest, constituted the acme of Maratha ambitions. Thus, when a full-fledged Maratha administration was established anywhere (and, if Muhammad Ali, author of *Mirat-iAhmadi*, is to be believed, it could on occasion be excellent), the country had already been so ravaged that the Marathas could only replenish their resources by extending the range of plunder.

I do not wish to enter into similar details for the Abdali or Durrani Empire of Afghanistan, which during the latter half of the eighteenth century came to include the whole of present Pakistan, as well as Kashmir. But in some essential features, especially the dependence upon plunder, it exhibited similar aspects.

One might then say that once the limits for plundering activities were reached, either because of geography, or of opponents, the tide was bound to turn; and civil war, that is really the plunder of the internal parts of these states, was thereupon bound to break out. This can be a plausible explanation of the break-up of both the Maratha and Afghan systems.

But here I should like to draw attention to another factor that might have introduced an element of exceptional economic strain precisely at a time when these states were otherwise vulnerable to centrifugal tendencies. In 1757, the British won the battle of Plassey and within seven years they were complete masters of eastern India. This conquest was not simply a mere political event. It changed the entire complexion of India's commerce. The revenues of Bengal and Bihar became the source of 'investments' of the English East India Company, and with these enormous resources, the English changed the entire direction of the exports of Bengal and Bihar, as well as Coromandel. The exports soon exceeded £5 million.[19] This complete diversion of commerce, must have resulted in the upsetting of the whole pattern of Indian commerce. The commercial decline of Gujarat and Agra, which imported silk and cotton stuffs from Bengal, was inevitable. Similarly, the overland trade through Afghanistan was bound to suffer. As the English advanced further inland at the beginning of the nineteenth century, the decline would become still more marked.

How adversely this economic process affected the political strength of the Maratha confederacy and the Afghan Empire is obviously difficult to establish with any degree of confidence. One is struck by the fact that the sudden collapse of the Afghan Empire, in 1809, should have followed so soon after the English advance up to Delhi in 1803. Elphinstone, who led a mission to the court of the Afghan ruler Shah Shuja and who was a witness to the dissolution of his authority, himself observed the decline of the trade and the abandonment of commerce by Afghan tribesmen in favour of agriculture.[20] The decline in commerce is thus established: What is still to be proven is its link with the British conquest on the one hand, and its role as a factor in the decline of the Afghan Empire. My plea is that both the processes occur in such sequence that, at least tentatively, the link ought to be accepted. Perhaps, closer scrutiny of the evidence would some day put us on surer ground.

Finally, a question about these 'transition regimes'. Why is it that when faced directly with British power, they attempted no, or very little, modernization? The case of Mysore under Haidar Ali and Tippu remained unique. Maratha *sardars*, like the Sindhias, would go no further than having some regiments trained and commanded by European officers.

What is singular is that at the ideological level the English influence should have made such little dent. It is true that information about western sciences begins to appear in some Persian works; but on inspection they are all found to have been written at the direction and wishes of an English official or clergyman. In the main, the Persian literature continued in its well-established grooves. Indeed, the eighteenth century saw its maximum progress in India. Checking through the works listed in C.A. Storey's monumental *Persian Literature: A Bio-bibliographical Survey*, Vol. I, I found that whereas there were only six Hindu writers who wrote one book each in Persian during the seventeenth century, there were during the eighteenth century no less than thirty-two Hindu writers who wrote as many as forty-nine books. This is a tribute to the strength of the cultural tradition bequeathed by the Mughal Empire. But it also partly explains, I think, why the new culture, coming from Europe, held so little attraction, and was, therefore, almost wholly ignored by the educated in India.

III

The author of *Siyar-al Mutakhirin*, himself a protégé of the English, presented in his work an idealized picture of the Mughal administration which he set before his masters as a model. He was writing in 1781.

The debate that subsequently occurred between Grant, Shore, and Cornwallis, reproduced in the celebrated *Fifth Report*, shows how to the new rulers, too, the rights and institutions established under the Mughal Empire were of abiding interest. Their claim to land-revenue, in particular, derived from Mughal precedent and practice. It has been urged that even the Permanent Settlement was not totally exotic and was rooted in the practice of the Mughal government in Bengal during the seventeenth century.[21] Munro's Ryotwari system was even more clearly a development of the Mughal system of *zabt* assessment that he found in vogue in areas seized from Mysore. Asiya Siddiqi has commented on how the British administrators of the Ceded and Conquered Provinces greatly relied upon Indian land-revenue expertise, which, as reflected in a work like *Diwan-pasand*, was simply a survival of Mughal land-revenue practices.[22] In so far as the Mughals had established a uniform system of administration all over the country, and a single official language (Persian), the English were helped thereby in creating an administrative machinery that was not too varied in character to render centralized control difficult, and yet was in some harmony with existing conditions.[23]

While saying all this, I should like to refer to a parallel. When the Spaniards captured the Inca emperor of Peru and stepped into his shoes, they used the highly centralized structure of the Incas to quickly establish and extend their rule. But it can hardly be said that the Inca Empire survived in any form through the Spanish colonization. Similarly, the entire basis of British rule in India was so different from that of the Mughal Empire, that one can hardly speak of the former as being in any sense a continuation of the latter. The conception of the revenues of the country, as gross profits of the English East India Company, was the basic principle on which English dominion was founded; and the drain of wealth to England, through public as well as private channels was the ultimate object to be realized. Thus the survival of the Mughal Empire was subverted to a new use, and not employed to resurrect anything resembling the old Empire. That empire had its own inequities, but these, to be fair to it, were of a different form and content altogether.

NOTES

1. William Irvine, *Later Mughals*, ed. Sarkar, 2 vols, and J. Sarkar, *Fall of the Mughal Empire*, 4 vols, *passim*.

2. J. Sarkar, *History of Aurangzeb*, III, Calcutta, 1916, 283–364.

3. Satish Chandra, *Parties and Politics at the Mughal Court, 1707–1740*, Aligarh, 1959, pp. xliii–xlvii.

4. Irfan Habib, *Agrarian System of Mughal India, 1556–1707*, Bombay, 1963, pp. 317–51.

5. Cf. M.N. Pearson in *IESHR*, IX, 114 and n.

6. The estimate for 1850 is that of J. Russell (*Fontana Economic History of Europe*, vol. I, p. 36) and for 1700 that of André Armengaud (ibid., vol. 3, p. 27).

7. Shireen Moosvi, *IESHR*, X, 194.

8. Tavernier, *Travels in India,1640–67*, tr. Ball, ed. Crooke, London, 1925, II, p. 2.

9. Phyllis Deane and W.A. Cole, *British Economic Growth, 1688–1959*, Cambridge, 1962, p. 7.

10. Irfan Habib, *Technology and Economy of Mughal India*, Devaraj Chanana Memorial Lectures, 1971 (mimeo).

11. Irfan Habib, *Enquiry*, NS III (3), 55.

12. On the composition of the Maratha army, see Satish Chandra, *IESHR*, X, p. 217 and n. Cf. Irfan Habib, *Agrarian System*, pp. 346–51.

13. Cf. Irvine, *Later Mughals*, II, 352 (Sarkar's addendum).

14. Azad Bilgrami, *Khizana-i Amira*, Kanpur, 1871, p. 47.

15. Mohibbul Hasan Khan, *History of Tipu Sultan,*Calcutta, 1951, pp. 344–7.

16. Philip Calkins in *Journal of Asian Studies*, xxix, pp. 799ff.

17. Cf. Z. Malik in *IESHR*, IV, pp. 269–70.

18. Cf. M.N. Pearson in *IESHR*, IX, pp. 118ff.

19. The British imports from 'East India' amounted to £5,785,000 in 1797–8 (Deane and Cole, *British Economic Growth*, p. 87). These imports included imports from China; but the China trade was itself financed by exports from Bengal.

20. Mountstuart Elphinstone, *An Account of the Kingdom of Caubul*, London, 1839, I, pp. 383, 387–8, etc.

21. Irfan Habib, *Agrarian System*, pp. 175–9.

22. A. Siddiqi, *Agrarian Change in a North Indian State*, Oxford, 1973, pp. 178–9.

23. See the perceptive remarks of Eric Stokes in *Past and Present*, no. 58, pp. 144–5, 146–7.

The Structure of Administration*

CHETAN SINGH

The history of a region such as Panjab cannot be described merely in terms of *zamindars, jagirdars* and the Mughal imperial system thriving upon agrarian surplus.[1] Nor would it be sufficient to project regional history as an autonomous process of commercialized agriculture, petty commodity production and the growth of a money-economy. Not only was the region subjected to influences that were common to the whole Mughal empire; it was also considerably affected by changes which swept across other parts of the world. The significance of the larger geographical context of the region must be borne in mind for a proper appreciation of the factors which influenced the course of events.[2]

Topographical characteristics and the other historical factors which contributed to the regional identity of Panjab, also influenced the organisation of its administrative divisions. As mentioned earlier, the region under study stretched across one entire *suba* and considerable portions of two others. It included within its span two *suba* headquarters. Due to the clear-cut delineation of *suba* boundaries there would be a tendency to assume that the administrative sub-divisions of these *subas* did not overlap in any way. Yet administrative convenience came to recognize the many integrating forces which were knitting the region into a closer unit. Local society and polity were subjected to a variety of stresses and the administrative system responded by transgressing the formal administrative divisions and sub-divisions of the Mughal governmental system.

* Excerpts from Chetan Singh, *Region and Empire: Panjab in the Seventeenth Century*, Oxford University Press, New Delhi, 1991, pp. 8, 30–55.

GENERAL ADMINISTRATION

(i) *Suba headquarters*: The manner in which the suba administration functioned has been explained by numerous scholars.[3] To recount it here in detail would be repetitive. Panjab does not appear to have been strikingly dissimilar from other regions in this respect. The *subadar* was the general administrative head of the suba and performed a wide range of duties. The actual position and power of the subadar, however, depended upon the emperor's favour and thus varied from person to person. The provincial *diwan* who ranked next in importance was primarily a financial administrator. Despite his considerable powers and his direct link with the chief diwan (*Diwan-i-Ala*) at the Mughal court, the provincial diwan could hardly match the subadar in importance. The latter was normally appointed from amongst the highest nobles of the empire and his personal ranking in the mansabdari was invariably higher than that of the provincial diwan. Given this difference in their personal and hierarchial status, the diwan must have found it difficult to escape the influence of a dominating subadar.[4]

Another official of importance in the *suba* was the *bakhshi* who frequently performed the additional function of the *waqai-nawis*. This office had its origins in the growing complexities of the imperial army and the *mansabdari* system. The provincial *bakhshi* was responsible for the recruitment of soldiers, regulations pertaining to their maintenance and inspection, and for the branding of horses. The payment of salaries was made through him.

The judiciary was represented in the suba by an official who often acted both as *sadr* and *qazi*. As sadr he supervised the land grants made to religious and needy people and regulated religious activities. As qazi he headed the provincial judiciary and recommended names for appointment of subordinate qazis. These two offices were, however, not inseparable. Different officials could be appointed to hold them separately.[5]

Any administrative peculiarities that may have existed in Panjab can best be revealed by investigating the practice of some of the above-mentioned institutions in the region.

Subadars: The cities of Lahore and Multan which lay within Panjab were both administrative centres of strategically important provinces, and the *subadars* appointed here were nobles of considerable influence. Apart from the suba of Kabul, it was the subas of Lahore and Multan which were regarded as frontier provinces and were normally kept strongly garrisoned. The movements of Khusrau towards Panjab during his rebellion against Jahangir, and of Dara Shikoh during the war of succession, point to the strategic importance of the region for any ruler of Hindustan.[6]

Of the two the subadari of Lahore was more prestigious if the rank and status of the subadars is any indication. The city of Lahore functioned at times as the imperial capital thereby acquiring greater importance. The *mansab* of the subadar of Lahore was normally higher than that of his counterpart in Multan. The *zat* rank of the Lahore subadars usually stood at 5000 or 6000, while that of the subadars of Multan was often below 3000 zat and in very rare instances rose above 5000 zat.[7] Militarily, however, the difference was not so obvious. Despite the lower zat rank of the Multan subadars, their *sawar* holding was relatively high, though not as high as that of the subadars of Lahore. The relatively high sawar strength of the Multan subadars meant that despite their lower zat status they were able to carry out their military functions effectively, and these functions were very important to a frontier province. Moreover, the difference in status between the two subadaris was not officially recognized. There are instances of subadars who served in both these provinces. There were nobles who had served as subadar of Lahore prior to their being assigned the subadari of Multan, suggesting thereby that the subadari of Multan was not officially regarded as inferior to that of Lahore.[8]

Princes of the blood, too, are known to have held the subadari of these provinces, and the highest mansabs were, probably, held by them. Aurangzeb as governor of Multan and Thatta held the mansab of 15,000/12,000 (8,000 × 2 – 3 h).[9] Such high ranks, however, were not held by the other nobles. From available evidence we know that the highest mansab held by a subadar of Lahore during our period of study (apart from the princes) was that of 10,000/9,000 (7,000 × 2 – 3 h) held by Ali Mardan Khan in 1640–1. As for the subadari of Multan, Mirza Ghazi Beg Tarkhan held the rank of 7,000/7,000 × 2 – 3 h, during the early years of Jahangir's reign.[10] Among the lowest mansabs held by a subadar of Lahore was that of 2,000/1,400 held by Dilawar Khan Kakar in 1605–6. In Multan the lowest ranking subadar was, probably, Abu al Nabi Uzbeg with a mansab of 1,500/1,000 in 1610–11. Despite this low rank the latter two subadars were full-fledged governors of their provinces.

The emperor on occasion permitted the princes and some high ranking nobles to administer the provinces of which they were subadars, through *naib*s (deputies), while they themselves continued to reside at the imperial court. In such cases the *naib-subadar* normally had a lower mansab than that held by a full-fledged subadar and he merely acted on behalf of the regularly appointed subadar. Of such cases we have numerous examples. Qasim Khan, the son-in-law of Itimad-ud-Daulah, acted as the latter's naib in suba Lahore from 1618–19 to 1623–4 and was a mansabdar of 1,000/400. Asaf Khan (6,000/6,000) who was the subadar of Lahore between 1625 and 1628 administered the province through his son and naib Abu Talib, who was succeeded as naib by Baba Inayatullah. However, no information about their mansab rank is available. Between 1645 and 1650, Lahore was once again administered by naibs succeeding one another, this time on behalf of Dara Shikoh. One of these naibs, Saiyid Sultan (1649–50) was a mansabdar of 1,500/200. Towards the end of Aurangzeb's reign, Munim Khan the naib of Prince Muhammad Muazzam in Lahore held the rank of 1,500/1,000.[11]

In suba Multan, too, naib-subadars are known to have been appointed. In 1628–9, Abu-l Baqa/Amir Khan the naib of Asaf Khan had a mansab of 2,500/–1,500, and was succeeded as naib in 1630–1 by Najabat Khan Mirza Shuja whose zat was 2,000. Dara Shikoh who was appointed to the subadari of Multan in 1652–3 administered the province through naib-subadars, and Shaikh Moosvi Gilani one of his naibs was a mansabdar of 1,000/1,400. The fact that the suba of Multan was ruled less frequently through naibs than suba Lahore may imply that fewer subadars of Multan were of sufficiently high status to be permitted this exceptional privilege. It might also suggest that the subadari of Lahore had acquired a higher status symbolically, such as those of Bengal and the Deccan.

In keeping with established Mughal policy, the imperial officials were periodically transferred. It appears that the policy of transfers was, in principle, directed towards preventing any particular section of the Mughal nobility from becoming too powerful in a region.[12] This policy of regular transfer was also followed in the case of subadars, and it was only occasionally that they were allowed to stay as subadars in one suba for a long duration. Only nobles of an exceptionally high standing were permitted to remain in one post for long periods. The longest term, of about ten years, in suba Lahore seems to have been that of Wazir Khan during the reign of Shahjahan. Judging from available evidence, even a term of five years as subadar could be considered a long one. On the other hand, there are numerous instances of subadars being transferred after one year or even earlier. In suba Multan, the seven-year governorship of Qulij Khan Turani seems to have been the longest tenure ever. As against Lahore, a fewer number of subadars remained in Multan for the relatively long term of five years. Moreover, the average tenure of governorship in Multan hardly ever exceeding three years, was shorter than in suba Lahore.

As the subadar was invariably appointed as the executive head of one suba, the peculiar instance of Ali Mardan Khan deserves mention. He was the subadar of Lahore in 1639–40. In addition, he held the subadari of Kashmir. This, however, was an exceptional case.

The regularity of transfers and their repeated mention in medieval chronicles could create the impression that the Mughal 'bureaucracy' were unable to develop regional moorings. This impression may not be entirely true.

Familiarity with the regions seems to have been a major consideration in making appointments to these provinces. While some of the nobles posted in Panjab belonged to the suba itself, others had, through their long service in the region, acquired substantial familiarity with the region. Names such as Ghazi Beg Tarkhan, Dilawar Khan Kakar, and Khwaja Main indicate the local roots of some of the subadars.[13] The repeated appearance of certain names as appointees to various positions within our region of study suggests that, though transfers did occur often, officials either remained within the region or were transferred back frequently. This was a way of utilizing the regional experience of these officials.

Najabat Khan Mirza Shuja who was appointed as the subadar of Multan in 1638–9 had earlier held the deputy-governorship of the suba in 1630–1. Some others like Qulij Khan Turani, Said Khan Bahadur, and Lashkar Khan served as subadars of Multan for at least two tenures each.[14] In suba Lahore, however, we find fewer subadars serving a second term. The only definite instances we have are those of Princes Muhammad Azam and Muhammad Muazzam.[15] Even here they must have been represented by *naib*s acting on their behalf in the province.

The fact that familiarity with the region weighed considerably in making the appointments is also illustrated from a number of cases of intra-regional transfers. Said Khan Bahadur was subadar of Multan in 1641–2 between his two terms at Lahore. Mukarram Khan Mir Ishaq, who served as subadar of Multan during the reign of Aurangzeb had, on an earlier occasion, been the subadar of Lahore. Conversely, Qulij Khan Turani was made the subadar of Lahore in 1643–4 after he had twice held the subadari of Multan. Bahadur Khan, the subadar of Lahore in 1655–6, too, had been subadar of Multan earlier in 1648–9. Even amongst the naib-subadars, we find that Saiyid Abdul Razzaq Gilani who had been Dara Shikoh's deputy in Multan (1654–5 to 1656–7) also served in the same capacity for Dara Shikoh at Lahore in 1656–7. This, however, is more easily understandable, considering that the relationship between the subadar and his naib was such that the removal or transfer of the latter naturally followed that of the former.

Thus, despite the regular transfers of the subadars, their experience and knowledge of the regional peculiarities does not seem to have been totally lost to the Mughal administration. Nor does the system of transfers appear to have achieved, its objective of preventing officials familiar with a region from building up strong vested interests, particularly in the case of the more influential mansabdars.[16]

Though the subadar was the superior official in Lahore, it appears that the charge of its fort or *qiladari* was separate from the subadari of Lahore even if the *qiladar* functioned under the general guidance of the subadar. Information regarding the qiladari of Lahore is rather meagre, but from two definite instances it can be gathered that this position was not held by mansabdars of very high rank.[17] There was, however, the case of Amanat Khan who, perhaps, functioned simultaneously as the subadar and qiladar of Lahore during the reign of Aurangzeb.[18] Virtually all the references to the qiladari of Lahore as a separate charge pertain to the first six decades of the seventeenth century. As threats to the imperial power in the region increased due to the north-west frontier problem, and the agrarian disturbances within Panjab assumed serious dimensions, it is likely that both the subadari and qiladari of Lahore were held by a single person in the subsequent period.[19]

Friction between officials in the suba was likely to have existed both with respect to their official functions and personal relationships. Such disputes arising out of internal rivalry, in case they directly involved the subadar, were quite likely to end in the latter's favour on account of his pre-eminent position in the suba. Such disputes, however, did not seriously disrupt administrative functioning. One such instance, nevertheless, occurred in Lahore in 1679–80, when a conflict between the *kotwal* and subadar on the one hand and the *qazi* on the other, resulted in the latter being killed. Immediate action was taken by the emperor to restore order in the city.[20] It is possible that towards the latter part of the seventeenth century such instances of rivalry increased, as imperial supervision was relaxed.

Diwans and bakhshis: The position of the diwan vis-à-vis the subadar has been briefly mentioned. In the specific context of Panjab it appears that the diwans could hardly escape the influence of the governors (as in the classical framework of Mughal provincial administration), even though the importance and independence of the former's position had the backing of imperial regulations.

The mansab rank of persons appointed as diwans was considerably lower than of those appointed as subadars. Since their inequality was reflected in their emoluments and the number of troops maintained by them, the realities of a corresponding social status could hardly be wished away by making the diwan administratively independent of the subadar. Even a cursory glance at the few names we have in the list of diwans of Lahore and Multan reveals that in position and rank, the appointees to this office were rarely at par with the subadars. The three diwans, about whose ranks we have information, were mansabdars of 1,000 zat only.[21]

It seems quite likely that persons of differing capabilities were required for the two offices. The diwan, unlike the subadar, had few military functions to perform. Besides, involvement in financial administration would hardly be an occupation of interest to a man seeking power and military splendour. The repeated appointment of persons such as Bihari Mal and Rai Sabha Chand as diwans in Panjab seems to suggest that the persons appointed to the positions of subadar and diwan were usually individuals of differing capabilities.[22] On the other hand, there were persons who seem to have held the office either of diwan or *faujdar* with equal ease. Dianat Khan who was the diwan of suba Lahore during

1630–1, went in 1631–2 as the faujdar, diwan, and *amin* of Sirhind. Murshid Quli Ali Mardan Khani having served tenures as diwan in Lahore as well as in Multan, became the faujdar of Kangra in 1645–6. Amanat Khan who has already been mentioned as a qiladar and possibly subadar of suba Lahore is believed to have functioned as a diwan of the province as well. In suba Multan, Shaikh Moosvi Gilani the diwan and bakhshi in 1651–2, was later in 1656–7 appointed as the naib-subadar of Dara Shikoh in the same province.[23]

Once again it can be noticed that despite the repeated transfers of these officials they were often reappointed to positions within Panjab, at times exchanging positions with one another. This holds true not only with regard to subadars and diwans, but also for the other subordinate officials. Among the few persons we know as having definitely held the positions of bakhshi of the two subas constituting Panjab, we find the familiar names of Shaikh Moosvi Gilani and Murshid Quli. Muhammad Shafi served as bakhshi during the reign of Jahangir first in suba Lahore and then in suba Multan.

(ii) *Local administration*: At the local level the jurisdiction and functions of the officials do not appear to have been very clear cut. As in the case of the suba headquarters, so, too, at local levels there was a separation of fiscal and administrative functions. But in the case of the local government not only was there a division of functions, there was also a difference in the area that was under the jurisdiction of officials performing these two functions.

For fiscal purposes, the subdivisions of the suba were sarkars, followed by parganas or mahals. The mahal normally consisted of a number of villages often termed mauzas.[24] The diwan of the sarkar was responsible for its land revenue administration and was aided by a number of officials both at the sarkar and pargana levels.

At the pargana level the land revenue administration was headed by the *amil* or *amalguzar* who had to ensure that cultivable land was increasingly brought under regular cultivation and the assessed revenues collected. He, with other officials, was responsible for the local treasury and in charge of payments made to quasi-government officials like *chaudharis*, *muqaddams*, *qanungos*, etc. Regular records were to be maintained by him. Though there is known to have been an *amin* earlier at the *suba* level, in the reign of Shahjahan an *amin* was appointed to every mahal and charged with the responsibility of assessing the revenue demand (*jama*). The *karori* was made responsible for collecting the revenue, maintaining revenue records and sending them to the revenue department. He was one of the officials connected with the local treasury. Among the subordinate officials of the pargana was the *karkun* who maintained an independent record of land measurements (apart from the *patwari*) and also registered daily receipts. Though the pargana treasury was controlled by a number of local officials in order to prevent the misappropriation of money, it was the *khizanadar* or *fotadar* who was most actively engaged in managing it.

There were also quasi-government officials like the *chaudhari* and *qanungo* who were local residents and whose position was normally hereditary. They were actively engaged in revenue administration at the lower level.[25]

The hierarchy, designations, and functions of these subordinate officials in the pargana did not remain the same throughout the seventeenth century. We have already mentioned the setting up of an amin in every mahal and this was later followed by the combining of mahals to create a *chakla* administered by an *amin-faujdar*.[26] Moreover, despite the creation of this well organised hierarchy of officials and the clear allotment of functions, revenue administration does not appear to have always followed this pattern. In numerous instances officials were appointed to territories irrespective of the formal pargana, sarkar, and even suba boundaries. The mention of certain officials as diwan, amin and faujdar of a region encompassing areas not only from different sarkars, but also from different subas, is evidence of the flexibility that the system permitted.

Faujdars: From the point of view of general administration, though the sarkars in Panjab were extensive doabs lying between the rivers, it is difficult at present to say whether each doab of Panjab (meaning thereby the sarkar) was under the administrative charge of one official. Most of our information pertains to the appointment of faujdars who were not necessarily the administrative heads of sarkars.[27] Amidst this confusion regarding the position of the faujdar, P. Saran argues that 'there were two classes of posts to which faujdars had been appointed as far back as the reign of Sher Shah. Firstly, as regular heads of districts or sarkars and secondly on special duty, either in cases of emergency or for purposes of military defence of forts and frontier outposts'.[28]

Regarding the functions of the *faujdar*, Abul Fazl notes that he should assist in the collection of revenue from disaffected and rebellious assessees or collectors if the need so arise, and also suppress and root out recalcitrant elements from his jurisdiction. The nature of his job entailed, therefore, the proper maintenance of his troops which constituted the local militia.[29] These general functions mentioned by Abul Fazl should, nevertheless, be seen in the context of the two categories of faujdars mentioned by P. Saran. This suggests that there did exist some functional differences between the two. Both categories of faujdars appear to have existed in Panjab as well.

Among the faujdars of Panjab more frequently mentioned in our sources are those given the charge of strategic forts and frontier areas. In suba Lahore the faujdari of Kangra appears to have been of particular significance.[30] The importance that was attached by the Mughals to the fort of Kangra and its environs emerges from the fact that some of the faujdars were close relatives of the subadars of Lahore, a way of ensuring that the cooperation of the subadar would be readily available to the faujdar of Kangra should such a contingency arise.[31] The simultaneous appointment of relatives to these positions was not coincidental, because the removal of the faujdar of Kangra in such cases coincided with the transfer of the related subadar of Lahore.[32]

It is possible that this association of some faujdars with the Lahore subadar resulted in the former being entrusted with the administration of a larger area. Khanazad Khan and Mir Khan (who held faujdaris at the same time as their fathers were subadars of Lahore) were appointed faujdars of both Kangra and Jammu. The former was appointed in 1640–1 and the latter immediately after the war of succession.[33] On account of the geographical proximity of Kangra and Jammu it is likely that these areas were occasionally administered by one person in the subsequent period. The largest mansab held by a faujdar of Kangra–Jammu was, probably, that of 3,500/3,000 held by Mir Khan. Surmising from the limited information regarding the faujdars of Kangra, it appears that few of them were less than 2,000 zat, with some of them even being 3,000 zat.[34] The faujdars who were, however, in charge of merely the faujdari of Jammu did not rank so high in the mansabdari hierarchy, and appear to have even been mansabdars of 1,500 or 1,000 zat.[35]

Since the faujdaris of Kangra and Jammu were of strategic importance to the Mughal Empire, it is likely that mansabdars appointed to them were provided with increased support. This was done by granting conditional (*mashrut*) mansabs meaning thereby an increased *mansab* which was to be held for the duration of the official's appointment as faujdar.[36] Contemporary chronicles do not always say much about the regular mansabs of appointees to faujdaris, much less about the details of their conditional mansabs. There is the instance of Mukarram Khan, the subadar of Lahore who held a mashrut rank of 300 sawar on account of his additional charge of the faujdari of Jammu. This conditional rank was withdrawn when the faujdari was transferred from his charge.[37] A document from the reign of Aurangzeb provides the example of Munim Khan, the faujdar of Jammu and naib-subadar of Lahore (1706–7) having a mansab of 1,500/1,000 of which 500/600 were conditional or mashrut.[38]

Kangra was among the few faujdaris in Panjab where apart from the faujdar, specific mention is made to the appointment of a qiladar for the fort of Kangra.[39] This assumes greater significance when, upon closer scrutiny, his mansab ranking emerges higher than that of the qiladar of Lahore.[40] This can be explained by the fact that the presence of the subadar at Lahore enabled the qiladar to draw upon the garrison already stationed in the fort if the need arose. The qiladar of Kangra, on the other hand, on account of his distance from the suba headquarters, had to be virtually self-reliant. At least initially he would have had to defend the fort only with the local force at his command.

Once again among the faujdars of Kangra are to be found names of officials who held charge of other positions within Panjab at different points of time. Najabat Khan who was faujdar of Kangra on two occasions (1630–1 to 1634–5 and in 1642–3) had earlier been naib-subadar of Multan in 1630–1 and full-fledged subadar of that province from 1638–9 to 1640–1. Similarly, Murshid Quli Ali Mardan Khani, faujdar in 1645–6 had previously served as the diwan of suba Lahore (1639–40) and suba Multan (1640–1).[41] There were others who belonged to the Kangra region itself, such as Raja Suraj Mal, Rajrup and Mandhata.

The faujdari of Attock was somewhat similar to that of Kangra due to its military and political significance.[42] Most of the other faujdaris of suba Lahore (belonging by and large to the second category, i.e. those created mainly for ensuring that recalcitrant assessees were made to pay revenue and that law and order was maintained) find only passing mention, in contemporary records. Mung, Rasulpur, and the area between Jandala and Lahore[43] and also those of Bhera and Khushab, Nurmahal and Sultanpur were among such faujdaris.[44] However, there were some other faujdaris to which more frequent references are made in our sources, these being Sialkot, Gujrat, Eminabad, Jalandhar and Sirhind. These latter faujdaris were among the more important ones of the region. Jalandhar was important because it opened to the hill areas and was among the most fertile parts of Panjab. Sirhind, apart from being commercially important functioned as a gateway to the Mughal capital.

At times these areas were held as separate faujdari charges by different appointees while at others two areas were merged and entrusted to one faujdar. Yusuf Chelah, the faujdar of Eminabad in 1655–6 and appointed to Sialkot in the same year, held these faujdaris as separate charges. So was the case with Mir Ahmad Khan at Eminabad during Aurangzeb's reign and Ganga Dhar, faujdar at Sialkot till 1653–4.[45] Yusuf Chelah was in both instances noted as being appointed to the faujdari and amini of his charge.[46] With the handing over of both these functions to one official during the reign of Shahjahan it can be suggested that many subsequent appointments to the faujdari, were likely to have required the appointee to function as the amin as well.

As against cases such as those of Yusuf Chelah, Iradat Khan (Azam Khan Mir Muhammad Baqir) was made the faujdar of Sialkot and Gujrat during the reign of Jahangir.[47] Firoz Rustam Khan, a mansabdar during Aurangzeb's reign, was entrusted with the faujdari of the Chenab-Ravi doab.[48] Another dual charge of a different nature was that of Rai Sabha Chand, the diwan of Panjab, who was also appointed simultaneously the faujdar of Sialkot.[49] Similarly, even the faujdari of Jalandhar while sometimes held as a separate and single charge was on occasion combined with some other faujdari, more often that of Sirhind.

While Kangra represents a typically military faujdari, the faujdari of Sirhind was of a very different nature. The faujdars appointed to Sirhind were persons more familiar with revenue administration than with military work. Rai Kashi Das, Dianat Khan and Todar Mal Afzal Khani, were among the persons we know as having been in charge of Sirhind. Most of the area under the jurisdiction of the faujdari was probably constituted by zamindaris which paid in the land revenue regularly and hence required the faujdar in charge to maintain only a minimal military force. The mansab rank of the faujdars of Sirhind was possibly for this reason lower than the mansabs held by many other faujdars.[50] The designation given the officials in charge of Sirhind was often that of diwan, *amin* and *faujdar*.[51] The first two charges were primarily concerned with the assessment and collection of revenue. As the faujdari part of the duties in Sirhind were not very important, it could be suggested that during the first half of the seventeenth century, the sawar rank of the faujdars of Sirhind was not very high, in instances where they were in charge of Sirhind alone.[52]

Todar Mal Afzal Khani appears to have been the most prominent mansabdar of Sirhind. Starting as diwan, amin, and faujdar of Sirhind in 1639–40, he was in 1640–1 also given the faujdari of Lakhi Jangal. Later (1647–8) we learn that he was the diwan, amin, and faujdar of Sirhind, Dipalpur, Jalandhar and Sultanpur. As late as 1659 he was still the faujdar of Sirhind, if not of the whole area.[53] From this it becomes apparent that Todar Mal's jurisdiction included territories not only from different sarkars, such as Sirhind, Bet Jalandhar, and Dipalpur but also from three subas, viz., Delhi, Lahore, and Multan. This, probably, was an exceptional case, but it does reveal the flexible character of the faujdari jurisdiction. The functional flexibility of the faujdari is evident in the appointment of the faujdar of Sirhind to the simultaneous charge of Dipalpur and Lakhi Jangal (and perhaps Jalandhar) which created a military responsibility in addition to the financial and revenue work that constituted his main function at Sirhind.[54] However, the primary reason for giving Todar Mal control over such a large area seems to have been his success in extending agriculture and populating the *khalisa* lands of the region.[55] It is, therefore, likely that his main concerns were revenue and finance, other imperial officials providing military support in areas where it was required. This was probably why his mansab rank, though the highest among faujdars of Sirhind, was not really commensurate with the vast area placed under his charge. This disparity suggests that his control over the area was not like that of a faujdar over his faujdari but more like that of a diwan or amin over the revenue administration.[56] Paucity of information, however, prevents us from drawing any definite conclusion.

Hisar-Firoza (in suba Delhi) seems to have formed a separate faujdari in south-eastern Panjab. Though it was regarded as the jagir of heir-apparents to the Mughal empire, we have virtually no information about its faujdars.[57]

Southwards, in the parts of Panjab which lay within the *suba* of Multan, the most important faujdari was that of Lakhi Jangal.[58] Though it contained some well-settled agricultural areas, turbulent tribal elements were also to be found within its jurisdiction. Their suppression was an important duty of the faujdar of the region, and mansabdars appointed to it were, probably, men of considerable military experience. Concluding from the limited information available, it seems that the highest ranking mansabdar to hold the faujdari of Lakhi Jangal was Prince Muhammad Muizzuddin (10,000 zat), the son of Prince Muhammad Muazzam, towards the latter part of Aurangzeb's reign. The highest mansab held by a noble as faujdar of Dipalpur-Lakhi Jangal was, probably, that of 4,000/4,000 by Mubariz Khan Rohilla in 1644–5.[59] On the other hand, the lowest ranking mansabdar to be appointed as faujdar of Lakhi Jangal was Todar Mal Afzal Khani with a rank of 1,000 zat, though he had a sawar holding of 1,000 (× 2 – 3 h) in 1642–3. In 1647–8, however, his mansab was increased to 2,000/2,000. Nevertheless, even this does not place him among the higher ranking faujdars of Lakhi Jangal.[60] Towards the end of the seventeenth century this faujdari assumed greater importance due to the tribal unrest it witnessed. The subsequent appointment of Prince Muhammad Muizzuddin as faujdar testifies to the significance that Aurangzeb attached to it.

Though Lakhi Jangal seems most commonly to have been held by faujdars as a separate charge, the exception of Todar Mal who held it together with Sirhind, Jalandhar, and Sultanpur has already been noted. Two similar exceptions are the cases of Sardar Khan who was the faujdar of both Lakhi Jangal and Tihara in 1634–5, and Khawwas Khan who succeeded him to this dual charge in the same year and, probably, held it till 1640–1. The jurisdiction of the faujdari in the last two cases included territory from suba Multan as well as suba Delhi.[61] Once again the flexibility of faujdari jurisdictions becomes evident.

The other important faujdari of suba Multan was that of Bhakkar. This area, though not strictly part of the area of my concern seems to have been administratively integrated with the region under study.[62]

The faujdars, therefore, appear to have been the most powerful local authority after the governor and the diwan. Besides military and political power, they sometimes had a measure of control over revenue matters. There also existed a fair degree of flexibility in the creation of faujdaris and the kind of functions they performed. In fact, the personal influence of the mansabdar concerned may have much to do with the manner in which faujdaris were reorganised.[63]

REVENUE ADMINISTRATION

The fiscal divisions and the official machinery involved in the assessment and collection of land revenue has already been briefly mentioned. There is hardly any information in our sources regarding the functioning of these officials with specific reference to Panjab. Most of the available information suggests that the revenue system of Panjab was quite similar to that which prevailed in other parts of the Mughal empire. Though variations existed in different regions of the empire, there is little to suggest that any such peculiarities existed in Panjab.

There was one fiscal division which had less to do with revenue administration and more with the rationality of calculating the jama of different places. This was the *dastur*-circle which is perhaps of significance from the point of view of studying the economy of the region. The importance of the *dastur*-circle derived from the fact that it was the largest division where uniformity in the asessed revenue demand was to be found. While on the one hand the mauza and mahal were rather small in extent to enable us to discern a pattern in the existing revenue divisions, the sarkar was too large, it was the dastur-circle (though not a part of the provincial sub-divisions) which lay somewhere in between and revealed far more. Fundamental to the nature of the dastur-circle was the fact that it consisted of a group of mahals which had the same revenue-rate (dastur). This was a reflection of a similarity of agricultural conditions in the area that constituted the circle.[64]

The Ain-i-Akbari gives us the details of the dastur divisions. Certain interesting features emerge from these. In the suba of Lahore, most of the mahals assessed for revenue were to be found in the north-west. The broad uniformity in the agricultural conditions of this part of Panjab becomes evident from the fact that the whole of it was divided into only eight dastur-circles.[65] Furthermore, each of these circles included a large number of mahals and was fairly large in terms of geographical extent.[66] For the Indo-Gangetic Divide, however, the picture was somewhat different. This area which lay in suba Delhi consisted of ten dastur-circles which were generally smaller than those of suba Lahore and were constituted by a fewer number of mahals.[67] The two sarkars of

Hisar-Firoza and Sirhind alone were divided into eight circles, thereby revealing the diversity of agricultural conditions. As a result, while some of these dastur-circles may have witnessed agricultural practices similar to those of the northern parts of *suba* Lahore, in others the conditions were, probably, very different. We have little information regarding the dastur-circles in the suba of Multan. The *Ain-i-Akbari* mentions only the dastur-circle of Dipalpur.[68]

Interestingly, in the normal revenue organisation there was no official machinery which conformed to the dastur-circle whether for assessment or for collection, even though the entire circle had a common revenue-rate. To add to its peculiarity this revenue division often transgressed not only sarkar but even suba boundaries. This can be gleaned from an examination of the mahals included in the list of dastur-circles provided by Abul Fazl. The dastur-circle of Patti Haibatput, for instance, included mahals from the subas of Lahore and Multan.[69] Moreover, while sarkar boundaries followed the rivers a single dastur-circle could include mahals which lay on either side of the rivers. This feature is true of all the riverine tracts of suba Lahore, irrespective of the sarkars within which they lay.[70] The dastur-circle, therefore, apart from being an area of common revenue assessment was also a recognition of the actual agrarian conditions which existed in different parts of the region.

The question of land revenue assessment need not be examined in detail as earlier researchers have dealt with it at length.[71] The general emphasis was on the assessment of revenue by measurement of the area. Large parts of Panjab which lay in the subas of Lahore and Delhi are, therefore, believed to have been measured and assessed. It has been suggested that for the suba of Lahore the measured area mentioned in the statistics of Aurangzeb's reign when compared with that in the *Ain-i-Akbari* is practically the same and that by the time of Aurangzeb, 'nine-tenths of the villages are shown to have been measured'.[72] For the part of Panjab which lay in suba Delhi, a similar comparison reveals an increase of one-third over that of the *Ain-i-Akbari*. In the suba of Multan, however, it was only the sarkar of Dipalpur which was thus measured.[73]

The collection of revenue was entrusted to a hierarchy of local officials. The manner in which the land revenue was assessed and the demand thereafter expressed in cash makes it apparent that money played a fundamental role in the economy of Mughal India. The fact that land revenue, the primary source of income for the Mughal state, was collected in cash is an indication of the, extent to which the cash-nexus had been established. The state's responsiveness to fluctuations, in the money economy, was remarkable. The level of prices determined the value of the peasant's crop and consequently the amount of surplus he would have with him to pay his dues in cash. Though the revenue demand was made to him prior to the produce being brought to the market, his real ability to meet the demand depended upon the value of his crop in the market. Abul Fazl informs us that on several occasions the emperor had to remit a portion of the revenue demand in some areas as the abundance of grain had caused a fall in prices.[74] The converse could also be true, resulting therefore, in an increase in government demand.[75]

One of the factors which influenced the level of prices in an area was the presence of the Mughal court, attended by innumerable nobles and their hordes of retainers and hangers-on, apart from the considerable military garrison which was constantly with the emperor. The Mughal court comprised, in fact, a large shifting population which provided a large market for grains. It was for this reason, perhaps, that during Akbar's reign while revenue concessions were made in many parts of the empire such as the subas of Oudh, Delhi, Allahabad, and Agra or at least in some of their sarkars, there is little reference to such concessions being made in suba Lahore.[76]

It is possible that on certain occasions, the emperor remitted a part of the revenue even in the case of suba Lahore, but most of the references in our sources to such remissions pertain to the years when the court happened to be located in Lahore. This resulted in higher grain prices in the city and the need for giving this concession there did not arise.[77] To the contrary, it occasioned an increase of revenue demand in the suba.[78]

The areas from which revenue was appropriated by the state were divided into broad heads: jagir, khalisa, and *paibaqi*. The ratio of these categories of land varied from time to time.[79] The jagirdars did not, however, employ as many people for revenue collection as were employed in the khalisa lands.[80] This often encouraged the practice of revenue farming (*ijara*) which could have permitted a greater oppression of the peasantry.[81]

A smaller portion of the land revenue came under the head of revenue grants.[82] According to Abul Fazl these were granted to, 'inquirers after wisdom', to those who 'practise self denial', and 'have renounced the society of men'; to the 'weak and poor...' and to 'honourable men ... unable to provide for themselves by taking up a trade'.[83] Numerous such grants were, probably, made in Panjab especially to support the large number of religious men who had made many of the region's towns their homes; towns such as Sirhind and Pakpattan.[84] The separate column under the head of *suyurghal* in the revenue statistics of the *Ain-i-Akbari* denotes the amount of revenue that was set aside for grants of this nature.[85] The grantees were not necessarily given these grants in their places of residence and it appears that certain areas were set aside from which grants of this nature were made.[86] This explains why certain mahals had a very large portion of their total revenues mentioned under suyurghal.[87] Compared to many of the other subas of the empire, the amount given up to suyurghal in suba Lahore was far less.[88] Considering their insignificant holdings the possessors of these revenue grants could hardly have had any remarkable impact upon the functioning of the land revenue system.

The system was regulated by means of well understood principles which were basic to its proper functioning. Governmental revenue demand was assessed according to established methods and not left to the whims and fancies of the local officials. Similarly the collection of revenue was, in theory, confined to the appropriation of the assessed demand and anything in excess was considered illegal.[89] Officials involved in revenue administration were specifically exhorted to encourage the extension of area under cultivation so as to increase the revenue of the state.[90] The state in some cases even took positive steps to aid the peasant in bringing new land under cultivation, by advancing (*taqavi*) loans for purposes of seeds and cattle.[91] The peasant on his part was expected to cultivate all the land he had been assessed for, and to pay his dues regularly. Once his dues were paid his right to cultivate the land was assured and his position secure. His claim to till the land was so strong that he could even reassert it after a gap of some years.[92] The zamindars for fear of losing their tenants refrained from oppressing them to a point where they would abandon their land. Though this fear acted as a restraining factor upon the zamindars and the official revenue collectors, in the event of the peasants fleeing their lands the law was heavily against the latter. The imperial regulations demanded that peasants who had abandoned their lands were not to be sheltered by anyone.[93] Under normal circumstances, however, the seventeenth century was a period of surplus land and shortage of cultivators, thereby placing the peasant in a far better position than was to be the case later.

The maintenance of an effective revenue machinery contributed immensely to the stability and integrity of the colossal Mughal empire. Though formal rules and regulations went a long way in its establishment and growth, the norms and conventions that emerged with the passage of time were equally significant.

NOTES

1. Muzaffar Alam, *The Crisis of Empire in Mughal North India*, p. 11. The relationship and balance between these three power centres (being complementary and contradictory at different points of time) forms an important part of his argument.

2. A similar argument has already been forwarded by Frank Perlin, 'Proto-Industrialization and Pre-Colonial South Asia', p. 33.

3. An authoritative work on this subject is, P. Saran, *The Provincial Government of the Mughals, 1526–1658*, Allahabad, 1941.

4. By way of comparison of the considerable difference in their status we can mention Dianat Khan, who was the diwan of Lahore in 1630–1 with a *mansab* of 1,000/250, at the same time that Wazir Khan was *subadar* of Lahore with a mansab of 5,000/5,000 (3,000 × 3– h); (2,000 × 1–3h). It is difficult to envisage that Dianat Khan would be in a position to do very much that was contrary to the wishes of Wazir Khan. Refer Muhammad Salih Kamboh, *Amal-i-Salih*, Ghulam Yazdani (ed.), Calcutta, 1912–46, (4 vols), see vol. II, pp. 11, 309; Samsam-ud-Daula Shah Nawaz Khan, *The Maathir-ul-Umara, being biographies of the Muhammadan and Hindu officers of the Timurid sovereigns of India from 1500 to 1780, A.D.*, H. Beveridge (tr.), revised annotated and completed by Baini Prashad, Calcutta, vol. I, 1911–41 and vol. II, 1952. See vol. I, pp. 484, 982; P. Saran, op. cit., p. 168. He adds that the nature of the two positions being different, people of 'different capacities' were appointed to them, 'very rarely a *diwan* was appointed *subadar* or vice-versa'.

5. P. Saran, op. cit., p. 344.

6. For the movements of Khusrau in Panjab and the subsequent campaign to suppress his rebellion, see Beni Prasad, *History of Jahangir*, Allahabad, 1973, pp. 128–35. Regarding the marches of Dara in this area as well as Sindh during the war of succession see Jadunath Sarkar, *History of Aurangzeb*, Calcutta, 1973 (first published in 1912), (5 vols.), see vol. II, pp. 275, 284.

7. Refer Table II-A (i) and Table II-A (ii). [In *Region and Empire: Panjab in the Seventeenth Century*, Oxford University Press, New Delhi, 1991.—Ed.]

8. Said Khan Bahadur, who was *subadar* Lahore front 1640–1 to 1641–2, was appointed *subadar* Multan in 1642–3 for one year, before being reappointed once again to Lahore. Mukarram Khan who served as *subadar* Lahore from 1683–4 to 1686 went at a later date to Multan. Refer attached tables: II-A(i) and II-A(ii). [In *Region and Empire: Panjab in the Seventeenth Century*, Oxford University Press, New Delhi, 1991.—Ed.]

9. Jadunath Sarkar, *History of Aurangzeb*, I, p. 63.

10. Information about the positions and ranks of the governors is drawn from the existing limited source material. It is quite likely that a later *subadar* held a larger *mansab* considering the fact that throughout the seventeenth century the size of *mansab*s held by nobles was constantly increasing.

11. The sources from which all these details have been obtained are mentioned in Table II-A (i) and II-A (ii). [In *Region and Empire: Panjab in the Seventeenth Century*, Oxford University Press, New Delhi, 1991.—Ed.]

12. Abul Fazl draws an interesting analogy when he writes, 'It is not hidden from the hearts of the far-seeing and the clear-sighted that the spiritual garland-twiners of sovereignty (i.e., kings) resemble gardeners. As gardeners adorn gardens with trees and move them from one place to another, and reject many, and irrigate others, and labour to rear them to a proper size, and extirpate bad trees and lop off evil branches, and remove trees that are too large, and graft some upon others, and gather their various fruits and flowers and enjoy their shade when necessary, and do other things which are established in the science of horticulture...' This Abul Fazl writes in the context of the removal of the Atka Khail from *suba* Lahore by Akbar. *Akbarnama*, II, pp. 486–7.

13. Ghazi Beg Tarkhan was *subadar* Multan in the beginning of Jahangir's reign. Dilawar Khan Kakar and Khwaja Main were *subadar*s of Lahore in 1605–6 and 1655–7, respectively. See Table II-A(i), II-A(ii). [In *Region and Empire: Panjab in the Seventeenth Century*, Oxford University Press, New Delhi, 1991.—Ed.]

14. Qulij Khan Turani was *subadar* Multan from 1631–2 to 1637–8 and from 1640–1 to 1641–2. Said Khan Bahadur was there from 1641–2 to 1642–3 and from 1645–6 to 1647–8. Lashkar Khan served as *subadar* here, once in 1658 and the second time from 1668–9 to 1670–1, Table II-A(ii). [In *Region and Empire: Panjab in the Seventeenth Century*, Oxford University Press, New Delhi, 1991.—Ed.]

15. Prince Muhammad Azam was appointed subadar Lahore in 1680 for the first time and for his second tenure served from 1689–90 to 1691. During his second tenure Lutfullah was the naib. Prince Muhammad Muazzam was appointed to the subadari in 1700 and once again in 1705. Munim Khan acted as his *naib* during his second appointment, Table II-A(i). [In *Region and*

Empire: Panjab in the Seventeenth Century, Oxford University Press, New Delhi, 1991.—Ed.]

16. See Chetan Singh, 'Centre and Periphery in the Mughal State: The Case of Seventeenth-Century Panjab', *Modern Asian Studies*, Vol. 22, No. 2 (1988), pp. 299–318.

17. Yusuf Aqa the qiladar in 1658–9 was a mansabdar of 1,000/400, and Amanullah Khan who probably succeeded him held a mansab of 1,000/200. See Table II-D(i). [In *Region and Empire: Panjab in the Seventeenth Century*, Oxford University Press, New Delhi, 1991.—Ed.]

18. Amanat Khan was appointed to this charge at a time when Aurangzeb was present in Panjab. This may explain why his mansab stood only at 1,000/200. It is also possible that Amanat Khan was never a full-fledged subadar at all, due to the emperor's presence in that *suba* for that period.

19. For unrest in the north-west of Panjab and regarding developments in Panjab proper, Sarkar makes some observations. See Jadunath Sarkar, *History of Aurangzeb*, Vol. III, pp. 142–60, 199–211.

20. The subadar, Qawamuddin Khan, was summoned to court and Prince Muhammad Azam was appointed in his place. Lutfullah acted there as Azam's naib. The kotwal, however, was more severely treated and was executed in Lahore. See Saqi Musta'd Khan, *Ma'asir-i-Alamgiri*, Jadunath Sarkar (tr.), Calcutta, 1947, p. 116.

21. Dianat Khan, diwan of Lahore in 1630–1 was a mansabdar of 1,000/250. Amanat Khan, diwan of Lahore during the late 1670s was a mansabdar of 1,000/200, and Shaikh Moosvi Gilani, the diwan and bakhshi of Multan in 1651–2 was still a mansabdar of 1,000/400 as late as 1656–7.

22. Rai Sabha Chand was the diwan of suba Lahore on two occasions, once in 1638–9 and for the second time in 1653–4. Bihari Mal served one term as diwan of Lahore in the late 1630s and a second term in the same capacity in Multan in 1638–9. *Amal-i-Salih*, II, p. 304; and III, p. 203.

23. Shaikh Moosvi Gilani is the only instance we have of a person functioning as both diwan and bakhshi. The normal appointment as bakhshi of a suba entailed an additional charge as *waqai-nawis*. See Table II-C(i) and II-C(ii). [In *Region and Empire: Panjab in the Seventeenth Century*, Oxford University Press, New Delhi, 1991.—Ed.]

24. See *Ain-i-Akbari*, Vol. II, pp. 298–301; 320–8, 331–5, where the divisions of the sarkar and mahals are recorded. The divisions continued till much later as we notice in the *Chahar Gulshan, in India of Aurangzeb*, Jadunath Sarkar, (tr.), Calcutta, 1901, pp. 125–30; N.A. Siddiqi, *Land Revenue Administration under the Mughals*, New York, 1970, p. 76. Though the terms pargana and mahal are used interchangeably, Siddiqi has clarified that 'whereas

the *parganas* denoted a fiscal-cum-territorial unit comprising a number of villages, the mahals in a more special sense signified a purely fiscal unit'.

25. See *Ain-i-Akbari*, II, pp. 46–53; N.A. Siddiqi, *Land Revenue Administration*, pp. 76–91.

26. Irfan Habib, *Agrarian System*, p. 277. An earlier experiment had been attempted during the reign of Akbar with the introduction of the karori system.

27. U.N. Day, *Mughal Government*, New Delhi, 1970, p. 80, regards the faujdar as the executive head of the sarkar; N.A. Siddiqi, op. cit., p. 76, however, says that the faujdari was a separate unit under the faujdar and quite distinct from the other divisions. The faujdari, according to him, could comprise a pargana and at times even a sarkar.

28. P. Saran, *Provincial Government*, p. 89. It must be mentioned that though this study may hold true for some other regions of the Mughal empire, in Panjab, apart from faujdars being in charge of either forts and frontiers or sarkars there were others who did not fall in any of these categories.

29. *Ain-i-Akbari*, II, pp. 41–2. Regarding the faujdari he writes that the Emperor 'apportions several parganahs to the care of one of his trusty, just and disinterested servants appreciative of what is equitable and faithfull to his engagements, and him they style by the above name'. (i.e. faujdar)

30. Kangra was also known and referred to by names as Kohistan-i-Shumali Panjab and Kohistan-i-Kangra. The faujdari of Kangra, hence, is also mentioned as faujdari-i-Koh Daman or faujdari-i-Daman-i Koh Kangra. Such references are scattered all over contemporary and later works, for example Kamgar Husaini, *Ma'asir-i-Jahangiri*, Azra Alavi (ed.), Bombay, 1978, p. 340; *Amal-i-Salih*, II, pp. 6, 209, 378, 425, 458; *Alamgimama*, I, p. 217; *MU* II, pp. 81, 365, 575, 778.

31. Khanazad Khan, the faujdar in 1640–1, was the son of Said Khan the subadar of Lahore in 1640–3 (with a break in between as subadar Multan). Khanjar Khan, faujdar in 1644–5 was a nephew of Qulij Khan, subadar Panjab in 1643–6. Mir Khan, faujdar after the 1658 war of succession was the son Khalilullah Khan, the subadar of Lahore at this time.

32. Both Khanazad Khan and Said Khan were removed from their respective offices in 1642–3. The same seems to have happened with Khanjar Khan and Qulij Khan in 1645–6. In fact, it is specifically mentioned in the *Amal-i-Salih*, II, p. 425, that because Qulij Khan was the subadar of Panjab, Khanjar Khan was appointed to the faujdari of Kangra.

33. See Table II-E (i) and II-E (ii). [In *Region and Empire: Panjab in the Seventeenth Century*, Oxford University Press, New Delhi, 1991.—Ed.] On the other hand we also know of Iraj Khan who as faujdar in 1649–50 held this dual charge at a time when suba Lahore was with Dara Shikoh.

34. Refer Table II-E (i). [In *Region and Empire: Panjab in the Seventeenth Century*, Oxford University Press, New Delhi, 1991.—Ed.] Though Najabat Khan possibly, held a higher *mansab* in 1642–3 on account of his having been subadar of Multan earlier in 1638–9 with 4,000/4,000, there is no definite mention that he was appointed to Kangra with the same *mansab*.

35. See Table II-E (ii) [In *Region and Empire: Panjab in the Seventeenth Century*, Oxford University Press, New Delhi, 1991.—Ed.], The cases of those with higher mansabs are those of Qawamuddin Khan, the *subadar* of Lahore from 1678–9to 1680–1 who was also made the faujdar of Jammu, and Mukarram Khan subadar of Lahore in 1695 who was also faujdar of Jammu for some time.

36. See Athar Ali, *Mughal Nobility under Aurangzeb*, pp. 41–2. When the mansabdar was no longer in charge of a post requiring a mashrut mansab, he was reverted to the original *mansab* he had held prior to this appointment to that post.

37. *Akhbarat* (Sitamau transcripts), Aurangzeb, 38th Regnal year 23rd Shawwal corresponding to 27 May 1695, p. 467.

38. Ibid.., 51 Regnal year, Sha'aban, p. 175. Munim Khan also being the *diwan* of Prince Muhammad Muazzam held a *mashrut* rank of 100 *sawar* on that account. That much of his conditional rank was because of the *faujdari* of Jammu, becomes clear from the statement in this document that in January, 1707, '500/ 100 out of his conditional *mansab* for the *faujdari* of Jammu were made unconditional'. We see that the entire increase in the *zat* is derived from his holding the office of *faujdar*.

39. Quite possibly, many of the forts of the other *faujdari*s had regularly appointed qiladars. The qiladar of Kangra fort is mentioned more often due to the prominence of the fort and the importance attached to its capture during the reign of Jahangir. Another place where reference is made to the appointment of a qiladar is Attock, which was a kind of frontier post for the Mughals and a strict vigilance was kept on the river-crossing.

40. Yusuf Aqa, qiladar of Lahore in 1650–1 was a mansabdar of 1,000/400 and Amanullah Khan qiladar of Lahore in 1658–9 held l,000/200. The qiladars of Kangra held mansabs as follows:

Alf KhanQiyamkhani	1620–1	1,500/1,000
Safi Khan	1656–7	2,000/1,000
Raja Mandhata	1670–1	1,000/1,000

41. Compare attached tables.

42. For purposes of levying taxes on imports and exports, however, Attock was of some importance. *Akhbarat,* Aurangzeb, 38th R.Y., 17th Jammadial-Awwal, p. 361.

41. *Akbarnama,* III, p. 921. These appointments appear to be new and we are told that faujdars at these places had been appointed in order to control the zamindars. The latter were, perhaps, not paying revenue regularly.

44. During the war of succession (1658) we learn that Khanjar Khan was the *faujdar* of Khushab and Bhera. *Alamgirnama,* I, p. 198; *Khulasat,* p. 513. During the reign of Aurangzeb, Misri Afghan with a *mansab* of 1,500/1,000 is mentioned as the *faujdar* of Sultanpur. We learn about the *faujdari* of Nur Mahal on account of the appointment of Iradat Khan (Mir Hidayatullah) as *faujdar* in the reign of Bahadur Shah. *MU,* I, p. 684.

45. See Table II-E(iv) and II-E(v). [In *Region and Empire, Panjab in the Seventeenth Century,* Oxford University Press, New Delhi, 1991.—Ed.].

46. These references being derived from the *Amal-i-Salih* (see Table II-E (iv) in *Region and Empire: Panjab in the Seventeenth Century,* Oxford University Press, New Delhi, 1991.—Ed.) it seems that this combination of functions pertains to the creation of the new position of *amin-o-faujdar* during the reign of Shahjahan.

47. *MU,* I, p. 315; Bhakkari. *Dhakhirat,* II, p. 200. Sialkot and Gujrat are located on opposite banks of the river Chenab. They were parts of two different sarkars.

48. *Alamgimama,* II, p. 219. This appears to have been a very large area including both Sialkot and Eminabad, which arc also mentioned in some cases as been separate faujdaris. In this case, however, they seem to have been combined in order to constitute one faujdari. The jurisdiction of this faujdari may have coincided with the sarkar.

49. *Amal-i-Salih,* III, p. 203. The combining of some of these charges may also be seen in the light of the fact that their revenue was probably allocated for the maintenance of the Kabul soldiery. This was the case at least in the early years of Bahadur Shah's reign. Refer *Akhbarat* (Sitamau Transcripts), Bahadur Shah, 5th R.Y., Vol. II, pp. 399, 439–40. 459.

50. Compare Tables II-E(i) to II-E(ix).[In *Region and Empire: Panjab in the Seventeenth Century,* Oxford University Press, New Delhi, 1991.—Ed.].

51. There were also some other designations. Abdul Karim is mentioned having been the *thanadar* and *mutassadi* of Sirhind and at a later date Abdul Nabi is referred to as the *nazim.* See Table II-E(vii). [In *Region and Empire: Panjab in the Seventeenth Century,* Oxford University Press, New Delhi, 1991.—Ed.]

52. Dianat Khan at Sirhind in 1631–2 was a mansabdar of 1,000/400. Todar Mal Afzal Khani seems to have been the only faujdar of Sirhind having more than 1,500 sawar, and this was due to the large area he had been made responsible for. In other faujdaris there were some mansabdars with a sawar rank of 2,000 and even 3,000. See Table II-E(vii). [In *Region and Empire: Panjab in the Seventeenth Century,* Oxford University Press, New Delhi, 1991.—Ed.]

53. See Table II-E(vii). [In *Region and Empire: Panjab in the Seventeenth Century,* Oxford University Press, New Delhi, 1991.—Ed.]. The *hasil of* the area under his jurisdiction stood at 50 lakh rupees. Refer *Amal-i-Salih,* III, p. 7.

54. The Dipalpur and Lakhi Jangal region was not entirely an area, with a subservient *zamindari.* Most of the faujdars appointed here were those with sufficient military experience.

55. *Amal-i-Salih,* II, p. 345.

56. In comparing the mansabs of the faujdars of Lakhi Jangal, it emerges that many of the *faujdars,* though in charge of Lakhi Jangal alone, had higher mansabs than Todar Mal, who was in control of a larger area along with Lakhi Jangal. Therefore, the military control over this area may have been with some other officials.

57. The two references in the *Tuzuk,* I, pp. 157, 310, are not very helpful. In 1609–10 Saif Khan Barha was appointed faujdar of sarkar Hisar with a mansab of 2,500/l,350. In 1615–16 Muhammad Husain was appointed as faujdar with a mansab of 500/400. During the reign of Shahjahan, Hisar Firoza was, for some time, under Muhammad Ali Khan, who during the first half of Aurangzeb's reign attained a rank of 2,000/1,000. See *MU,* II, p 113; Athar Ali, *Mughal Nobility under Aurangzeb,* p.194.

58. Though the faujdari was called Lakhi Jangal, its headquarters were probably in Dipalpur. Refer also Irfan Habib, *An Atlas of the Mughal Empire,* Sheet 4A. Therefore, those mansabdars mentioned as faujdars of Dipalpur, were also probably faujdars of Lakhi Jangal and vice-versa.

59. This rank was attained by him in 1637–8 and in the normal course of events he was likely to have held the same rank in 1644–5 or even been promoted to a higher one.

60. Refer Table II-E(viii). [In *Region and Empire: Panjab in the Seventeenth Century,* Oxford University Press, New Delhi, 1991.—Ed.].

61. Irfan Habib, *An Atlas of the Mughal Empire,* Sheet 4A.

62. Yusuf Muhammad Khan Tashkandi, the faujdar of Bhakkar till 1638–9 went as subadar Multan the same year. Jan Nisar Khan, faujdar Lakhi Jangal in 1632–3 was faujdar Bhakkar in 1638–9. Abdul Razaq Gilani, the naib of Dara in Multan (1654–5 to 1656–7) was appointed *faujdar* Bhakkar in 1661–2. Refer Table II-E(ix). [In *Region and Empire: Panjab in the Seventeenth Century,* Oxford University Press, New Delhi, 1991.—Ed.]

63. Chetan Singh, 'Centre and Periphery in the Mughal State', pp. 299–318.

64. See W.H. Moreland, *The Agrarian System of Moslem India,* Delhi (reprint), 1968, p. 86.

65. See *Ain-i-Akbari,* II, p. 118. A comparison with other subas can further clarify this fact. The suba of Allahabad had 9 sarkars and 15 dastur-circles.

Suba Oudh with 5 sarkars had 12 dastur-circles, suba Agra with 12 sarkars had 27 dastur-cirlcles, and suba Delhi with 8 sarkars had 28 dastur-circles. *Ain-i-Akbari*, ii, pp. 96, 100, 103–4, 111.

66. Ibid., II, p. 118, for the number of mahals listed under each circle. Irfan Habib, *An Atlas of the Mughal Empire,* Sheet, 4B, has plotted the extent of these circles.

67. *Ain-i-Akbari*,II, pp. 111–12.

68. Ibid., II, p. 121.

69. While Qasur and Patti Haibatpur were in suba Lahore, the mahals of Firozpur and Muhammadot were in *suba* Multan. See *Ain-i-Akbari*, Vol. II, p. 118. See also Irfan Habib, *An Atlas of the Mughal Empire*, Sheet 4A.

70. *Ain-i-Akbari*, ii, p. 118; Irfan Habib, *An Atlas of the Mughal Empire,* Sheet 4A.

71. The most impressive among these being Irfan Habib, *Agrarian System,* pp. 196–235.

72. Ibid., p. 16. Measured area also included cultivable waste and fallows.

73. Ibid., pp. 14, 16, 17.

74. See *Akbarnama*, III, pp. 749, 812, 875. He leaves no scope for doubt why the revenue remission was made. He says that, 'On account of the extent of cultivation, and the goodness of the administration, prices fell very low and many cultivators were unable to pay the government revenue.'

75. Ibid., III, p. 116. In the events of the 43rd regnal year, it is noted that, 'when Lahore was for sometime the seat of government, the imperial officers increased the government share in the proportion of ten to twelve on account of the high prices'.

76. The sarkars of Sirhind and Hisar-Firoza which were part of Panjab but in the suba of Delhi are, however, mentioned as being given some concession in 1590. Refer *Akbarnama*, III, p. 875.

77. The reference to remissions pertain to the 31st, 33rd, and 35th regnal years of Akbar, at a time when the emperor was co-incidentally in Lahore or some other part of Panjab.

78. This, as we have noted earlier, happened in the 43rd regnal year. See *Akbarnama*, III, p. 116. Abul Fazl further notes here that, 'when it appeared that by the departure of the auspicious standards, prices returned to their former level, the just sovereign remitted the increase and small and great were much relieved'.

79. Irfan Habib, *Agrarian System*, pp. 257–73. The question is dealt with in detail.

80. Ibid., p. 284. Habib provides an instance where a representative of the jagirdar acted as amin, shiqqdar, karkun and faujdar simultaneously.

81. Ibid., pp. 284–5, 286–7. In Panjab we have the example of a *shaikhzada*

giving his *madad-i-ma'ash* land in ijara during the 1670s. Apparently, this was recorded through a deed in a *qazi's* court. See B.N. Goswamy and J.S. Grewal, (tr. & ed.) *The Mughal and Sikh Rulers and the Vaishnavas of Pindori,* Simla, 1975, Document 1. Though this is a reference to *madad-i-ma'ash* land, the giving out on *ijara* of *jagir* land must also have been common. The increasing oppression by *ijaradars* could force the peasant to abandon his land and migrate to another place. See also Muzaffar Alam, *Crisis of Empire in Mughal North India,* pp. 39–42.

82. These were known by numerous names such as *milk, amlak, suyurghal, aimma,* and most commonly *madad-i-ma'ash*. See Irfan Habib, *Agrarian System,* p. 298.

83. *Ain-i-Akbari,* I, p. 278.

84. The mention of Sirhind and Pakpattan as the abodes of such men crops up very frequently in our sources. Revenue grants were also made to religious men in rural areas. See B.N. Goswamy and J.S. Grewal, (tr. & ed.), *The Mughals and the Jogis of Jakhbar,* Simla, 1967.

85. *Ain-i-Akbari,* II, pp. 298, 301, 320–8, 331–5. The proportion of revenue given to *suyurghal* varied in different sarkars. It has, however, been argued that these statistics do not include all grants made under this head and are hence not definite indicators of the amount that was alienated to such grantees. See Irfan Habib, *Agrarian System,* p. 313. Moreover, these statistics only represented the amount which would be subtracted from the regular revenue of tilled land and did not account for the income that could be derived from cultivable land that normally constituted half of the land given as madad-i-ma'ash.

86. *Ain-i-Akbari,* I, p. 279, 'The officers of the government on receiving this order, told off certain villages for this purpose'. *Akbarnama,* III, p. 343. 'The just lord of the earth ordered that the Aima lands should not be mixed up with the exchequer and jagir lands.'

87. *Ain-i-Akbari,* II, pp. 300–1. In sarkar Sirhind, two mahals had a very large revenue allotted to this head. Thara (Tihara) with a total revenue of 7,850,809 dams had 2,369,841 dams under suyurghal, and Thanesar with 7,850,803 dams had 2,069,841 dams under suyurghal. This worked out to about 30% and 26% of the total revenue of these mahals.

88. See Irfan Habib, *Agrarian System,* p. 314. While Delhi had 5.4% of its revenue under suyurghal, Allahabad had 5.2% and Oudh had 4.2%. Lahore registered only 1.8% of its revenue under suyurghal.

89. These illegal collections were, however, frequently made by local authorities, ibid., p. 247.

90. *Ain-i-Akbari,* II, p. 46. Referring to the amalguzar Abul Fazl notes that, 'He should strive to bring waste lands into cultivation and take heed that what is in cultivation fall not waste. He should stimulate the increase of valuable

produce and remit somewhat of the assessment with a view to its augmentation'.

91. *Ain-i-Akbari*, II, p. 46. He says that the amalguzar should 'assist the needy husbandman with advances of money and recover them gradually'. See also Irfan Habib, *Agrarian System*, pp. 253–5. Peasants in newly settled areas were given concessions of various kinds in the initial stages.

92. Irfan Habib, *Argarian System*, p. 114.

93. An order of Jahangir (November 1617) records that, '... it has so reached the sacred, sublime and exalted notice through the contents of the petitions of the karori and the faujdar of the pargana of Tahara that the tenants of some of the villages of the said pargana have migrated into the villages of the pargana of Bhatinda and that they (agents) have given them shelter and have not surrendered (them) to the karori and the faujdar. It is necessary that as soon as they receive the honour of the knowledge and information of the contents of the glorious and auspicious mandate, they should not detain a single individual of the pargana of Tahara in that mahal'. *Descriptive List of Farmans,Manshurs and Nishans addressed by the Imperial Mughals to the Princes of Rajasthan*, Bikaner, 1962, p. 36.

The Formation of a Regionally Oriented Ruling Group in Bengal, 1700–1740[*]

Philip B. Calkins

Thirty years ago, Hermann Goetz wrote an essay entitled, "The Crisis of Indian Civilisation in the Eighteenth and early Nineteenth Centuries," in which his primary concern was to try to understand the eighteenth century in its own terms and thus to reclaim some element of usefulness and creativity for an age which at that time was traditionally depicted as one of dark depravity. He argued that the important historical contributions of eighteenth century India were not in the realm of political or economic development, but rather in the refinement of aesthetic appreciation—that the eighteenth century was, in fact, an age of political and moral decay and produced an over-ripe and 'overrefined' aesthetic sensitivity which was characteristic of that sort of period the world over and which had its own peculiar, but very real value in the development of the cultural civilization of India.[1]

Professor Goetz's defense of eighteenth century Indian culture was quite persuasive, but perhaps the price which must be paid for that kind of defense is too high; for it is becoming increasingly apparent that far too little attention has been paid to those political and economic changes which Goetz was ready to dismiss as having only a negative value. "Indian life in this critical time," he said, "exhibited all the morbid characteristics of a late, decaying civilisation."[2] When one looks at the center of the empire, at the courts of the emperors who succeeded Aurangzeb, much of what Goetz argued appears to be valid. But what about the provinces? Was the same sort of decay evident in the political life of the provincial

* Reproduced from Philip B. Calkins, 'The Formation of a Regionally Oriented Ruling Group in Bengal, 1700–1740', *Journal of Asian Studies*, Vol. 29, No. 4, August 1978, pp. 799–806.

governments—and especially of those which developed into successor states? The closer we look, the more evidence we can find that political and economic affairs were conducted vigorously and constructively at the local and provincial levels in many parts of India. The case of Bengal cannot be said to have been typical, but at least it is one example of a provincial administrative system which appears to have grown stronger, not weaker, after the death of Aurangzeb, and where an elite ruling group which was representative of the political realities of the day coalesced and maintained rather high standards of administrative efficiency.

During the seventeenth century, the Mughal system of government was highly centralized. The government of Bengal was organized on the standard Mughal model, and was staffed at the upper levels by *mansabdars*—officials who were appointed by the central government and were transferred at frequent intervals from one province to another. The central government retained strong control over the provincial administration, both by transferring these mansabdars and by maintaining a system of checks and balances within the province. The political structure in Bengal was somewhat peculiar, however, because almost all of the land was controlled at the local level by indigenous landholders, who were called *zamindars*. These *zamindars* played an unusually important role as revenue collectors and keepers of the peace. By controlling them, the Mughal provincial officials indirectly controlled lesser landholders and, finally, the cultivators.

The *zamindars* were the highest level of landholders, and were responsible for remitting the revenue for their lands directly to the provincial government. Below the *zamindars* there were various levels of intermediate landholders, who collected revenue from the landholders beneath them, and at the lowest level, directly from the cultivators, and transmitted the revenue up through the system to the *zamindars*. The available evidence indicates that most of the zamindaris were relatively small during the seventeenth century, which meant that it was not very difficult for the Mughals to control them.[3] Also, since most zamindaris were relatively small, the system of intermediate landholders within the zamindaris tended to be less stratified than it became when larger zamindaris developed, with more room in them for the organization of a system of sub-tenures.

As the imperial government at the center of the empire weakened during the eighteenth century, the administrative system of Bengal was adapted, with reasonable success, to account for the changing power relationships. Briefly, we can say that the shift in the focus of political power from the center to the province was accompanied by a shift in the balance of power within the province. From a position of strong dominance, the Mughal mansabdars became relatively less powerful within Bengal as they became entrenched there, since they could no longer depend upon the support of imperial forces from the center. Essentially, the price they paid for their independent actions within Bengal was that they had to contend with the other forces inside the province without help from outside, and send revenue regularly to Delhi. At the same time, a group of larger and stronger *zamindars* began to emerge and take over more of the responsibilities of government. Thus a partnership between the Mughals and the more important members of the indigenous landed ruling group developed. But the partnership was not complete until a third group, which represented the larger commercial and financial interests within Bengal, was brought into the ruling councils and began to play an important role in financing the administrative reforms which accompanied the shift in the focus of political power.

In order to understand the way in which the political order of Bengal was changing during the first half of the eighteenth century, it is necessary to review some of the political events of the period, and to establish the connection between, provincial and imperial politics and the revenue reforms which were instituted in Bengal shortly after 1700. The story begins, in fact, with the introduction of the revenue reforms which resulted from the emperor Aurangzeb's urgent need for additional funds to finance his war against the Marathas. The emperor's demand for more money was directed particularly to Bengal, and for a good reason.

If we compare the figures for the revenue demand of Bengal circa 1580 with those for the revenue demand of 150 years later, we find that the total increase for the province was about 22½ percent and that the increase was only about 15½ percent if areas which had not been assessed as part of Bengal in 1580 are excluded.[4] Compared to the increases in the revenue demand which were made in most of the provinces of northern India during the seventeenth century, this increase in Bengal was proportionately very slight.[5] In fact, the increase in the revenue demand within Bengal probably was not even large enough to compensate for the decline in the value of the rupee and the corresponding rise in agricultural prices during the seventeenth century.[6]

Why should Bengal have been different than other provinces? There is no reason to believe that Bengal was comparatively poor. Indeed, references in contemporary literature indicate that the province was considered to be a rich one.[7] In addition, we know that new lands were brought under cultivation, that trade with Europeans increased, and that silver was brought into Bengal in substantial quantities during the seventeenth century.[8]

The inference which we can make is that if the government was not collecting revenue at a rate commensurate with increases in production and in the quantity of silver which was available, then someone else was becoming more prosperous. The evidence suggests that a substantial proportion of the increased prosperity was enjoyed by three groups: those mansabdars (Mughal officials) who held *jagirs* (revenue assignments) in Bengal; the *zamindars*, who held title to the revenue-collecting rights from the Mughal government; and the intermediate collectors who held revenue rights between the village level and that of the zamindari. The *Risala-i-zira'at*, an administrative manual which was written about 1760, explains the situation clearly. The author states that the revenue demand which was instituted in the time of Akbar was never revised by actual assessment and that those who paid revenue to the government paid in accordance with the official rate of demand, while they collected in accordance with revised assessments, which were usually much higher than the rates shown in the revenue roll of the Mughals.[9] Consequently, the landholders and some Mughal officials were getting rich.

Given the circumstances of a province which was comparatively lightly assessed, it is not surprising that when the Emperor Aurangzeb was pressed for funds to carry on his war with the Marathas, he should have sent a man of proven administrative ability to Bengal with instructions that he was to try to increase the revenue of that province.[10] Murshid Quli Khan arrived in Bengal around 1700, and from the date of his arrival until his death in 1727, with the exception of a period of two years, he was the most important administrator in Bengal. First as *Diwan* and later as *Nazim* (governor), he carried out the reforms which were to form the basis for the revenue assessment and administration of Bengal until the British conquest.

Murshid Quli assured his position in relation to the emperor by providing the essential service for which he had been sent to Bengal: increased revenue collections. The figures for the actual amount of revenue collected each year for the period from 1700–1722 indicate that the collections rose from Rs. 11,728,541 to Rs. 14,115,363—an increase of just over 20 percent in 22 years, compared to an increase of about 22½ percent during the entire 17th century.[11] But the process of increasing revenue collections led to important changes in the landholding and political structure of Bengal which were to result, I would suggest, in the formation of a new, regional ruling group. Briefly, these changes might be described as an increase in the size of a few zamindaris and a consequent decline in the total number of zamindaris, the increased importance of the larger zamindaris within the political system of the province, and the enhancement of the financial and political roles played by moneylenders and bankers.

Murshid Quli Khan's primary aim, at least during the first ten or twelve years of his administration, was to increase the revenue collections. Since the level of the revenue collections was considerably less than the official revenue demand in 1700, the new diwan could move a long way toward accomplishing his objective if he merely raised the level of the collections so that it equalled the level of the demand. Thus, he had to tighten the reigns of the revenue administration so that some of the profits which the jagirdars, *zamindar*s, and intermediate collectors had been taking could be taken instead by the government.

The eighteenth-century Persian chroniclers describe three principal means by which he proceeded toward his goal: first, he transferred many of the jagirs of the mansabdars from Bengal to Orissa, thereby freeing rich lands in Bengal for inclusion in the *khalisa* portion of the revenue collections, which went directly to the government, in exchange for less productive lands in Orissa.[12] At the same time, freeing the jagir lands in Bengal made it easier for Murshid Quli Khan to send in his investigators in order to enhance the revenue collection in those areas. Second, Murshid Quli insisted that the *zamindar*s pay their revenue in full. If they could not or would not, they were imprisoned and sometimes tortured, and investigators were sent out to determine whether the *zamindar*s had been cheating the government and to seize whatever revenue they could find.[13]

Murshid Quli's third method of enhancing the revenue payments was to send his investigators and collectors into all of the revenue-paying areas of Bengal, whether or not they belonged to defaulting *zamindar*s, in order to make a detailed survey.[14] Whether the survey was actually conducted at the village level, as the chronicles claim, is doubtful. No documentary evidence of such a detailed survey has survived, and there is evidence in the form of zamindari *sanads* which indicates that the provincial government's revenue records normally did not extend below the level of the lowest intermediate landholders. Mughal government accounts indicate that the government was interested primarily in collecting money from the *zamindars* who were responsible for collecting from the intermediate landholders, who in turn paid the revenue for relatively large blocs of land which were considered to be units normally under almost exclusive control of the landholders.

Thus, when Murshid Quli Khan began to enhance the revenue demand, it meant that government pressure was primarily applied to the *zamindars* and intermediate landholders and only indirectly upon the peasants. The result was that a zamindar either had to bring his revenue payments up to the required level or lose control of his zamindari—either to the government, or to a moneylender. If the zamindar defaulted and the government took over his zamindari, a frequent procedure was to grant the zamindari rights to someone else—usually another zamindar—who was presumed to be capable of meeting the government's demand for revenue.[15] A consequence of this policy was that the weaker or less efficient *zamindars* and intermediate collectors tended to lose their landholding rights.

In addition, since Murshid Quli adopted a policy of conciliating and encouraging particular *zamindars*, who were allowed to build up enormous holdings by the purchase of other zamindaris and from lands which were assigned to them by the Nazim, this period also saw the growth of a few very large zamindaris. Rajshahi is perhaps the most obvious example of a zamindari which grew to enormous size between 1700 and 1727. Although their rise was not quite as spectacular, the zamindaris of Dinajpur, Nadia, and Burdwan also appear to have profited as a result of Murshid Quli's policy.[16] By the time of his death in 1727, the fifteen largest *zamindaris* were responsible for almost half of the revenue of the province.[17]

Thus, Murshid Quli's reforms tended to depress the weaker and less efficient *zamindars* and intermediate landholders (although they often retained their position as landholders at a lower level in the system), while allowing the stronger and more efficient ones to survive. Essentially, he had converted a large and less stratified base of small landholders into a smaller but more stratified base of larger—and therefore more powerful—landholders. By 1727, the *zamindars* as a group definitely represented one of the major political forces within the province. But they were not the only group whose economic and political status were affected significantly by the revenue reforms; some bankers and moneylenders profited as well.

According to the *Risala-i-zira'at* many relatively small moneylenders, called *mahajans*, made a practice of loaning money to *zamindars*, often with the idea that the *zamindars* could be driven so far into debt that the moneylenders eventually could gain either temporary or permanent control of the zamindaris.[18] Of course, the opportunities of the moneylenders to entrap the *zamindars* were multiplied once Murshid Quli began to increase the pressure on the *zamindars* to pay their revenue in full.

The most notable example of a banking house which was the direct beneficiary of Murshid Quli's revenue policy is that of the Jagat Seths. It was almost certainly the patronage of the Nazim which allowed the Jagat Seths to build the richest banking house in Bengal, if not in India, and to become the treasurers for the provincial government by the 1730's. The house of Jagat Seth made a large part of their profits by collecting interest on loans which they made to *zamindars* who could not pay their revenue.[19] Essentially, the banking house acted as a guarantor for many of the larger *zamindars*, assuring the government that their revenue would be paid, regardless of their financial condition at the time when the revenue was due. It would appear, then, that the structure of money-lending operations in Bengal was parallel to the landholding structure, with relatively small mahajans to service the smaller *zamindars*, and larger moneylenders developing as the larger zamindaris emerged.

While the political and revenue structure within Bengal was shifting during the period of Murshid Quli's administration, the political situation within the empire as a whole was also changing. Although an attempt to become independent was not feasible, Murshid Quli did find that the hold of the center was becoming weaker than it had been under Aurangzeb, so that he had more freedom in which to maneuver within Bengal.

He used his freedom to consolidate his position within Bengal by gaining the loyalty of officials, *zamindars*, and financial interests. In the case of officials, he ensured loyalty mainly by appointing relatives and devoted followers to important offices, and by excluding from Bengal any potentially hostile mansabdar.[20] In the case of the important *zamindars*, as we have seen, loyalty was commanded on the basis of the fact that he helped them to increase their holdings, and probably because he did not inquire too closely into the administration within their zamindaris—as long as they paid their revenue. Finally, the bankers and moneylenders had many opportunities for profit and, in some cases, they were aided by the official sanction of the government.

It was obviously Murshid Quli's intention to remain in Bengal, and to try to ensure the succession of one of his relatives to the Nizamat of the province. Although events did not work out exactly according to his plan, Murshid Quli's political base in Bengal was secure enough, and the balance of power between Delhi and Bengal had shifted enough so that the Nizamat was passed on to a member of his family, Shuja' ud-Din Muhammad Khan, when Murshid Quli died in 1727—a maneuver which never would have been tolerated during the days of a strong, central imperial government.

Shuja's position was somewhat different than Murshid Quli's had been. Although he was probably a competent administrator, he had neither the prestige nor the exceptional ability of his father-in-law. In addition, as the period of time which he and his family had spent in Bengal lengthened and they became more firmly entrenched, the importance of their connection with Bengal became greater, and their ties with the empire weakened. An unspoken but real understanding between Delhi and Murshidabad seems to have been reached: Shuja' continued to send the imperial revenue to Delhi, and the emperor allowed him to do more or less what he liked in Bengal.

Given this situation, Shuja's position in Bengal naturally became increasingly important to him, and since the price he paid for his semi-independent position was reliance upon his own troops and the knowledge that he dare not ask for aid from outside the province in the event of internal troubles, the power of the *zamindars*, bankers, and local military commanders within Bengal became relatively greater. We have an indication of these changes in power relationships in the fact that upon becoming Nazim, Shuja' released the *zamindars* who had been imprisoned by Murshid Quli Khan, executed the two notoriously harsh officers of the former Nazim, and sent large amounts of money— in effect a bribe—to Delhi.[21] Soon he appointed an advisory council of four men, which included Jagat Seth Fateh Chand, the head of the banking house.[22]

During the 1730's, then, the government of Bengal began to look more like government by cooperation of the dominant forces in Bengal, rather than the imposition of rule from outside. In terms of revenue administration, there are two indications of the effects of this changing balance. First, the new taxes (*abwabs*) which were levied were figured as a percentage of the existing revenue demand, and thus did not require detailed assessment below the zamindari level.[23] Consequently, the government could not be as well-informed about revenue conditions at the local level as it had been under Murshid Quli. Second, the available evidence suggests that, up to 1757, the records available to officials of the provincial government were fewer and less detailed for the period after 1727 than they were for the period of Murshid Quli's administration.[24]

Thus, during the 1730s, the government was getting very little new information concerning the revenue capacity of some areas of Bengal—particularly areas within the large zamindaris. It seems that Murshid Quli Khan's policy of encouraging the growth of large zamindaris was beginning to have bad effects. As long as the land was changing hands, the government was likely to acquire information concerning its capacity to pay revenue; but once a pargana became a part of a large zamindari, it was unlikely that the government would obtain much new information about it. The policy of levying *abwabs* only made the situation worse, from the point of view of the government, and led to a further decline in the power of the government over the big *zamindars*.

It would appear, then, that the power of the Nazim declined somewhat during the 1730's, while the power of the *zamindars* and bankers increased. In 1739, a series of events occurred which, I would suggest, revealed the extent to which the administrative structure and political balance of power in Bengal had changed. In that year the power of the *zamindars* and financial interests of the Jagat Seths became evident when they helped Alivardi Khan to depose the new Nazim, Sarfaraz Khan. Sarfaraz Khan was deposed not only because he was an inefficient administrator, but also because he alienated the most prominent banker and some of the most prominent Mughal officials in Bengal, and thereby drove them into the arms of his ambitious rival and best military commander, Alivardi Khan.[25] The cooperation of this group in their deposition of the Nazim revealed the growing interdependence of the groups they represented, and was a logical extension of the increasing degree of cooperation between the groups during the previous twenty or thirty years. In a very broad sense, we might say that the coup of 1739 was brought about because the interests of the principal landholders, bankers, and many military men coincided. It was this coalition of interests which continued to govern Bengal until the military intervention of the British began to destroy the system.

The provincial government was not strong enough to withstand the attacks of the British that began seventeen years later, nor could it have survived a concerted attack by a strong and centralized force from Delhi, such as had existed in the seventeenth century. However, the new balance of power in Bengal made it possible to deal successfully with the immediate problems of internal stability and protection against attacks by other Indian forces. Alivardi's takeover actually was a move toward stability, since the result was to replace a man of rather modest administrative and military ability with a man of considerably greater ability. During Alivardi's reign, the source of instability came from outside—from the attacks of the Marathas—and although the Marathas were disruptive, it cannot be said that even they destroyed stable government in Bengal. Before his death, Alivardi had come to terms with them, and it appears that he had convinced them that it was not worth their while to continue their attacks on Bengal.

Thus, it appears that there was an orderly transformation of the political structure in Bengal between 1700 and 1740. The decline of imperial power brought changes in the provincial system, but it did not bring chaos, decadence, or even, perhaps, a decline in administrative efficiency.

NOTES

1. H. Goetz, *The Crisis of Indian Civilisation in the Eighteenth and Early Nineteenth Centuries* (Calcutta, 1938) p. 5.

2. H. Goetz, p. 16.

3. See James Grant, "Historical and Comparative Analysis of the Finances of Bengal," in: *The Fifth Report of the House of Commons on the Affairs of the East India Company*, W. K. Firminger, ed. (Calcutta, 1917) vol. II, pp. 176–91. Grant's account of the records for the Mughal revenue assessment of Bengal up to 1728 indicates that it was only during the eighteenth century that some zamindaris became so large that the assessment was organized around them,

rather than on the basis of territorial units which had been defined by the Mughals.

4. James Grant, pp. 176–91.

5. See Irfan Habib, *The Agrarian System of Mughal India* (Bombay, 1963) pp. 399–407 for the *jama'* figures for the *subah*s of the empire from 1580 to 1709. In many *subah*s, the increase amounted to 100 per cent or more.

6. Irfan Habib (*Agrarian System*, pp. 392–4) demonstrates that the value of silver (the metal which was used as a basis for the coinage of the empire) declined during the seventeenth century. Taking the gold and copper prices of the silver rupee given in the *'Ain-i-Akbari* (circa 1580) as a base of 100, the value of gold was close to 150 in terms of silver by 1700, and the value of copper was above 200. Since the inflation of prices in terms of silver appears to have been caused largely by the importation of that metal by European traders, and since much of the import trade came through Bengal, it is reasonable to assume that the rate of inflation was at least as high for Bengal as for the empire as a whole. The increase in the revenue demand within Bengal, however, was not great enough to compensate for the decrease in the value of silver during the seventeenth century.

7. S.N. Sen, ed., *Indian Travels of Thevenot and Careri* (New Delhi, 1949) pp. 96–7; Francois Bernier, *Travels in the Mogul Empire*, trans. A. Constable, 2nd ed. revised by V.A. Smith (London, 1916) pp. 437–40; Ghulam Hussain, *Riyaz-us-Salatin*, ed. Abdul Hak Abid (Calcutta, 1890) pp. 222–3, 246.

8. Irfan Habib, *Agrarian System*, pp. 384–94, on the importation of silver. On the settlement of new lands, see H. Blochmann, "Contributions to the Geography and History of Bengal," *Journal of the Asiatic Society of Bengal*, vol. XLII (1873) p. 228, and J. Beames, "Notes on Akbar's Subahs: Bengal," *Journal of the Royal Asiatic Society*, vol. 65 (1896) p. 127.

9. *Risala-i-Zira'at*, Edinburgh Univ. MS 144, fol. 8b.

10. Abdul Karim, *Murshid Quli Khan and his Times* (Dacca, 1963) pp. 19–23.

11. Appendix no. 6 to John Shore's "Minute on the Rights of Zamindars," West Bengal Govt. Archives (Calcutta), Board of Revenue, *Proceedings*, April 2, 1788, vol. 127, pp. 539–40.

12. Ghulam Hussain, *Riyaz-us-Salatin*, Abdul Hak Abid, ed. (Calcutta, 1890) pp. 245–6.

13. Salim Allah, *Tawarikh-i-Bangalah*, trans. by F. Gladwin as *A Narrative of the Transactions in Bengal* (Calcutta, 1788) pp. 26, 36.

14. Ibid., p. 26.

15. The general process is described in *Risala-i-Zira'at*, ff. 7a–9b.

16. A brief account of the growth of these zamindaris is given in N.K. Sinha, *Economic History of Bengal* (Calcutta, 1962) vol. II, pp. 119–22.

17. See James Grant, pp. 194–8, for a list of these fifteen zamindaris and their revenue assessments.

18. *Risala-i-Zira'at*, fol. 7a–b.

19. J.H. Little, "The House of Jagat Seth," *Bengal: Past and Present*, vol. XX (January–June, 1920), pp. 121, 133; and Ghulam Hussain, *Riyaz-us-Salatin*, p. 289.

20. F. Gladwin, *A Narrative of the Transactions in Bengal*, p. 40.

21. Ibid., pp. 74–5.

22. Ibid., pp. 79–80.

23. F.D. Ascoli, *Early Revenue History of Bengal* (Oxford, 1917) pp. 27–8, 57.

24. Beginning with the *sadr* revenue roll of 1728, the major zamindaris were listed as revenue-paying units.

25. J.H. Little, "The House of Jagat Seth," pp. 150, 181–4.

From *The Crisis of Empire in Mughal North India**
Awadh and the Punjab, 1707–1748

Muzaffar Alam

THE ZAMINDARS, THE JAGIRDARS AND IMPERIAL DECLINE

A close examination of the Persian sources brings to light a large number of rebel *zamindars* besides the well-known categories of so-called *mufsids* (disturbers) of the early-eighteenth century: Sikhs, Jats, Marathas, and Afghans. *Zamindars* of different denominations mounted the rural uprisings (each with its own logic) but all sought greater share in power over, and thus in the revenues of, their region. In some cases, it was a strong landholding community seeking to establish some form of dominance over its region. In several cases in Awadh rural pressure took the form of the *zamindar* beseiging a fortress (*ihdas-i qilacha*) and mobilizing his kinsfolk and an armed retinue (*jami 'at-o-sipah*). One or more *zamindars* would thus proclaim the central position of their clans and villages in the area—*pargana* or a group of *parganas*—where they had *zamindaris*.

These revolts were organized and led by powerful *zamindars*. But their goals were limited. The scale of their mobilization against imperial power could not transcend the divisions of their caste and community. The Mughals could handle the Awadhi *zamindars* either by a show of strength, using the other local elements against them or by extending concessions to the powerful rebels. Rural resistance in the Punjab, however, was less tractable. This difference has been examined in

* Excerpts from Muzaffar Alam, *The Crisis of Empire in Mughal North India, Awadh and the Punjab, 1707–48*, New Delhi, Oxford University Press, 1986, 13–17, 299–318.

terms of the history of the two regions, including the nature of their relationships with the centre.

Even though not always directed against the state, these uprisings corroded the basis of imperial authority, sometimes through linkages with imperial court politics. In the emerging political situation, service and loyalty to imperial authority ceased to count, for it was not the emperor but the nobles in the region who began to dictate state actions. Thus, the imperial assistance available to provincial nobles and· the local officials for coping with local problems depended more on their individual influence with powerful nobles at the centre, and less on their loyalty to the emperor. Thus were the beginnings of the new *subadari* in Awadh and the Punjab made.

In the context of rapidly diminishing imperial authority at local levels, I have examined certain administrative developments which had originated with a view to enabling the nobles to meet local challenges effectively. Among such developments were the *jagir-i mahal-i watan* and the long-term *jagir* holdings aimed at augmenting the strength of the nobility. These developments violated the classical Mughal concept of imperial authority, as seen in the seventeenth century, undermined the prospects of its survival, and reinforced the course of provincial autonomy.

SOCIAL AND POLITICAL BASE OF EIGHTEENTH CENTURY PROVINCIAL STATES

As the play of various factors is examined the period of my study separates into four phases, 1707–13, 1713–c. 1722, c. 1722–39, and 1739–48. In the first two phases, the issues are those of imperial authority vis-à-vis the governors and the local potentates, and the slow pull to provincial independence; in the latter two phases, the issues relate to the working of the new *subadari*, sometimes called the 'successor state', the extent of its independence from the imperial centre and its relations with the emerging system of regional powers.

The period of our study appears to have witnessed an emerging sense of regional identity which buttressed both political and, to a degree, economic decentralization. This sense of identity or provincial obduracy followed and accompanied economic prosperity in the regions. Different regions of the empire gained in strength in the wake of relative peace and political stability under the Mughal system in the seventeenth century. Intra-region as well as inter-region trade in local goods, artifacts, and food grains sustained a network of towns and money markets of varying sizes throughout the empire, linking some of the regions together with strong ties of economic interdependence. Conditions were thus generated for economic unity among these areas, irrespective of their political and military relations with each other. In a measure, the economic developments of the regions took a course independent of their political detour, even though their political unification under the Mughals had a bearing on this course.

The provinces of Awadh and the Punjab were among such regions. Economic developments in these provinces, as we shall see later, resulted in not only a rise in the revenue figures but also in the emergence and affluence of a number of towns, with a chain of routes to link them to the long-distance trade. The prosperity of these regions was to the obvious advantage of the *zamindars* who enjoyed dominance in rural production; it also benefited the merchants who controlled and regulated the markets. The *zamindars* in our period, as 'local despots', were in an almost uncompromising conflict with the imperial authorities. They had allied with the Mughals and accepted their subordinate position either in the face of the fear of the invincible Mughal or with an objective of protecting and promoting their individual interests vis-à-vis the others within the region. Since they now found themselves strong enough, they were up in arms. But as their goal was narrow and parochial, they failed to incorporate the interests of other regional groups in their programmes, and thus fight the imperial power. They relied on support from peasants and smaller *zamindars* of their own castes and in many cases their interest remained limited to their kinsfolk in the villages; the townsmen and traders also became victims of their fury.

In addition, the enrichment of the region generated conflict among the various local groups, as they each tried to maximize their profits at the expense of the other. The *madad-i ma'ash* holders made a bid to turn their grants into *zamindaris,* without forfeiting their existing privileges and perquisites. The *jagirdar* too aspired to a permanent holding so that he could build his own base in the region.

Conflict and absence of coordination between the local elements enabled the Mughal nobles to establish their hegemony over them and to mobilize the regional resources to emerge as a focus of power in the region. The political formations in these areas remained within the Mughal institutional framework.

However, it would appear that Awadh and the Punjab differed radically from each other in the social and economic bases of the problems in the period under review. In fact, even earlier the leaders of the agrarian uprisings in these two provinces did not have the same programmes, slogans, and perspectives. Besides, the *jagir* holdings in the Punjab were large in size and the *jagirdars* were powerful nobles who were unwilling to accept the authority of the governor. Further, the location of the Punjab—exposing it to developments in and invasions from Persia and Afghanistan—did much to shape the course of its history. These factors in combination with the nature of its relations with the centre and the interest of the *wazir* and a number of his Turani associates in the province constricted the growth of the new *subadari* in the Punjab. In contrast, the governor of Awadh was able to make fresh arrangements both with the local potentates and the petty *jagir* holders in the province, providing a new social basis for his rule, and thus establish the new *subadari* on firm ground.

Governorship during this period was consolidated at the initiative of the then incumbent; the office became hereditary ultimately and the province began to be designated as the 'home province' (*suba-i mulki* and *dar-ul-mulk*) of the governor. It, however, remained a *suba* (province), part of empire, replete with imperial symbols. The governor, despite his attempt, was unable to shake off the Mughal centre completely. These powerful new *subadars* continued to seek links with one or the other group at the court.

THE IMPERIAL COURT IN THE EIGHTEENTH CENTURY

One may ask why the new *subadar* wanted this support from the imperial court or, in other words, why the symbols of empire continued to be persuasive, even though the power which had promoted them decayed. We shall see that the social and political realities of the eighteenth century continued to require reference to at least a semblance of an imperial centre. Our period saw not only the collapse of central government, but also a re-stabilization in certain regions and this was achieved almost wholly within the Mughal institutional framework. Disintegration of the empire did not mean the drying up of all sources of growth in society. But no region was in a position to maintain itself in complete isolation of other areas. Despite decentralization and the regional rulers' war against each other, the regions remained integrated through trade and monetary transactions.[1] Again, in the conditions of unfettered political and military adventurism which accompanied and followed the decline of imperial power, none of the adventurers was strong enough to be able to win the allegiance of the others and then replace the imperial power. All of them struggled separately to make their fortunes and threatened each other's position and achievements. Only some of them, however, could establish their dominance over the others. When they sought institutional validation of their spoils, they needed a centre to legitimize their acquisitions.

The Mughal emperor and his court provided the safest such centre, since it had long been generally accepted as a source of all political power and authority; but now it was too weak and ineffective to resist the adventurers' ambitions and was also unable to restrict regional developments. It is significant that even after the total collapse of the central government, the governors of the virtually independent provinces continued to make serious efforts to obtain offices at the Mughal court. Considered from the perspective of the Mughal court, this phase of politics has been seen either as mere factionalism in the nobility,[2] sometimes attributed to the 'crisis' of the period,[3] or as a kind of recurrence of an earlier pattern.[4] This study suggests that court politics in the 1740s, the last phase of our period, could well be linked to the conditions emerging in the provinces, particularly the ambitions of political and military adventurers who sought a standing at the centre, in order to secure firmly their positions in the regions. Ambitious individuals, like the governors of Awadh, or groups like the Marathas, looked for positions at the court after they had established their dominance over local groups in the regions in order to reinforce and secure their regional bases. This shift from control of peripheries by the centre in the seventeenth century to control of centre by the provinces is significant. But such was the myth and influence of Delhi that no regional power could replace it as the centre in the eighteenth century.

CONCLUSION

The stresses resulting in the disintegration of the Mughal empire towards the last phase of the period of our study, were first reflected in the crisis of the relations between the emperor and the nobility. When the *zamindars* in the regions resisted the authority of the centre effectively, the nobles in control of provinces began to see this as a threat to their fortunes and sought more powers. The emperor did not view this as a systemic crisis but as a mere extension of the old problem of the entrenched position of dominant sections of the nobility and tried to counter this by encouraging the newer elements

However, the problem of the nobility at this stage was no longer linked to one or other group of the nobles. It concerned the organization and the emoluments of the entire class of the nobility and percolated down to officials on lower rungs as well. It was closely linked to the challenges that the emperor and the state officials began to face in the regions. The emperor believed wrongly that by reasserting his position as the source of all power and patronage he could recover the waning prestige of the empire. While, on the one hand, the emperor was unable to evolve innovative solutions outside the well-established framework of the emperor-noble equations, the nobles' urge for additional powers, on the other, indicated that the principle of the emperor as the source of all authority was no longer tenable.

The provincial governor's attempt to combine his authority, ultimately, with all powers and offices in the province marked a virtual rejection of the authority of the imperial centre. The process of change began when the old and established nobles (the *khanazads*) tried to make up for the loss of their prestige at the centre by seeking additional powers in the provinces. They were allowed this privilege in consideration of their eminent position in the hierarchy of the nobility. But this did not represent the aspiration of the *khanazads* alone; it was part of a wider problem of the provincial administration, reflected in the second phase of our period in the changing position of the governor. At the beginning of this phase, the governors of Awadh enjoyed some additional authority, even though they could not claim the eminence and the influence of their predecessors. Soon the governor sought a major break from established Mughal convention in Farrukh Siyar's reign when he made an effort to maintain a longer term of office, to extend his authority to a province in the neighbourhood and, above all, to control provincial finance. In 1716, the governor even resisted the conferment of executive and military powers by the imperial centre on the provincial *diwan*. This was obviously incompatible with the imperial control of the province and the Mughal system of 'checks and balances'.

The appointment of Girdhar Bahadur in 1719 perhaps amply illustrates the change in the attitude of the nobles posted in the province towards imperial authority. Girdhar himself chose the province. This was in keeping with developments at the court where nobles and not the emperor had come to dictate the course of state action. It eroded the very basis of imperial authority. To such governorships we can trace the beginnings of the new *subadari* and provincial independence in the eighteenth century.

This change was, however, also conditioned by the nature of relations between the nobles in control of provinces and the central authorities. The emperor, during the first phase, saw the governors' plea for extended powers as a threat to imperial power founded on their claims to high position as *khanazads*. He allowed them to govern the provinces with special privileges in order to keep them at a distance from the court. But the emperor was unable to resist the erosion of his power, since his authority rested on support from the nobles. The emperor was compelled to reconcile with one or the other faction of the nobility, whom he considered to be less ambitious and who, to him, appeared to be willing to help him keep, at least, the myth of the imperial aura intact. During the second phase in Farrukh Siyar's time when the *wazir* aspired and threatened to take over the central position from the emperor, the latter allowed the governor of Awadh to control provincial finance. The governor in this particular case was Chhabele Ram, a supporter of Farrukh Siyar in his battle against the *wazir*, and the purpose was simply to increase his strength vis-à-vis the *wazir* and his faction and not to enable him (the governor) to meet the extraordinary situation in the province. Chhabele Ram also sought the *subadari* for a long term in order to build a base in case of his and his master's defeat against the *wazir* at the centre. The case of Chhabele Ram set a precedent. Yet in 1719 when Girdhar Bahadur, the governor of Allahabad, was allowed to take the charge of Awadh with extended powers, it was not in consideration of the problems of administration in the province. The *wazir*, at this stage, was keen that Girdhar should leave Allahabad where he had revolted and had thus threatened the passage from the eastern provinces to the centre.

The process is also illustrated from the case of the Punjab. As the governor did not belong to the faction of the *wazir*, he received little support from the centre. Instead, the *wazir* tried to replace him by a man of his own faction, incited the local chiefs to rise against him and, if possible, to eliminate him. The governor survived, in a large measure, due to his association with a kin group, opposed to the faction of the *wazir,* at the centre. In return, however, the governorship with extended powers in the Punjab came to be virtually shared with those leaders of his group who held offices at the centre.

In the governor's struggle for additional powers there was a case for a political framework flexible enough to accommodate the interests and aspirations of the different components of the ruling class in the province together with a lose imperial unity. But with the centre unable to guarantee provincial security, the governor had to work it out himself in alliance with emerging local forces. In fact, the emperor and central authorities, vulnerable as they were to factional politics at the court, had become the channel for extending such politics to the provinces. The centre now acted as a force for destabilization rather than stabilization in the provinces.

Thus, there was a rapid decline in control of the centre over the various departments of local administration following invariably the governor's estrangement with central authorities. Not only was the governor utterly disrespectful of the centre during the second phase, but the persons in charge of the provincial and local offices that he aspired to control had to encounter his hostility. On the other hand, the central authorities overlooked cases of dereliction, irregularities and even serious offences by those local officials who were intended or were posted in the province to be a check on the governor. Accordingly, the composition of the local officials kept changing to suit the interests of one or the other party in power at the centre, often in total disregard of the requirements of the offices in the province.

Crippled imperial control over local administration manifested itself in the misappropriation of revenue by local officials which resulted in a conflict, for instance, with the agents of the *jagirdars* and the *amils* of *khalisa*. Again, the *faujdar*'s indifference to the difficulties of the news-writers, which posed a problem in obtaining details from the *mahals*, seriously affected the working of local administration. As a result, in a number of cases, the centre was either uninformed or ill-informed. Moreover, in a number of instances from the Punjab, the news-writers took the side of the governor in the latter's clashes with the centre; they remained in office in spite of imperial orders to the contrary.

The office of the *qazi* operated until the end of our period, but it tended to become hereditary in Awadh from almost the beginning of the eighteenth century. In some cases, the *qazis* complied with the orders of their transfer, but they illegally retained the *madad-i ma'ash* granted to them against their services.

The *jagirdars* became primarily concerned with the protection and promotion of their own interests. They resisted implementation of imperial regulations and defied the practice of frequent transfers. The extension of *watan jagir* to non-*zamindar mansabdars* created more difficulties for the functioning of the administration. Most of such *mansabdars* in Awadh obtained positions in or around their *watans* and they remained idle, hardly attending to their work. Some of them retained their *jagirs* and collected revenue even after they had become physically disabled and of no use to the state. It would appear that the *jagirdars* were not content with the terms and conditions of their service. Their resistance of imperial principles was evident in their attempt to hold on to their *jagirs* and treat them as hereditary rights. The tendency was seen at work not only in and around the provinces under review but also in the areas dominated by the Marathas and the Rajputs.

The local and organized regional resistance against the centre expressed itself in widespread agrarian uprisings, mounted in Awadh by the dominant Rajput *zamindars*; while in the Punjab, socially and politically, an increasingly important community took over the leadership of these revolts. The agrarian risings were not a new phenomenon in our period. The *zamindars* who were in control of rural production and producers, had never welcomed the state extraction of almost the entire surplus from the villages, leaving them only a marginal share. There was always a lurking fear, as indeed often the reality, of the *zamindars'* resistance to the local officials. But a notable feature of the *zamindar* risings in our period was the remarkable speed with which they recovered from a defeat and re-engaged themselves against the Mughals. In Farrukh Siyar's reign a number of military expeditions against *zamindars* in Awadh reportedly ended in the victory of the Mughals. Yet the prime concern of Girdhar Bahadur and later of Burhan-ul-Mulk was to suppress the rebel *zamindars* or, at least, to seek a strategy to arrive at some kind of accommodation with the dominant landed communities in the province. This indicated the wide popular base of resistance and also the extent of the resources at the command of their leaders. The strength of the armed bands under their command and also the fortresses they had under their control is to be particularly noted in this connection.

The intensity of the *zamindars'* resistance in our period followed economic growth and the prosperity in our regions in the seventeenth century together with an imperial decline. A number of old settlements in southern Awadh appear to have become notable for trade and artisanal production, while a number of others were emerging as new centres of important *zamindaris*. By the middle of the eighteenth century the central and southern districts of Awadh were apparently linked with the towns on the south banks of the Ganga in the provinces of Agra and Allahabad. The entire area was endowed with rich soil and good natural irrigation, favouring a particularly productive agriculture. The available *jama* figures suggest a remarkable rise in revenue from the end of the sixteenth century.

There is a possibility that the swollen *jama* figures showed merely the magnitude of state demand and that they represented a readjustment following the increase in prices in the seventeenth century. There is, however, enough evidence to lead us to believe that the rise in *jama* figure in our region cannot be explained simply in terms of the price hike of the seventeenth century. We have reports that the intermediaries' collections from the peasants had risen more substantially in proportion to their payments to the state. The *jama* seems to have borne some relationship with the performance of agriculture.

Two different processes which complemented and gained momentum from each other in the course of the seventeenth century proved to be of enormous profit to the *suba* of the Punjab and the adjoining areas. One was the impressive agriculture following the Jat settlements in the areas which combined regular rainfall, rich soil and extensive fields of river basins. These Jat settlements were connected with the great route which carried the trade of the country east and south of Delhi with the Punjab and beyond with Persia and Central Asia. The region also had an opening through the Indus to Lahari Bandar. The second process was the emergence in the Punjab on and around the trade routes of a number of towns with the merchants who specialized both in inland and foreign trade. All this resulted in the prosperity of the province in the seventeenth century which the contemporary Punjab historians speak of so boastfully and which is reflected in the fantastic increase in revenue, in particular, from the bazaar levies and tolls.

The growth in these regions led to a dislocation of existing agrarian relationships. In some cases, the dominant *zamindar* and the peasant castes emerged from their original settlements and began to make encroachments into the *zamindari* areas of the others, while in the others a *zamindar*–peasant clan struggled to bring under their control the entire territory around their area of residence. Their resistance in such cases was not necessarily directed against the state, but certainly against the rule, the order and the class positions the state protected and promoted. At any rate, the *zamindar* risings predominantly signified a challenge to the imperial power from regional and local communities.

The Mughal imperial power rested on a balance between the interests of different regional and local magnates on the one hand and the ambitions of the Mughal emperor and his nobles and the other *mansabdar*s on the other. This coordination or the alliance between the two with the emperor as the dominant partner was possible due to the social conditions of the country, which never allowed local and regional elements to act in unison. They were divided among themselves on caste, community and territorial lines and were perpetually at war with each other. Their strength was limited even though each of them tried to subjugate the other. There were certain traditions which guided and regulated their actions and inter-caste and community relationships, while most of them also had a history and memory of having served as intermediaries under the Sultans of Delhi. These factors minimized the possibility of rising above the narrow limits of their communities and territories. They were thus not only weak enough to be vanquished by a power above community and limited territorial considerations, but were also in need of a 'paramount' power under whose umbrella their individual positions were guaranteed.

The Mughals on the other hand were not bound by any such considerations which prevented them from building an empire that allowed for these local loyalties. And, as they came from an area which had long social and trade contacts with the subcontinent, they could also appreciate the implications of and respond accordingly to an extraordinary phenomenon of the time, namely the expansion of India's external trade following the advent of the Europeans with the precious white metal from the New World. The empire responded to the widening network of money and commerce connecting the peripheries with the heartland of Hindustan. The traders and the money dealers welcomed a system which could reinforce, augment and regulate the economic integration of the territories and the communities under the jurisdiction of their operations. Artisans and the producers also were in need of stable extended markets.

However, the same factors eventually provided nourishment to the process of political 'decentralization'. The Mughal alliance with the local and the regional magnates had been uneasy. The conflict between the two had not been resolved entirely. Whenever the *zamindar* found an opportunity he raided and tried to demolish the bastions of imperial power in the region. In a highly differentiated society, the expansion of artisanal production, urban development and the region's integration into a wider market network in the seventeenth century was to the obvious benefit of the upper strata of the local communities. The strength acquired following the prosperity of their regions enabled them to challenge Mughal claims in the face of declining imperial authority. They were now rich enough to afford the weapons and the provisions necessary to wage a long war against the Mughals. The *zamindar* uprisings in the early-eighteenth century were widespread, demonstrating the breakdown of the alliance between them and the Mughals as well as the region's resistance against control by the centre.

But the *zamindar*s fought for a very limited cause, and their strength was often impaired by their internal social differences. The agrarian revolts were often organized on caste and community lines and were a threat to those rural sections which did not belong to the caste or creed of the rebels. A large number of the *zamindar*s and peasants were constrained to seek help from the Mughals. There is also evidence of the support of some *zamindar*s and peasants to the Mughals in their military expeditions against the rebels. This is amply illustrated from the case of Mansa Ram, a Bhumihar *zamindar* of Gangapur, who mobilized his community behind the Mughals against the turbulent Rajputs to eventually found a raj in Benaras. It is also not unlikely that the rebels in Awadh, for instance, submitted after they won some privileges from the nawab. Their social conditions did not allow them to fight beyond a point, lest the others join hands with the Mughals and crush them and take over the leadership of the locality.

Again within the village and the *zamindari* centres there were social groups, namely the *madad-i ma'ash* holders, with interests, attitudes and objectives sharply different from those of the rebel *zamindars*. The *madad-i ma'ash* holders were the ideologues and traditional supporters of the Mughal state and subsisted in principle on the revenues alienated from the states' share in the produce. By the beginning of the eighteenth century they constituted a considerably strong social force, being in control of large land-holdings and sometimes were assertively present in local *zamindari* and money transactions. By the virtue of their ideological position they were in conflict with the *zamindars,* but now that they had become rich and powerful while also enjoying the full support of the state, their position was anomalous. They not only provoked but also restrained the strength of the rebels. As symbols and representatives of imperial power, they became victims of the wrath of the *zamindar.* The *madad-i ma'ash* holders were, however, a local social group and were vulnerable to the shifting fortunes of the region. For instance, they were a source of trouble for the imperial authority in Awadh in the early-eighteenth century.

The merchants and the other urban sections also suffered at the hands of the rebel *zamindars*. Long distance trade and money transactions were closely linked with political stability which, in the prevailing circumstances when economic integration had followed the political unification, could be thought of only through the maintenance of imperial authority. The traders and also some artisans sided with the Mughals and thus invited the hostility of the rebels. Trade and urban properties like the offices of the *qazi* and *kotwal* became targets of their raids since they were believed to represent the Mughal power in the region.

The *zamindars* thus could rarely think beyond the limited goal of a greater share in political power and revenues for themselves and their communities, even if their actions became part of a larger regional endeavour to become independent of the political control of the centre.

The feeling of uncertainty and apprehension among the officials posted in the region was inevitable. As the support from the centre, if available, was of little value, most of them rejected imperial authority and in some cases even colluded with the rebels.

In these circumstances, the Mughal governor sought additional powers and as he earned these through a course of confrontation with the central authorities, his success depended more on his ability to meet the demands of the region, including the *zamindars,* the *madad-i ma'ash* holders and the local and provincial officials. The governor aspired to establish his dominance over them which often led to virtual rebellion against the centre. By bringing the powers of the *diwan* and the *faujdars* under his control, the governor tried to strengthen himself to tackle the problems of local administration. And as he could arrive at some arrangement with the leaders of the rebels, and protected and promoted with some success the interests of the different local elements, he saw the possibility of refurbishing the Mughal power in the region through some changes in the existing political alignments including his own relations with the centre. This meant a longer if not a permanent tenure of his office, which was denied to him as the centre still insisted on the old pattern of its relations with the province.

The governor thus defied the directives from the centre and refused to leave the province, as he built and mobilized the resources of the region which enabled him to survive independently of the centre. Burhan-ul-Mulk remained in Awadh in spite of the emperor's order of his transfer to Malwa. Later, after his death, Safdar Jang succeeded him by the virtue of his blood relations with the deceased. In the Punjab Abd-us-Samad Khan, the governor, appropriated the revenues of the *khalisa mahals* earmarked for the maintenance of the army on the borders. Abd-us-Samad Khan refused to leave Lahore to take over his assignment in Kabul. Instead, he and his son, Zakariya Khan, together managed to control the Mughal Punjab and the *suba* of Multan towards the third phase of our period. This, in a measure, indicated their appreciation of the social and commercial links of the two provinces. Later, after his father's death, Zakariya Khan combined the governorship of both the provinces virtually on account of hereditary rights.

In all matters relating to the province, the governor did what he thought would further his interests in the region. Burhan-ul-Mulk showed no regard for the legitimate possession of the office of governorship of Allahabad, since he aspired to hold the province as a buffer zone between Awadh and the Baghela and Bundela chieftaincies. He added to the difficulties of Muhammad Khan Bangash against the Bundelas, as the Bangash chief had a base in the neighbourhood. The governor of Awadh was friendly towards the Bundelas even when they had entered into an offensive alliance with the Marathas against the

Mughals. Relations between Awadh and the Marathas were independent of any regard for the centre. Political alignments in the region came to be guided by the factors which threatened or were believed to promote the position of the governor. Safdar Jang thus financed an imperial campaign against Ali Muhammad Khan of Anola, his potential rival in the region, while the *wazir* of the empire, who also had his *jagirs* in the area, was kept in the dark about the objectives of the expedition.

Yet, it was not possible for the governor to be completely free from the centre. The imperial tradition was not totally forgotten. The emperor was the source of all claims to authority, even though he himself was effectively divested of power. The nobles, including those in control of virtually independent provinces, defended him, provided he did not imperil their interests in the regions. As late as 1739, Burhan-ul-Mulk and Nizam-ul-Mulk arrived at the centre from Awadh and the Deccan respectively to defend the emperor against Nadir Shah. Safdar Jang refused to act on an imperial order to defend the Raja of Jaipur against the Marathas; he went half-heartedly to Patna to help Ali Vardi Khan of Bengal; but he could not avoid taking active interest in court politics.

Again, the *jagirs* of the nobles posted at the centre or in any other provinces, restricted the freedom of the governor. Together with the agents of their *jagirs*, these nobles also had their associates among the local rural and urban gentry. Indeed, the *jagir* system had added considerably to the problems of the governor in the earlier phases of our period. The practice of the *jagirdar* having *faujdari* right over his *jagir mahal* had amounted to legitimizing dual authority in the province. It had imposed limitations on the exercise of powers by the regular provincial officials. Similarly the recently modified *jagir* set-up encouraging and creating a long-term interest of the nobles in their *jagirs* jeopardized the governor's endeavour to build a base in the province.

The governor thus had to be in touch with the developments at the centre. Burhan-ul-Mulk developed and maintained political equations with some nobles at the court, whose response to his overtures showed little concern for the damage he had caused to the emperor's authority in Awadh. His attempt to establish links with one or the other faction at the centre was evidently because he appreciated that it was necessary for his independence in the province. When the road passing through Allahabad, Bindki, Kora to Delhi was disturbed, he readily undertook the responsibility of the safe passage of the Bengal treasury through Awadh to the centre. This, he hoped, would compensate for his defiance of the imperial order, increase his prospects of bargaining for greater power and also enable him to show formal obeisance to the emperor. Burhan-ul-Mulk also envisaged an increase in the financial base of the *nawabi* rule when the imperial highway between Buxar and Delhi was diverted from the Allahabad-Bindki route to the one that passed through Lucknow and Bareilly.

The cases of the attempts of the new governor to continue his association with the centre highlighted the necessity of maintaining the imperial frame. The semblance of empire had to be sustained, for it suited the individuals and the groups who had hitherto constituted the empire and were now in power in the regions. He who had greater ambitions in the regions aspired to a higher and stronger position at the court. This brought the regional powers including the Marathas and later the British into direct contact with court politics.

The kind of power politics that emerged in different parts of the Mughal empire in the eighteenth century explains in part the need of emphasizing the imperial symbols. In order to survive and thrive in the absence of the long accepted legitimate and fairly effective imperial organization of the Mughals, each of the newly emerged regional powers looked for and seized the opportunities to subordinate the others, at least, in its neighbourhood. But each of them also resisted, or, at least, had the ambition or ability to fight any such endeavour of the other. To the victorious among them when they sought institutional arrangement of their spoils, it was convenient to accept and maintain the legitimizing authority of the Mughal centre which had in fact collapsed and come to coexist with their ambitions and positions in the regions.

The necessity of maintaining the symbols of the political unity of the regions of the erstwhile empire may perhaps be sought more in the realm of the economy of the period. By the 1720s when the symptoms of political disintegration were all too evident, the different parts of the empire were economically integrated by inter-regional trade along the coastal as well as the inland routes. The economic and monetary institutions of the seventeenth century which had led to the expanded network of commerce and the distant credit markets survived the collapse of the Mughal empire, and amid the political turmoils of the eighteenth century, kept a large part of the erstwhile empire inter-connected.

The decline of the Mughal empire was thus manifested in our regions in a kind of political transformation, in the emergence and configuration of the elements of the new *subadari*. However, as the beginnings of the new *subadari* are to be seen more in the context of the history of the region, the developments in and around Awadh and the Punjab provide explanation for its stability or weakness in these provinces. The genesis for the emergence of 'the successor state' was present in both the provinces, but in the Punjab it ended with chaos at the close of our period while Awadh saw a stable dynastic rule.

Geographical continuity of the Punjab with the frontier province and the emergence of a strong power beyond Kabul in the face of the rapidly collapsing Mughal centre together with the actuality and the lurking dangers of foreign invasions influenced the political developments in the province. Zakariya Khan's special equation with the centre also mattered considerably. Almost the entire 'Turani' kin group had a claim to whatever independence and stability these provinces had acquired under Abd-us-Samad Khan and Zakariya Khan.

Burhan-ul-Mulk and Safdar Jang, however, did not allow the interests of any court party to determine the course of the developments in Awadh, even though they were involved in court politics in varying measures during their tenures as governors. In this they were facilitated also by the fact that they were not ethnically tied with any dominant faction at the court. They assessed the problems of the province and experimented with solutions almost independently.

Since the nobles influenced provincial politics and administration through the local agents in their *jagirs* in the province, an attempt to change the *jagir* administration was among the first measures Burhan-ul-Mulk took to establish his rule in Awadh. Even though *jagir* was still a symbol of imperial control over the region, it had in actuality come to signify, the extent of the nobles' strength, sometimes threatening to emerge as a quasi *zamindari*. Due to the pecuniary benefits and influence that their position and continued association with the noble *jagirdars* implied, these agents, not infrequently local people, often endangered the strength of the governor. To convert the entire *jagir* into *khalisa* was not possible, for it amounted to inviting the hostility of the nobility. Burhan-ul-Mulk therefore brought their agents under his control by taking over the right of collection of revenue of the *jagirs* from the *jagirdars*, and he minimized interference in his schemes by non-Awadhi sections of the nobility. He was now able to distribute patronage to the local service gentry and also to hold in check revenue defalcators. An important feature of the new *subadari* in Awadh was thus realization of the revenues and then payment to the *jagirdars* by the officials who were in direct control of the governor. By the end of our period, the governor in Awadh also succeeded in reducing to the minimum the number of the large sized *jagirs* of outside nobles; quite a considerable number of the officials and military men who had *jagirs* in Awadh were in the service of the governor himself.

On the other hand, the *jagirs* in the Punjab remained very large in size, assigned to the powerful nobles including those belonging to the governor's kin group. In addition, a consider\able amount from the revenues of the Punjab was earmarked for the imperial hospitals, imperial food houses and, above all, for the imperial armed forces posted on the north-west frontiers. This implied constant outside interference, even when the centre was weak and the governor had virtual control over the finance of the province.

The governor in Awadh also integrated local groups into the provincial administration and army. There is sufficient evidence to suggest the emergence of regional elements in various positions in the Awadh administration and army. A large number of Awadhis, especially from urban areas, were in Mughal service, posted in different regions of the empire. With the decline of imperial authority in these regions and the inevitable decrease of avenues of promotion in the empire, we can legitimately presume, that these Awadhis sought their fortunes at home. Our sources convincingly show their reluctance and even refusal to accept offers outside Awadh. There is also evidence to suggest a definite and positive response from local groups to the political stability and opportunities that *nawabi* rule in Awadh ensured. This the Shaikhzadas demonstrated effectively in their defence of the *nawabi* against the invasion of the Farrukhabad Afghans and, subsequently, in their invitation to Safdar Jang, to come and take possession of Lucknow despite an imperial *farman* to the contrary. The Shaikhzadas, the Afghans and certain sections of the Hindus can be said to have formed a very loosely organized 'regional ruling group' in Awadh. But we must note that Burhan-ul-Mulk and Safdar Jang were outsiders and that the Qazilbash formed substantial part of the Awadh army in the middle of the eighteenth century.

In providing a firm foundation to the new *subadari* in Awadh, equally important was the governor's success in reducing, if not totally removing, the rural tension that ensued with the changes in the position of the *madad-i ma'ash* holders. The strength and the impact of the *madad-i ma'ash* holders are indicated in the shifts in Burhan-ul-Mulk's policy towards the *madad-i ma'ash* holding. He began with an uncompromising sternness, but ended with nominal assessment, lending legitimacy to their behaviour as virtual *zamindar*s. The insignificance of the size of their shares in the revenues notwithstanding, they had close social links with the Shaikhzadas in imperial service and thus with, the nobility, and the imperial court. The new *subadar* perhaps eventually recognized the necessity of using influence in the furtherance of the state's interests. Even though we have not discussed it, the context of the foundation and the configuration in Awadh in our period of the Sunni *madrasa* syllabi (*Dars-i Nizams*) which was to bring to its fold the future *madrasa* system in India needs careful analysis. The claims of the *madad-i ma'ash* holders in the late-seventeenth and eighteenth centuries may be seen in the light of their authority and ability to legitimize or otherwise social and political actions. Azad Bilgrami's observation (which typified their reaction) on the rise of Maratha power indicated their enthusiasm to contribute as also their response, to the stability implied by *nawabi* rule in Awadh.

The arrangement with the *zamindar*s, however, was a singular achievement of the Awadh government. Until the end of our period, the provincial government was opposed by one or the other *zamindar*, nevertheless its victory over the local problems was, in a large measure, due to the support of the *zamindar*s. Baiswara, a centre of constant threat to Mughal power, appears to have turned into a base of *nawabi* power in Awadh. The *zamindar*s were reconciled through a contract (*ta'ahhud*) which empowered them to engage in the collection of revenue and the payment of the stipulated sum to the government together with some kind of military and administrative authority over the territories under their jurisdiction. The contract combined in it the elements of the earlier Mughal attempt of both conceding some autonomy to the *zamindar*s as well as absorbing them in the imperial service. To such *ta'ahhud*s can be traced the rise of some of the rich *ta'alluqadari*s of eighteenth-century Awadh.

Such *ta'ahhud* also contributed, in a certain measure, to the decay of the institution of *faujdari*. The decay of the *faujdari* as a bulwark of imperial authority had set in with the new *subadar*'s acquisition of *faujdari* rights over the province. The new *subadar* began to appoint his own men as his deputies, not infrequently from among the local elements in different areas of the province. These deputies, often referred to as *naib*s and *nazim*s, were different from the Mughal *faujdar*s in that they combined both executive and financial powers.

The governor of the Punjab, unlike Burhan-ul-Mulk and Safdar Jang, could not reach accommodations with any section of the rural magnates. His failure stemmed, to a great extent, from the nature of the problems in the province. The problems in Awadh emanated from the movement and uprisings of the regional and quasi-regional magnates to secure, at least, a greater share in political power and revenues. The governors in Awadh made use of their weaknesses and planned to take over the leadership of the resistance against the centre. In this they were helped a great deal by the continued growth in and around Awadh from the seventeenth to the eighteenth century. Not only did the revenues of the province almost double in our period, but the governor was also able to augment his strength by adding to his domain a large rich area of the neighbouring provinces of Allahabad and Agra.

Indeed, the entire region of Awadh and the adjoining districts experienced remarkable growth in the eighteenth century. In the Benaras region, Benaras city was particularly noted for its wealth and money. Azamgarh, Bhadohi and Mirzapur flourished in this region amidst a number of bazaars and *ganj*s. The *jama* in the region rose by over 107 per cent and continued to rise under the Benaras raj in the mid-eighteenth century. In the early 1730s, Burhan-ul-Mulk collected twenty-five to thirty lakh rupees in *sarkar* Kora which had earlier seen one of the severest rural uprisings in the Gangetic plain under Bhagwant Udaru. No governor or *faujdar* could subjugate Bhagwant Udaru and realize state dues from the *zamindar*s. In 1745 the Mughal emperor demanded one crore rupees from Ali Muhammad Khan, an *ijaradar*-cum-*zamindar* of a few *pargana*s in the Moradabad-Bareilly region. Ali Muhammad Khan did not pay the amount on the strength of the *wazir*'s support to him, but the sum demanded of him indicated his capacity and the riches he had accumulated from *ijara* and his military adventures in the region. The rise in *jama* in this region was almost incredible—over 247 per cent. In 1745 when Amir Khan, the erstwhile governor of Allahabad, died his assets were assessed at fifty to sixty lakh rupees. In the same year, Safdar Jang is reported to have spent forty lakh rupees on the marriage of his son, Shuja-ud-Daulah, while according to one report he paid more than three crore rupees to Nadir Shah from the Awadh treasury to obtain the *subadari* in 1739–40 and to prevent him from attacking Lucknow.

In a measure, the problems in Awadh represented administrative breakdown and a dislocation of the political and social balance at the local level. The legend that on Burhan-ul-Mulk's query, the *qanungo* indicated the gap between what the *zamindars* actually collected from the peasants and what they paid to the state is significant.

The Sikh uprisings, on the contrary, which spearheaded the local and regional resistance to the Mughal rule in the Punjab, were fraught with weaknesses. The Sikh movement reflected a deep-rooted antagonism between the Mughal state and its beneficiaries on the one hand and the various categories of smaller *zamindars* and the peasants on the other at a stage where any attempt at reconciliation and compromise failed to operate effectively. The Sikhs had also begun to put forward a claim to rulership and were not to be contented with less than the total overthrow of Mughal rule and the establishment of their power in the province. The high sounding title of *Sachcha Badshah* and the symbols of *degh, tegh* and *fath,* therefore, continued to inspire the Sikh leaders even after the ruthless execution of Banda and his seven hundred comrades in 1715. The chiefs of the Punjab also looked for an opportunity, which they seized in the wake of foreign invasions, to totally throw off their obeisance to Mughal authority. The new *subadar* in the Punjab was, thus, unable to make any arrangements with the *zamindars,* nor there is any evidence to suggest that he could effect any changes in the administrative set-up of the province.

Zakariya Khan did try to build a base for the new *subadari* by associating the Khatris, a dominant trading community of the Punjab, with the provincial government. The Khatris and the Turanis, the faction to which the governor of the Punjab belonged, seem to have been in association with each other even at the centre. But the Khatris themselves suffered heavily in the wake of the decline of trade and urban centres in the Punjab by the middle of the eighteenth century. Trade had contributed a great deal to the prosperity of the Punjab in the seventeenth century. The trading centres and towns concentrated on and around the great land route which linked the Mughal empire through Kabul and Qandahar with Persia and Central Asia. These towns were, in turn, connected with the rich agricultural settlements in the Indo-Gangetic plains and the sub-Himalayan zones of the province. The trade of the Punjab also had an opening through the Indus to Lahari Bandar.

The trade with the countries beyond the north-western frontiers was brisk and made up for the loss of what may have accrued to the economy of the region due to the silting of the Indus in the seventeenth century. The Punjab appears to be in a flourishing state even in the early eighteenth century. Banda's concentration on the townsfolk showed the wealth in the cities for which our sources contain incontrovertible evidence. The Sikhs under Banda could plunder Rs 60,000 from Garhi Pathanan. In 1714, the deputy *faujdar* of Jammu misappropriated Rs 33,000 of the collection of the *mahals* of the *walashahis* in the *chakla*. In 1716, the *rabi* collection of *pargana* Sialkot amounted to Rs 6,00,000 out of which Rs 2,50,000 were reportedly misappropriated by the *faujdar*. The Shalharias of the *pargana* readily offered to pay Rs 5,000 for the release of two of their *zamindars* who had been imprisoned by the local *amil* for non-payment of revenue. Mirza Muhammad's evidence for the end of Farrukh Siyar's reign clearly shows that the office of the *amini faujdari* in Jalandhar was keenly sought and was still profitable, but, of course, only for those who could muster sufficient strength to collect the revenue.

However, political developments beyond the north-west frontiers, as well as the Maratha inroads into western and upper India, disturbed this trade. The revenues of the province fell sharply in Muhammad Shah's reign, the decline being the heaviest in the income from the bazaar levies and tolls. The dislocation of the economy led to great sufferings to the urban communities including the Khatris and thus shattered one source of social support for the new *subadari* in the Punjab. The governor did not possess enough resources to make arrangements with any other groups of local magnates. The Sikh movement continued to challenge the Mughal power, now, greatly reinforced by the dispossessed *zamindars*, impoverished peasants and the pauperized lower urban classes.

There were variations in the regions of our study in the nature and growth of the conditions in which set in the process of the formation of the new *subadari* in the early-eighteenth century. Conditions emerged in Awadh favouring the foundation and consolidation of a regional state under the aegis of a Mughal noble. On the other hand, the dislocation of the economy of the Punjab led to a change in the character of popular uprisings against the Mughals in the province, with the liquidation of all prospects, whatsoever, of accommodation between the provincial government and the Sikhs. One can speculate that the narrow religious and caste bond of the Sikh movement, absence of a positive political programme and hostility to urban communications must have also had their own share in the political chaos in the Punjab in the mid eighteenth-century.

It is therefore difficult to find a single explanation commonly applicable to the problems at the Mughal empire in all its regions and provinces. It is also difficult to accept the view that by the end of the seventeenth century the Mughal empire was faced with an insurmountable crisis owing to the very nature of the Mughal mechanism of administration. We may perhaps look more profitably to the conditions in the early-eighteenth century in which the empire disintegrated into the regional principalities in north India. In some regions the land still yielded riches if it was collected either by show of strength or tactful dealings with the intermediaries. The growing tendency among the nobles and officials to hold *jagirs* on a permanent/ *quasi*-permanent basis, the struggle to convert the *madad-i ma'ash* holding into *milkiyat,* the emergence of the *ta'alluqa, ta'ahhud* and *ijara* contract as the most acceptable forms of government, and the consensus among the regional powers to maintain the Mughal imperial symbols to obtain legitimacy and thus stability and security of their spoils—all indicated the eighteenth-century endeavour to make use of the possibilities for growth within existing social structures.

NOTES

1. See Chapter 1 of *The Crisis of Empire in Mughal North India, Awadh and the Punjab, 1707–48*, n. 56.

2. Jadunath Sarkar, *Fall of the Mughal Empire*, Vol. I, 1971, New Delhi, Orient Longman Limited, pp. 1–25.

3. Z.U. Malik, *Reign of Muhammad Shah: 1719–1748*, 1977, Bombay, Asia Publishing House, pp. 182–9.

4. Satish Chandra, *Parties and Politics at the Mughal Court, 1707–40*, 1982, Delhi, Oxford University Press, p. xviii.

From *Rulers, Townsmen and Bazaars** North Indian Society in the Age of British Expansion, 1770–1870

CHRISTOPHER A. BAYLY

VARIETIES OF EIGHTEENTH-CENTURY REGIMES IN THE GANGES VALLEY

Most of the regional and local powers gained autonomy between 1735 and 1762.[1] Aurangzeb's attempt to revive the Mughal empire had foundered through over-expansion before 1700. Faction plagued the ruling elite in Delhi in the 1710s and 1720s. But the seismic shocks to the old structure came in the late 1730s when the revenues of the rich provinces to the south of the capital were rapidly drained away into Maratha pockets. The weakness of the empire was cruelly displayed in 1739 when it was defeated by a Persian invasion under Nadir Shah, and contemptuously confirmed by the Afghans under Ahmed Shah who created a power vacuum in the great plains with their defeat of the Marathas in 1761. Between these two dates, the viceroys of the old Mughal provinces of Bengal, Awadh, and Hyderabad surreptitiously diverted the centre's revenue to their own purposes and set themselves up as virtually independent monarchs. During the same period, two further regimes were carved out to the north and east of Delhi by Afghan military adventurers who had once served the empire as mercenary soldiers. These became the principalities of Rohilkhand and Farrukhabad. There were significant distinctions in organisation and culture between these first two categories of Muslim successor state: the independent Mughal *satrapy* or province, and the new conquest state. But first a political form

* Excerpts from Christopher A. Bayly, *Rulers, Townsmen and Bazaars, North Indian Society in the Age of British Expansion 1770–1870*, New Delhi, Oxford University Press, 2010, pp. 15–17, 35–7, 459–72.

more typical of the century must be considered. This represented the determination of the local Hindu landholders of the east of the region to stand forth as rajas in their own territories.

PROLOGUE: WAR AND SOCIETY IN
EIGHTEENTH-CENTURY INDIA

Fairly recently the historiography of eighteenth-century India resembled that of the European Dark Ages before Henri Pirenne or the Thirty Years' War before the intervention of the economic historians. The picture was derived from the melancholy tales of contemporary European travellers to upper India and reinforced by the self-congratulation of later amateur historians among Indian officials who told of anarchic conditions and the decline of cultivation. It was embellished with the quatrains of those Indian writers who bewailed the decline of past glories with the bitterness of the unemployed scholar, the small literary elite of Mughal India mourning the passing of the old Delhi, 'city famed throughout the World, where dwelt the chosen spirits of the age'.[2] With the emergence of nationalism, the Black Legend of the eighteenth century was enlisted in the service of imperial ideology. H.M. Elliot, for instance, berated those young Indians who wished to return to 'that dark period' of independence, 'when the bare utterance of their ridiculous fantasies would have been attended not with silence and contempt but with the severer discipline of molten lead or impalement'.[3] Yet even the nationalist writers of the early years of the present century were ambivalent about the immediate pre-colonial past. Most condemned its leaders for the betrayal of the Indian nation; some were doubtful about the advantage of rule by Muslim potentates. Hermann Goetz was one of the few historians who saw anything admirable about the century. But the cultural renaissance in the miniature painting, music, and architecture of the period was, for him, but the sweetness of decay in the body politic.[4]

A more varied and interesting picture has now emerged from closer archival work. As in other dark ages, the darkness of eighteenth-century India was in large part the shadow cast by the massive historiographies of earlier and later periods. New analyses of the political systems of the period have led to the view that the conflict which contemporaries saw signalled the emergence of powerful 'successor states' which gained a closer control over rural resources and inherited the political style of the Mughal empire. Studies of the regional principalities of Bengal, Hyderabad, and Awadh suggest that the turbulent events of the century heralded not the final dissolution of the Mughal polity as much as the emergence of regional dynastic rulers who initiated new cycles of growth and regeneration. Some are tempted to go further and claim that the cries of alarm and despair issuing from the elite were no more serious than those to be heard in seventeenth-century Istanbul or early nineteenth-century China. They were witness to a cyclical realignment rather than the collapse of a political culture. Indeed the Mughal empire did not fall, it was simply swallowed by a larger political organism.[5]

These new approaches have the great advantage of deriving from Indian sources and have helped to dispel many distortions inherent in European judgements of Indian affairs. For instance, the annual conflicts over the size of a territory's annual land-revenue between a regional authority and local magnates can be seen as a kind of ritualised political bargaining rather than an irrevocable slide into anarchy. So, too, in time, the feared danegeld (*chauth*) which the Marathas levied from their conquered territories was often transformed into a revenue system as detailed and even more efficient than that of the Mughals themselves. A start can also be made in revaluing the social movements of the period. To the rulers of Delhi and Agra, the Jat warriors who pressed into their territories from the south-west were rebels and bandits; to the incoming British, they were a stubborn source of resistance poised across a main artery of defence and trade up and down the Gangetic plain. But if the Jats are looked on as a social rather than as a political phenomenon, they appear more as one of the last great movements of pioneer peasant colonists which have periodically revitalised the agriculture of South Asia.

Nevertheless, there are some anomalies and omissions in the emerging consensus which stresses the positive aspects of political change and the continuities and balance within kingdoms. Most of the material so far available has come from the provinces of Bengal, Awadh, Benares, and Hyderabad. Yet these were dominions which even contemporary European observers recognised to be areas of relative stability. They were the satrapies of the old empire which gradually seceded from Delhi rather than those which openly revolted against it. How do we reconcile the evidence of stability and economic health in these areas with the picture of declining towns and falling rents which still emerges unmistakably from the once rich hinterland within 200 miles of Delhi and Agra? If contemporary conflict was on a relatively small scale, what was the cause of local agrarian dislocation? Indeed, what in more general terms was the relationship between political, commercial, and agrarian change in late eighteenth-century north India.

Part of the problem is the tendency of the older works to describe these changes in terms of a general pathology which attributed all signs of decline to 'native misgovernment'. For the changes observed could be of quite different origins. The effects of warfare, population scarcity or internal migration; the redistribution of capital, and periodic cycles of bad seasons: all these have been lumped together to portray an undifferentiated Time of Troubles. But the economic background has been almost as shadowy in some of the more recent works which set out to rewrite the political history of the century. Here we find valuable discussions of the relations between the rulers of the successor states and their chief landholders and bureaucrats, but the agrarian system remains in an economic vacuum, except in the work of Irfan Habib and some of his younger colleagues. Eastern Rajasthan is beginning to come into focus,[6] but the economic performance of much of the Ganges valley between 1740 and 1810, and its relation to political change, remains an open question.... We shall stress the flexibility and adaptability of the contemporary political economy and show how the withdrawal of resources from some areas was often matched by their reinvestment elsewhere. By emphasising the interconnection between economic and political change, it becomes easier to reconcile the picture of stability and commercial growth in some areas with the evidence of decline in others.

CONCLUSIONS

... One good starting point for an analysis of the society of eighteenth-century north India is its recently reconstructed political history. In many ways, it is better to think of decentralisation or of the commercialisation of power within the Mughal polity than of anarchy. Between 1720 and 1740 Mughal magnates began to amalgamate provincial offices which had once been separate and to found new dynasties. These regimes developed closer links with rural society and favoured the petty rulers of the countryside by allowing generous perquisites and remissions. Even the Hindu and Sikh warrior states which were in open revolt against the empire retained much of the Mughal revenue machinery and continued to operate within a loose imperial system of honours and legitimacy which still centred on Delhi.

Political decentralisation encouraged the growing economic vitality of small places away from the imperial capitals. Magnates and gentry employed by the regional states founded fixed markets and settled colonies of specialist cultivators around them. While the merchants of the great Mughal towns faced disorder, local traders extended their branch agencies to secure the flows of artisan products and provided advances for the fine crops which the local aristocracies and armies needed. Religious foundations continued to flourish as pious rulers displayed their faith in eclectic religious patronage. This pattern was widespread throughout India. Islands of high farming and commercial enterprise existed around the courts and camps of all the lavish-spending contemporary nobilities. The environs of Hyderabad were settled with new colonies of farmers. The Maratha princes encouraged cash-cropping and artisan ventures around their capitals at Poona, Nagpur, or Gwalior as their peasant parsimony gave way to Mughal luxury. Hyder Ali's Mysore was run like a huge estate.[7] Even in the far south the warrior *poligars* founded fort-mart centres which drew in petty local entrepreneurs and laid the foundations for later commercial enterprise.[8]

There was also another pattern which cannot be ignored. The desire to paint a more balanced picture of the 'Black Century' should not obscure the existence of large tracts where political change actually produced a serious decline in local commerce and agriculture. This decline was not necessarily the result of war itself; for the military engagements of post-Mughal India were generally small-scale affairs. Sometimes decline resulted simply from the orderly movement of aristocracies, capital or skills from one centre to another, and the subsequent realignment of trade and production. Physical movement was an integral part of the eighteenth-century social order and should not be regarded as a pathological feature. Sometimes, however, these patches of decline were the consequence of banditry or warfare in areas where agriculture was fragile and heavily dependent on artificial irrigation. This was the case in the tracts north and west of Delhi. But the drier areas near Madras, for instance, were also greatly at risk from an interruption in the repair of village water tanks like that that took place after the invasions of the Mysore rulers.

The first chapters of the book (*Rulers, Townsmen and Bazaars*) tried to rectify the picture of economic collapse without retreating to a stereotype of 'Traditional India' where cultural and political norms worked in an economic vacuum. First, it was suggested, the areas of decline were quite limited in extent. Secondly, their existence actually advantaged the richer and more stable territories which preyed on them. Thirdly, the farmers, merchants and aristocrats of the stable areas were already expanding outward to colonise the waste before the imposition of the British Peace at the beginning of the nineteenth century.

Most important, however, is the subtle social change which was taking place in the stable zones even during the most war-scarred decades of the century. The 'farming' to magnates of the perquisites of kingship— the commercialisation of royal power—had been a feature of the later Mughal empire. These regional dynasts pushed the process further. The new nobility was drawn from entrepreneurs who could mobilise both military forces and capital. And even regimes of pioneer peasants such as the Marathas, Jats, or Sikhs needed entrepreneurs of this sort once they had ceased to be expansive movements of plunder and protest and became settled kingdoms. However, the fortunes of these new magnates and fiscal barons themselves rested on the networks of skill and credit created by moneylenders, stewards, and service gentry—people whose families had long acquaintance with the management of bazaars and revenue papers.

These groups of intermediaries between state and agrarian society demonstrated great resilience during the political flux of the eighteenth century. But they also provided the British merchants and administrators with the keys to the vast resources of inland India. Much of the book has dealt with two sections of the intermediate classes: the trading community and the service gentry.

On the face of it, the eighteenth century was a bad time for Indian commercial towns and traders. Along the coasts, the British established an unshakeable hegemony. The old oligarchies of Indian Ocean trade which dated back before the time of Vasco da Gama were strangled by piracy and internal depredation. Ancient Gujerati houses declined in Bengal and their native western India at the same time as revolt against the Mughal empire severed their internal routes. Disruption of demand in the Ottoman and Iranian empires or in the Arab lands dealt a savage blow to the west coast ports, while the decline of the Dutch and wars in the extreme south marked the passing of an age here also.

But even for international trade and the coastal economies, this picture of collapse is too stark. True, indigo and cloth exports through Surat fell off, but Malwa opium was still sold in vast quantities throughout West Asian markets.[9] Coastal trade down the length of the Gujerat and Konkan coasts remained buoyant.[10] Cloth exports from eastern India to Europe and South-East Asia were still considerable in the second half of the century.[11] The hardy overland trade to Central Asia in gold and luxury produce often managed to reroute itself in the face of political turbulence. Thus the volume of shipping in Indian ports controlled by Asians remained surprisingly large in the early years of the nineteenth century. Only on the lucrative China routes were the Europeans utterly dominant. And even in Bengal where the Company and the agency houses were building up their own exclusive society, the death-knell of international trading ventures pioneered by local men awaited the Scottish and Marwari deluge of the mid-nineteenth century.[12] In fact, the reduction of Indian merchants to a position of dependence within the Asian trading world was not assured until after 1850 when the high-speed ship and the electric telegraph revolutionised commercial information and risks.[13]

During the eighteenth century great volumes of Indian produce continued to find their way to foreign markets albeit by different hands and through different ports than a century earlier. This helped to keep the inland trade routes moving. But there were also internal sources of commercial vitality. The vast trade of the Indian interior continued to dwarf its external trade. Of course, it is important not to exaggerate; in many areas, volumes may well have declined between 1720 and 1800. But what is striking is the rise of rich overland trade routes to compensate for the clogging of the great Mughal arteries. Indian trading institutions were well adapted to move nimbly in the wake of the new aristocratic consumers and protectors. The persistence of revenue payment in cash—and in similar orders of magnitude to those paid in the later Mughal empire—provides the simplest and most telling evidence of the capacity of the commercial community to adjust to new political conditions.

Yet the question at issue is not simply one of the shifts of routes or the percentage rise and fall of trades. More significant was the role of commercial people in society at large. For the 'Black Century' saw the redeployment of merchant capital within India, not its destruction. Increasingly, control of land or men became ineffective without access to silver, credit, and markets. The extraction of revenue from the peasantry was facilitated by the village trader. Revenue-farmers could not farm without merchants; and the dominance of the new magnates of the countryside was enforced in silver rupees as much as by the iron-shod staff. In an age of cash-hungry small states, it is not surprising that commercial people subtly extended their influence. Few aspired to the dangerous heights briefly commanded by the great Hindu merchants of Bengal, the Jagat Seths. But in many parts of the country, commercial men in cartel could 'command the state' in the matter of revenue.

This represented more than the emergence of a new elite within the politics of the successor regimes. The influence of the commercial houses straddled the realms of the petty states and linked up with new patterns of commerce in more stable parts of the countryside. It was the harbinger of a slow social change, not merely a cyclical modification in the composition of the ruling class. But at the same time, these developments did not amount to the emergence of an Indian bourgeoisie. Capital controlled by traders and revenue-farmers was becoming a junior partner in the politics of the land; kingship was being commercialised. But capital was not being applied directly in the creation of new modes of production, nor were landed magnates giving place to capitalists.

What we can see is the creation of a unified merchant class. Groups of entrepreneurs in money and credit were consolidating themselves yet more rapidly within the interstices of small, commercialised and bureaucratic monarchies. Their independence was expressed through corporate institutions and rights which were recognised by the rulers. Paradoxically, the disturbed conditions of the eighteenth century tended to increase the homogeneity and independence of these solidarities. The needs of revenue-extraction and the consumption of aristocrats in small centres pulled the great merchants of the towns into the bazaars and *ganjs*, and brought the petty traders of the localities into the cities. The decline of some of the old Muslim and Gujerati traders with their continental networks meant that local merchant groups united by culture and religion were able to control the whole hierarchy of centres from peasant market to urban entrepôt.

This was happening across the subcontinent. In many parts of the country, inferior merchant groups aggrandised themselves at the expense of the cosmopolitan oligarchs of the past. In our area it was Chaube Brahmins, Rajasthani Bohras, Agarwals and eastern Khattris who were to form the trading and urban elites of the future. In the Punjab it was the Nanakpanthi Khattris and Aroras associated with the Sikhs, who took over from their more Islamicised caste fellows. In the south, Kannada merchants and local Chettis slipped into positions occupied by the old Armenian, Jewish, and Vaishya firms. However, the story did not end here. It was from the groups of local merchants whose fortunes greatly improved with the commercialisation of power in the eighteenth century that much of India's modern industrial and business class has been recruited.

It is now a truism of colonial historiography that Europeans could not have established their trade and administration in Asia or Africa without the compliance of key people in indigenous societies. The book (*Rulers, Townsmen and Bazaars*) has tried to give such an assumption greater depth and precision in the case of India. We start from the proposition that the pace of 'expansion' and the form of the colonial relationship was determined mainly by the form of the society penetrated in the years before the full force of industrialisation was brought to bear on the non-European world.

To begin with, the theory and practice of Indian states—in particular their limited notions of authority or territorial integrity—were crucial. The coastal kingdoms of the fifteenth and sixteenth centuries had put up only intermittent resistance to the Portuguese interlopers because they did not consider sea trade and the 'business of merchants' to be important matters for kings[14] .... the relationship between trade and power was highly ambiguous. The notion of 'farming out' rights, including rights over trade and markets, was designed to raise cash. But the redistribution of rights and duties was also an expression of the corporate nature of kingship. This created a peculiarly loose-textured political system in which a ruler could alienate much of his revenue and control without affecting his status as a king. So in India merchant corporations could quietly service and encourage European interlopers with impunity. Yet, since trade required protection, the Europeans were forced gradually to assimilate the functions of the ruler themselves.

The British were able to exploit the ambiguous relationship between ruler and merchant in Indian political practice. But they were also advantaged by changes which had taken place since the Mughal heyday. The expansion of the merchant class and town-building under the successor states provided them with networks of facilities which transported their trade goods, supported their armies and underpinned their revenue systems. Without the trader–bankers of Benares or Surat, the British would have found it infinitely more difficult to succour their fragile outposts in Bombay and Madras from the surplus revenues of rich Bengal. Again, the high consumption of the new regional and local aristocracies of the Mughal decline provided capital to revitalise tracts which had fallen out of cultivation. The expansion of settled agriculture and commerce from the nodes of high farming to which they had retreated since the 1740s was beginning before the British established their Peace; and it occurred in areas where their writ did not run.

If the dynamic changes in Indian commerce and politics provided much of the force behind the British advance, they also limited its impact and formed its character. The Europeans did well enough out of India; but not as well as they intended. The relationship between trade and power which tempted them into formal control of the continent also locked them out of detailed management of agrarian production. The peasant family farm and the merchant family firm were sophisticated institutions which responded vigorously to the possibility of profit. But their perception of the meaning of profit was determined by the context of institutions within which they were set, and dominated by considerations of security. They were too well adapted to be swept aside by European business methods, but they signally failed to provide the basis for a capitalist transformation or even a revolution in cash-cropping.... In a sense then, it was the very sophistication of the internal market and merchant institutions which sealed the British out of their Indian agrarian societies.

Historians have been preoccupied with two processes which link pre-colonial society with the colonial period and supply an internal dynamic to Indian history. First there has been much consideration of the evolution over the long term of the institutions of caste.[15] Secondly, dominant groups of landholders and peasants in various parts of the country have been traced through from Mughal times to the present.[16]

This study has highlighted the evolution of two other groups. Primarily, it has traced the creation of a unified merchant class within a Vaishnavite and urban setting. But we have also isolated the development (and frustration) in parts of north India of a 'service gentry' against a largely Islamic and small town background. Both these themes seem capable of illuminating events as diverse and as separated in time as the decline of the Mughals, the rise of the Company, the 1857 Revolt, and the origins of nationalism and 'communalism'.

The term service gentry emphasised the dual role of these families as state servants and *rentier* landlords. The keynote of Mughal rule had been size and centralisation. The massive army required to buttress imperial control over half South Asia and much of Central Asia created a compact bureaucratic nobility and large cities. But over time, lesser soldiers and clerical servants of the empire began to accumulate power and resources away from the centres of imperial pomp, in small towns which had often started life as the residences of Muslim holy men and artisans. At first the emperors set their face against such a development, but the accumulation of land-rights went ahead regardless. In later years, the rulers came to see this rurally based gentry as an important ally in their incessant battles with the Hindu clan leaders. The gentry steered an uneasy course through the shoals of eighteenth-century politics. Yet eighteenth-century changes often extended their control of land-rights and production around their small town centres. Successor states provided them with patronage and protection; in turn, they offered military and clerical expertise. Sometimes they avoided the consequence of local political decline because, like the Hindu trading or priestly corporations, their networks ran all over the country. Many of the apparently rootless families of administrators gathered in the great cities kept one foot in small centres which they called home (*watan*) and to which they remitted money.

How widely across the subcontinent did this occur? Obviously, the class of service gentry was not as fundamental to the Indian social order as it was in China. But even in those areas where Muslim influence was weak, there were other groups in an analogous position linking state to agrarian society, yet vulnerable to changes in either. Throughout Hindustan, Bihar, and Central India, *qasbah* settlements of the classic sort existed; though families of Hindus who were skilled in the Persian court culture often stood alongside the aristocratic Muslim gentleman.

In the Punjab the eruption of the Sikhs levelled away many *qasbah*s and their denizens, but it created in turn its own class of literate pensioners settled in small centres. In Maharashtra in the eighteenth century there is evidence of the consolidation of a kind of gentry between the substantial peasant and the state,[17] though control of village office and perquisites was more important here than *rentier* landownership. True, in the long run the fickleness of state patronage and the limited yields of agriculture in the Deccan aborted the development of a cohesive gentry of office-holders. But the point is that even within this fragile system of pre-colonial Hindu states, there developed an intermediate class between state and the substantial peasant in the form of a group of hereditary office-holders.

In Bengal, again, where the Islamic gentry was weak (outside the immediate environs of the Muslim cities of Dacca and Murshidabad) we can find analogies among the Hindu superior people—the rural *bhadralog*.[18] By 1756, literate high caste men serving Muslim fiscal lords or Hindu rajas in the commercial tracts had established themselves as subordinate tenure-holders and had consolidated their position in semi-urban villages which they regarded as their homes. These Hindu service gentry did well out of the Permanent Settlement while at the same time they were tightening their grip on public office in colonial Calcutta. Thus, even the clerkly 'babu' of Victorian Calcutta—Macaulay's revenge as it seemed to many later administrators—did not spring fully formed from Britannia's helmet but bore witness to longer-term changes in the bazaars of rural Bengal.

The patchy emergence of this service gentry also aided the establishment of British rule and moulded the form of colonial society. The British could sweep away the rickety and 'corrupt' system of revenue-farming and turn fiscal lords into landholders. But they were only able to do this because they could recruit into their system sufficient numbers of the inferior servants of the old regimes. These provided the Europeans with skills to cut through the jungle of revenue management and with some ambivalent allies in rural society. But the perilous dominances of service gentry were also to provide an unstable element in the social politics of the later colonial period. Gentry frustration provided one of the ingredients for the combustible mixture of north Indian Muslim separatism after 1860. In Bengal, the *bhadralog* Hindu gentry, embattled in the professions and losing out in rural society, fought both the British and the rich farmers, sinking Bengali nationalism under the weight of terrorism, agrarian conflict, and communal hatred. Surely, the decline of the literate gentry in the colonial period was as important a feature of colonial politics and colonial nationalism as the rise of the 'rich peasant'. Both concepts are crude, but both are capable of discovering unities in the perplexing diversity of Indian social history.

Consideration of the link between the state, the intermediate classes, and agriculture suggests some new time-scales for Indian history. In the annals of events and policies, the old turning points—1707, 1757, 1802, and 1857—retain much of their importance. By contrast, in the slower moving agrarian economy the sea-change probably occurred after our period, in the 1890s. A widespread slowing in the pace of agricultural expansion about this time may have been related to the growing pressures of population on land. From here on the new rural elites took a bumpy *ride* through to the Great Depression of the 1930s when they were faced with a crisis originating outside India. But this work has argued that for large parts of urban society and for the intermediate economy of artisans, traders and service people in the countryside, it was the rapid decline of the old polity in the third and fourth decades of the nineteenth century which represented the first major break with indigenous forms.

In the Ganges valley the eighteenth-century pattern was coming under great pressure by the later 1820s. Decentralisation of power and resources gave way to a new British centralisation. The boosting up of local economies by kingly and ritual expenditure gave way to cost cutting and deflation. By coincidence, some of the *démarches* against superior landholders and large military forces came at the same time as a series of dismal harvests and the pressures on merchants and landowners were increased by a series of hiccoughs in the export trades. The 1830s saw widespread disruption, but the decline of the old order was a long-term process. In Awadh, for instance, the coup de grace was not delivered until after the Rebellion of 1857.

Historians of colonial rule have sometimes argued that capitalism rather than modern government was the most disruptive force unleashed by the European presence. In early nineteenth-century India commercial dislocation certainly derived from external crises. These partly reflected the rhythms of the European economics. The relentless drive for higher revenue yields by colonial officials and their retreat to a resolute philosophy of laissez-faire also reflected the distant nostrums of classical political economy. However, many of the weapons being used in the battle for the redistribution of India's resources had been fashioned by indigenous rulers. The real change was that whereas these earlier despotisms had been tempered by a political culture which insisted that rulers should offer service and great expenditures in return for high revenue demand, the British acknowledged few such restraints. The crisis of early colonial rule was a moral as much as an economic one.

Peasant economies are resilient. Soldiers and unemployed servants of declining rajas could often swell the ranks of agricultural workers. In time income from external trade filled the gap left by the decline of the old regime. Yet to a greater or lesser degree, the disruption of the regional and local kingdoms which had emerged after 1720 affected the performance of agriculture. Where new export trades developed rapidly or where there existed a landowning class deeply rooted in rural production, the effects were likely to be less than in tracts where service gentry, towns, and warriors had been predominant. In Hindustan, the Doab and west suffered more than the east. For similar reasons, Maharashtra's rural economy seems to have been deeply affected by political change. Sumit Guha has traced the origins of the prolonged price depression in the Deccan between 1820 and 1850 to the collapse of the Maratha aristocracy and the pressures on the institutions of rural credit unleashed by the colonial administration.[19] The contemporary price depression in Madras may have had similar origins. In Bengal also, the difficulties of the years between 1790 and 1820 appear to have arisen not only from forced land sales under the Permanent Settlement of revenue but also from the decay of the military forces which the Nawabi regime and the great landholders had placed in countless rural market places.

Changes in the theory and practice of Indian kingship were as important as the economic consequences of the demise of the old order. Indian peasant and merchant societies had their own organisations and sense of solidarity. But at the same time, the adjudication and patronage of rulers bound these units into wider groupings and mediated their conflicts. The end of royal patronage and the modification of old systems of urban and rural government sent out ripples of change which reached into even the most placid backwaters of community and religious life. Of course, this is not to say that the old regime had been unchanging. The sale of royal rights, the eruption of outside warrior rulers, the rise of the corporations, had all jarred relations between communities and changed the face of post-Mughal India in ways which brought despair to the poets and writers of the Delhi Silver Age. But the vigorous, opinionated government of the early Victorian years shook society even more aggressively with its peace than had the earlier warriors. The decline of the Muslim urban magistracy and the fading of royal and gentry power in the north exacerbated conflict between communities and economic groups. The Hindu–Muslim riots of the 1830s and the conflicts which boiled up in the Rebellion of 1857 have a common context here. But if we look to the south where royal Hindu power had been only lightly modified by Indo-Persian forms of government, similar changes can be seen. The uprooting of the *poligar* warrior chiefs in Tamilnadu and the decline of the Cochin and Travancore kingdoms along the Kerala coast exacerbated a whole range of religious and caste conflicts which helped give Madras Presidency its reputation for exotic social disorder in the later colonial era.[20]

If the decline of the old order in the middle third of the century proved a turning point in some parts of the economy and society, there were continuities elsewhere. Corporate groups of service gentry and merchants also came under pressure during these years. But the broad sweep of their development reached through from the pre-colonial era to the later nineteenth century when they proved the recruiting ground for two key elements of the Indian middle classes.

In many parts of Asia and the Middle East, the development of indigenous intermediate classes between the state and agrarian society provided the context for the establishment and ultimate demise of colonial rule. True, emperors, khedives, and other warlords occupied the front of the stage during the period of conquest and expansion; while towards the end of colonial rule, peasant rebellion gave a new dimension to nationalist movements. Yet the intermediate classes evolved throughout. In the early stages their form and outlook was crucial in determining the timing of European penetration. Later, the interests and ideologies of merchants and service gentry conditioned the speed with which colonial nationalists were prepared to enlist the volatile movements of the countryside in their struggles.

The complexity of the Indian subcontinent and the quirks of its historiography have made it difficult to establish continuities in social history. There have been a few admirable studies of sections of the service or merchant classes over the long term. But these have concentrated on families, clans, or castes as units, and it has been difficult to see how they relate to each other or to wider changes in the political economy. So far the sense that India had an indigenous history which persisted, albeit in a modified form, into the colonial period is much easier to grasp for rural society. We can now at least trace the slow development of some of the peasant brotherhoods of the Punjab, or the great notables of Awadh from the Mughal period into the India of the National Congress.

The book *Rulers, Townsmen and Bazaars* has attempted to forge a further set of links between eras which have been fractured by the history of events, and it has suggested some new approaches to the study of Indian society. The possibility that pre-colonial India could have developed an indigenous middle class, or indeed any significant intermediate group between the state and agrarian society was denied by the classical theorists. In their different ways, both Marx and Weber implied that the cellular, caste-based society of India frustrated the development of wider solidarities except the state itself; and this was largely an agency of plunder. The denial of pre-colonial 'structural change' and the emphasis on family and caste groups by recent writers has done little to challenge these views. Yet some revision is necessary. This study has suggested that from late Mughal times at least kin groups of merchant people and service gentry were bonded together in ways which strengthened their economic control and sense of identity. Moreover, the weakening of the state in the eighteenth century enhanced the significance of these wider solidarities.

Of course, gentry and merchant groups could not form in a context in any way as favourable as that provided by Roman and feudal law in Europe. But some features of the Indian social order did encourage the consolidation of intermediate classes. Privileged tenure associated with religious endowment, for instance, provided both gentry and merchant people with long-term income and association with the management of property in particular centres. Again, trading links and the institutions of the market which had to cross caste boundaries created a sense of moral community between merchant people, ascetics and Brahmins, which extended to religious and, ultimately, to political action.

By comparison with developments in the west, these were weak forces for social change. Where the disruption of trade was widespread or rulers particularly fickle and oppressive in pre-colonial regimes, intermediate classes could be uprooted. Later, the colonial state severely curtailed their power by resuming privileged revenue grants and snapping the link between the commercial classes and revenue management, Weber too was right in this sense: though corporate solidarities breached the bounds of clan and caste, it proved difficult for the intermediate elements of Indian society to meld together across the religious and historical divide which separated merchant and priest from Islamic service gentry. All the same, many distinct characteristics and institutions of the Indian middle classes of the later nineteenth century can be traced to the pre-British past. English education or the joint-stock company wreaked their changes on developing institutions and identities, not on a stagnant and fissiparous traditional society. Many features of India's recent history seem more comprehensible against this background. Whatever the merits of the press and parliamentary government, the persistence of the capacity for self-organisation outside the ambit of the state or the army owes much to the older tradition of solidarity represented by India's commercial and religious corporations.

NOTES

1. Zahiruddin Malik, *The Reign of Muhammad Shah 1719–48* (London, 1977).

2. See, e.g., *Zikr-i-Mir,* tr. Ralph Russell and Khurshid-ul Islam, *Three Mughal Poets: Mir, Sauda, Mir Hasan* (London, 1969), p. 35.

3. P. Hardy, *Historians of Medieval India* (London, 1959), p. 8.

4. H. Goetz, *The Crisis of Indian Civilisation in the Eighteenth and Early Nineteenth Centuries* (Calcutta, 1938), pp. 5–8.

5. J.C. Heesterman, 'Was there an Indian reaction? Western expansion in Indian perspective', in H. Wesseling (ed.), *Expansion and Reaction* (Leiden, 1978), pp. 31–58.

6. Dilbagh Singh, 'Ijarah System in Eastern Rajasthan 1750–1800', *Proceedings of the Rajasthan History Congress,* v. (1973), 60–9; and his Jawaharlal Nehru University Ph.D thesis which is soon to be published.

7. Asok Sen, 'pre-British Economic Formation', in B. De (ed.), *Perspectives in the Social Sciences,* 1 (Calcutta 46–119).

8. B. Stein, *Peasant State an Society in South India* (Delhi, 1980); D. Ludden, 'Ecological zones and the cultural economy of irrigation in southern Tamilnadu'. *South Asia.* VI (1978, 1–15: C. Baker, *An India Rural Economy, 1880–1955,* Oxford, 1984).

9. See Bombay Commercial Proceedings and Reports, 1780–1820, IOL.

10. S.C. Ghosh (ed.), *Journal of a Route through the Peninsula of Guzeraut in the years 1800–10* (New Delhi, n.d.).

11. D. Washbrook, 'Some notes on market relations and the development of the economy of South India, c. 1750–1850', Paper presented to Leiden workshop on Comparative Colonial History, 1981.

12. B. Kling, *Partner in Empire, Dwarkanath Tagore and the Age of Enterprise in Eastern India* (Berkeley, 1970).

13. M. Vicziany, 'Bombay merchants and structural changes in the export community, 1850–1880', in K. Chandhuri and C. Dewey (eds), *Economy and Society* (Delhi, 1979), pp. 103–96.

14. M.N. Pearson, *Merchants and Rulers in Gujarat. The Response to the Portuguese Sixteenth Century* (Berkeley, 1976).

15. Especially, F. Conlon, *A Caste in a Changing World. The Chitrapur Saraswat Brahmins, 1700–1935* (London, 1977); K. Leonard, *The Kayasths of Hyderabad* (Berkeley, 1978).

16. E.g., Metcalf, *Landlords*; Kessinger, *Vilayatpur*; Pradhan, *Jats of Northern India*.

17. F. Perlin, 'Of White Whale and Countrymen, *Journal of Peasant Studies*, v, 1978.

18. Ratnalekha Ray, *Change in Bengal Rural Society circa 1760–1850* (Delhi, 1979), pp. 32–33.

19. S. Guha, 'The Bombay Deccan 1800–1930' (unpublished Cambridge Ph.D. dissertation, 1981), chs. 1–3.

20. S.B. Kaufmann, 'Popular Christianity, Caste and Hindu Society in South India, 1800–1915'(unpublished Cambridge Ph.D. dissertation, 1980), ch. 5.

The Slow Conquest
Administrative Integration of Malwa into the Maratha Empire, 1720–60*

STEWART GORDON

THE EIGHTEENTH CENTURY, THE MARATHAS, AND MALWA

The eighteenth century in India has generally been described as a period of great turbulence, characterized by March and counter-march, rising and failing fortunes, and bewildering political intrigue. Many historians, focusing on this aspect, have dismissed the century as merely an unsavoury hiatus between the collapse of the Mughal Empire and the rise of British domination. Yet there was more to the century than the March and counter-march of armies. The other aspect of the period was the emergence of strong successor states in Gujarat, Bengal, Oudh, Malwa, Hyderabad, Mysore, and the Punjab. Recently, historians have begun exploring these successor states, looking both back towards the Mughal administrative and ideological heritage and forward towards their role as princely states in British India. There are also important issues within the century itself, such as the role of successor states in developing regional language and consciousness, and successor states as channels of economic and social mobility.

For historians prone to see only 'chaos' and 'anarchy' in the eighteenth century, the Marathas more than any other group typified the period. Thompson and Garratt, for example, termed them 'cool and insatiable robbers', a judgement based perhaps on their raids on Mughal supply lines and extractions of naked tribute (termed *chauth*, or one-quarter).[1] It

* Excerpts from Stewart Gordon, *Marathas, Marauders, and State Formation in Eighteenth-Century India*, New Delhi, Oxford University Press, 1994, pp. 23, 58–9, 60–1.

seems supremely ironic that these supposedly archtypical marauders, the Marathas, of all the successor states should have left the most complete administrative record, permitting the broadest questions and the most detailed answers....

CONQUEST AND THE NATURE OF SUCCESSOR STATES

....What, then, does this analysis of Malwa suggest about the nature of conquest in eighteenth-century India? To begin with, there were what might be termed 'threshold levels' of military forces required to threaten a province. With fifty troops, a leader might maintain a tenuous existence as a bandit, and occasionally hold a village to ransom, but he was no threat to a town or garrison and would have been successfully resisted by any larger zamindar. (The leader's best course would have been to hire his troops out to a zamindar or to a larger power, like the Mughals.) With between one hundred and five hundred troops, a leader might threaten smaller zamindars and Mughal garrisons in rural areas. Still, sustained existence was only possible with great mobility and somewhere a safe base camp during the monsoon. A force of this size would have been defeated by a force from a sarkár garrison. With one to five thousand troops a leader would be a contending force anywhere in the province. He could easily hold villages and zamindars to ransom and compete on about equal terms with a large Mughal garrison or town. He might be able to hold some small territory as a safe base, but his troops would still be too few to defeat a Mughal main force army. Any serious rival to the Mughals as a paramount power had to be able to field—at least occasionally—between five and ten thousand troops. No matter how clever the tactics or strategy, it took this number to either meet an army in the field or tie it down while cutting off supplies.[2]

During the first two decades of the eighteenth century, the Marathas could not field an army of anything like this size. Conquest, therefore, took a long time, and proceeded by identifiable stages. In the first stage, through most of the 1720s, the Maratha bands were probably less than a thousand men. The forays into Malwa avoided large towns and garrisons; they extracted movable wealth from villages in the countryside and relied on greater mobility to escape pursuit by sarkar-level garrison forces. They had no safe bases within the province and retreated to the Deccan during the monsoon. The raids must have undermined belief, particularly among the zamindars, in the ability of the Mughals to maintain basic law and order in rural areas away from garrisons.

In the second stage, the new leadership of the Peshwa made it possible to coordinate raids of perhaps 1,000 to 5,000 troops, occasionally larger. The pattern included yearly dry-season raids still usually avoiding large garrisons in favor of ransoming villages and smaller towns. The effect was to create at least ambivalent behavior, if not ambivalent loyalty, among the local zamindars. The regular raids denied revenue to the Mughals, paid the Maratha troops, and isolated the Mughal towns from the countryside. The opening of negotiations with a few large zamindars succeeded in establishing marginally safe bases within the disputed province.

The third stage, in the 1730s, saw regular attacks on garrisons and towns. Except for a few years in mid-decade, the countryside was conceded to the Marathas, and they tried—not particularly successfully—to solidify their control with tribute contracts with the zamindars. By and large, the Mughals waited in their forts for a main force to defeat the Marathas. Communications between *sarkar*-towns were often cut; trade suffered badly.

In the fourth stage, the Peshwa assembled about 10,000 troops to defeat a Mughal main force. After this battle in 1738, near Bhopal, the Mughal garrisons and towns rapidly fell to the Marathas. With the conceding of these enclaves, Mughal administration disappeared from the province. The battle also resulted in a Mughal sanad, granting the plateau to the Marathas. The victory was an impressive show of strength to local zamindars, and contractual tribute relations promptly began.

In sum, conquest was slow. It began with raids on movable wealth of villages; it proceeded from countryside to city, first unhinging the rural administration at the zamindar level. Towns and garrisons were first isolated, then attacked. Trade suffered badly. The final conquest demanded a force of some 10,000 troops, a defeat of a main force army, and the extraction of a Mughal grant.

Ironically, this rehearsal of raids and guerrilla warfare tells us almost nothing about the administration the Peshwa built to rule the conquered province. Within a few years of the crucial battle, Maratha revenue collecting apparatus was the exact antithesis of the marauding raid of the previous two decades. Malwa had come full circle. By 1745, it was the Marathas who held the towns and roads. It was their garrison troops who walked the ramparts and anxiously watched for marauders. Their civilian officials made surveys, collected revenue, tried cases, regulated bazaars. Now the Peshwa and his *kamavisdars* worried over and depended on the very communications and trade they had so recently disrupted, and committed themselves to the economic rebuilding of the province they had plundered.

If this Maratha administration sounds suspiciously Mughal, it should. This is perhaps the key point which a study of conquest can tell us about the nature of the eighteenth-century successor states. Any larger political entity had to be built up out of negotiations with hundreds of zamindars, village headmen, and indigenous revenue officials (*chaudhri* and *qanungo* in Malwa). At this interface between the Maratha conqueror and the representatives of the conquered, the terms of reference remained severely Mughal. Taxes were called by Mughal terms, assessed in a Mughal manner, paid in customary Muslim months. Maratha demands never exceeded the pre-existing Mughal settlement. Further, it was the normal practice that when the Marathas gave replacement *sanads* to zamindars, the duties and responsibilities were described in Mughal terms. Finally, when the Marathas established the basic apparatus of law and order—courts, rural, and urban police—both the terminology and function resembled their Mughal counterparts.

In spite of these Mughal continuities at the interface between conqueror and conquered, Malwa was not a makeshift copy of a Mughal province. Firstly, above the interface with indigenous officials, the administration was completely different from the prior Mughal one. A fundamental feature of the Mughal system was the unified military hierarchy to which all officials, civilian and military, belonged. Rank and pay were defined numerically; both were proportionate to the size of the unit a man commanded, and it was expected that any official would command his unit, if necessary. In contrast, the Marathas had no such ranking system or hierarchy. Further, the military commanders and civilian administrators were rigidly divided. Non-Brahmins, principally Marathas, were the commanders and Brahmins the administrators. Another fundamental feature of the Mughal system was the division of the empire into large units called subahs (Malwa was one); each was headed by a high-ranking official, termed a *subahdar*. The Maratha system, in contrast, had no subahdar, in fact no Malwa-wide administration; the plateau was divided into areas of 200–300 villages overseen by a single collector (kamavisdar) who reported directly to the Peshwa. The third feature of the Mughal system was the concentration of administrative and military power in sarkar towns (there were ten in Malwa). The Maratha military and administration seem more dispersed, with over thirty garrisons and centers in just the eastern half of Malwa (from which there is extant data). A fourth essential feature of Mughal rule was regular rotation of officials; each served only a few years in a province before being moved to another area. In contrast, the Marathas promoted longer tenure in a single area. As we have seen, tenures of ten years were probably common.

After the Maratha conquest, it was not just the administration that was different, Malwa was different. Some rural patterns were permanently altered. Many big zamindars suffered; some had been entirely displaced and many had lost a substantial part of their territory. In contrast, a few successfully resisted all Maratha incursions and paid only occasional tribute. Twenty years of warfare still affected the countryside; many areas only produced seventy-five per cent of the best Mughal collection.

Urban patterns were changed more profoundly. The Marathas did not simply take over the Mughal sarkar towns. Generally, they settled at towns which were not as important under the Mughals—Bhilsa, Mehidpur, and Sironj, for example—rather than Mughal Sarungpur and Shajapur. The Mughal trade from Agra to Surat never recovered. The Marathas patronized new capitals, such as Indore and Gwalior; British observers, in the 1780s, noted that these new Maratha towns were prosperous and thriving, while the Mughal ones decayed. The financial networks shifted from Mughal Agra to Poona, in the Deccan. New bankers, often Deccani Brahmins, moved the revenue south, rather than north. The new trade route (in Chanderi silk, for example) was to Poona and Bombay. Even with the Mughal heritage, it is by these links and changes that by 1760 we can call Malwa successfully conquered and integrated into the successor state we know as the Maratha State.

NOTES

1. Edward John Thompson and G.T. Garratt, *Rise and Fulfilment of British Rule in India*, London, 1934, p. 63.

2. These conclusions from the Maratha material fit well with the history of Dost Muhammad Khan, another military adventurer operating in Malwa

in the opening decades of the eighteenth century. He succeeded in setting up a small state in southeast Malwa. The fullest history of his activities is in a recent unpublished dissertation. O.P. Malhotra, 'History of Bhopal State from its Foundation up to AD 1819', Vikram University, Ujjain, 1968.

Index

Contributors

Muzaffar Alam is George V Bobrinskoy Professor, South Asian Languages and Civilizations, University of Chicago, Illinois, USA.

M. Athar Ali was Professor of History, Aligarh Muslim University. He passed away in July 1998.

Christopher A. Bayly is Vere Harmsworth Professor of Imperial and Naval History, St. Catharine's College, University of Cambridge, Cambridge, UK. He is also a trustee of the British Museum and Director of Centre of South Asian Studies, Cambridge.

Meena Bhargava is Associate Professor, Department of History, Indraprastha College for Women, University of Delhi. Her publications include several research articles and books.

Philip B. Calkins was formerly at the University of Chicago, USA.

Satish Chandra is Retired Professor, Centre for Historical Studies, Jawaharlal Nehru University, New Delhi. He was also Chairman, University Grants Commission. Currently he is the Secretary-General of the Society for Indian Ocean Studies.

Stewart Gordon is Senior Research Scholar, Centre for South and Southeast Asian Studies, University of Michigan, Ann Arbor, Michigan, USA.

Irfan Habib is Professor Emeritus, Department of History, Aligarh Muslim University. He is an elected Corresponding Fellow, British Royal Historical Society since 1997.

Karen I. Leonard is Professor and Chair, Department of Anthropology, University of California, Irvine, USA.

W.H. Moreland served in the British administration in India from 1886 to 1914. He wrote on the economic history of sixteenth and seventeenth century India.

Michael N. Pearson is Emeritus Professor of History, University of New South Wales, Australia.

John F. Richards was Professor, Department of History, Duke University, Durham, North Carolina, USA. He passed way in August 2007.

Chetan Singh is Professor, Department of History, Himachal Pradesh University, Shimla.